Agency of the Enslaved

Agency of the Enslaved

*Jamaica and the Culture of
Freedom in the Atlantic World*

D. A. Dunkley

LEXINGTON BOOKS
Lanham • Boulder • New York • Toronto • Plymouth, UK

Published by Lexington Books
An imprint of The Rowman & Littlefield Publishing Group, Inc.
4501 Forbes Boulevard, Suite 200, Lanham, Maryland 20706
www.rowman.com

16 Carlisle Street, London W1D 3BT, United Kingdom

British Library Cataloguing in Publication Information Available

Library of Congress Cataloging-in-Publication Data
The hardback edition of this book was previously cataloged by the Library of Congress
follows:

Dunkley, Daive A., 1973–
  Agency of the enslaved : Jamiaca and the culture of freedom in the Atlantic world /
D.A. Dunkley.
    p. cm.
  Includes bibliographical references and index.
  1. Slavery—Jamaica—History. 2. Slaves—Jamaica—Social conditions. 3. Liberty. I.
Title.
  HT1096.D86 2013
  306.3'62097292—dc23

                                                                    2012037650

ISBN 978-0-7391-6803-5 (cloth : alk. paper)
ISBN 978-0-7391-9741-7 (pbk. : alk. paper)
ISBN 978-0-7391-6804-2 (electronic)

⊖™ The paper used in this publication meets the minimum requirements of American
National Standard for Information Sciences—Permanence of Paper for Printed Library
Materials, ANSI/NISO Z39.48-1992.

Printed in the United States of America

For Summer Paige Dunkley,
my next chapter,
for you to know all that's within you

~

Contents

~

Acknowledgments

I owe my teachers of history a great deal and can only express my gratitude for their help in my transition into a practicing historian. My flaws are not theirs, of course, but my successes, if any, are certainly due to their teaching. This book is a small contribution to the work that they put into making me into an historian. I am referring specifically to the historians who taught me at the University of the West Indies, Mona, Jamaica: Verene Shepherd, B.W. Higman, Patrick Bryan, Carl Campbell, Sultana Afroz, Veront Satchell, Waibinte Wariboko, and Jonathan Dalby. This fine tutoring continued when I went to the University of Warwick to be supervised by Gad Heuman, and where I was also influenced by the work of Trevor Burnard and by the novelist and literary critic, David Dabydeen. Life also has a funny way of putting you in contact with influential people. One of these individuals was Robert Gavron, member of the House of Lords. His support of my work when this book was first conceived manifested in a generous grant to visit London to complete my research on the Anglican clergy. Without this support, a large part of this book would not have been possible. I owe a great deal to the staff of the libraries and archives that I visited. The list includes the Moravian Archives, the National Archives, and the Lambeth Palace Library, all in London, and the University of Birmingham Archives. I am also grateful for the fine help that I received from the staff of the National Library of Jamaica, Kingston, and the Jamaica Archives, Spanish Town.

Abbreviations

CO	–Colonial Office Papers, The National Archives, London
ECCO	–Eighteenth Century Collections Online
FP	–Fulham Papers (Colonial Correspondence), Lambeth Palace Library, London
HCPP	–House of Commons Parliamentary Papers (Online)
HLRO	–House of Lords Record Office, London
NLJ	–National Library of Jamaica, Kingston
TNA	–The National Archives, London
UBA	–University of Birmingham Archives, Birmingham

~

Tables

I submit it for what it is and no more: the memorandum of a crafts-man who has always liked to reflect over his daily task, the notebook of a journeyman who has long handled the ruler and the level, without imagining himself to be a mathematician.

—Marc Bloch, *The Historian's Craft* (1954)

~

CHAPTER ONE

Slave Freedom

An Introduction

This study is really about freedom, but because its focus is on the age of slavery in British-colonized Jamaica (1655–1834), the study examines slave freedom. Slave freedom is an entirely new concept in the history-writing on anywhere in the Caribbean during slavery. However, in some ways it is not so new. I define slave freedom as the knowledge and conviction of enslaved people that they were free. They held this belief in spite of enslavement, and demonstrated it through their agency and/or acts of resistance. These performances of agency and resistance have been examined by a number of historians and other scholars. This means that slave freedom has been explored, but without naming the concept of slave freedom. Slave freedom was not the pursuit of freedom or the attempts by the enslaved to undermine slavery. These were among the main means through which slave freedom was demonstrated or shown to be real. However, the goal was to show slave freedom or something that was much bigger, the assertion by enslaved people that they were free, and enslavement did not mean that they had lost their freedom or their sense of it.

During the age of slavery in British Jamaica, the only people who viewed slavery as the loss of the freedom of the enslaved were slaveholders, the colonial and British governments, the churches, and the abolitionists or antislavery campaigners located mainly in Britain. One of the main points of this study is that the concept of freedom in the history of the Caribbean, indeed the history of the entire Atlantic world, has been examined without adequate reference to the enslaved people. Slave freedom returns the scholarship on freedom to the people who fought the hardest, most frequently, and longest to show that they were free, and that like any other people, they had the right to live in freedom. They showed that slavery was wrong and unwise in every conceivable way, that is, socially, economically, and politically. When Plato, writing in *The Republic* many centuries ago, examined the concept of freedom, he was certain about one thing. It was indestructible. Plato's "doctrine of freedom," according to R.F. Stalley, revolved around the idea that freedom cannot be destroyed, and therefore cannot be made. It exists in the same way that humans exist, and in spite of attempts that might be made to undermine it or engineer its disappearance. Plato's well known denouncement of liberal democracy was not merely the attempt to undervalue the importance of freedom. Rather, Plato's goal was to show, as Stalley explains, that freedom is an internal belief, or a state of mind, or a state of grace. No form of government can create or destroy it, and it is visible in the human with the strongest sense of justice and fairness. As Stalley puts it, "a central strand in" Plato's "argument is the claim that only the just man is truly free."[1]

This "just man" is the human combined with the sense that he or she makes of the "*politeia.*" In this way, according to Stephen Taylor Holmes, the "*politiea*" or government gains importance in people's lives. This importance comes about through the choices that people have made. The "*politeia*" will have to resort to suppression in the absence of popular acceptance or consent. Suppression thus represents the abandonment of government by consent for autocratic rule. The weakness of this rule is evident in the same suppressive measures. People under autocracy have not lost their freedom. Autocracy is an attempt to bring about this loss, and acknowledges its inability to materialize this objective by becoming increasingly suppressive over time.[2] Similarly, Aristotle's "realms of freedom" offered an explanation of freedom as one of the "distinctive features" of humankind.[3] In other words, humans develop notions of self in order to shield their minds and bodies from external controls. At the same time, these notions are shaped by their experiences, though never in a direct sense. External factors serve to reinforce humankind's convictions, such as their belief in their freedom. The grossest of these external factors, such as slavery, reinforces the human belief in the rightness, fairness, justice, and wisdom of freedom. External factors aid the formulation of resistance, but they do not create notions of freedom. These notions themselves are and remain the foundations of resistance and/ or agency.

Since Plato and Aristotle, however, the concept of freedom in Western culture has been fully and essentially externalized. It has become an ideal, rather than a state or condition that is inherent in humans. It is now seen as a creation, following perhaps Western Christianity's promulgation of the story of the creation of the human at a point in time, and naturally, of course, since Christianity was and still is popular and powerful in Western culture. Freedom has been given a beginning, and an existence which, like human life, can be brought to an end, even with the triumph of liberal democracy in the West. This is, ironically, the implication of Francis Fukuyama's famous work *The End of History and the Last Man*. While Fukuyama's argument is that Western liberal democracy has triumphed over autocracy, and so the world is thriving toward a unitary end under the banner of liberalism, the implication is the acknowledgement that liberal democracy itself is still facing serious threats and can still be replaced. It must therefore remain on high alert, if it really hopes to retain or maintain its glorified and victorious position.[4] Essentially, freedom has been re-conceptualized as both makeable and breakable, and apparently due to mainly sociological scholarship. This scholarship, from Parsons, Mead, Blummer, and all the rest, is often based on the profound neglect of historical realities or the lived experiences of the people in the past. Historical sociologists, namely Orlando Patterson, have told us how to view freedom, and we have accepted this viewpoint without much apparent or effective resistance. Slavery has played a big role in this acceptance, at least in and because of the way that it has been discussed in the scholarship on the making of Western culture.

For example, Patterson, in *Freedom in the Making of Western Culture*, argues that freedom is "socially created," or basically "an invented value." Patterson advises us further that this was linked to the "specific pair of struggles generated by slavery" in the West.[5] This perspective undervalues the human capacity for self-conceptualization. People are presented as if they are mere robots, and as if their freedom was created not by them, but by slavery and its negation of this freedom. This notion of freedom as a created social value has also crept into historical scholarship on the making of the Atlantic world, and unfortunately it is still there. Edmund S. Morgan's recent *American Slavery, American Freedom: The Ordeal of Colonial Virginia* is a consummate example. Morgan rehashes Patterson's inextricable link between slavery and freedom. Freedom is depicted as impermanent, though important. Even this latter quality, however, is due to the effects of enslavement.[6] The nonsense of this dynamic is laid barest if we should ask the simple counterfactual question that, if slavery was absent, would there be no freedom? A better title for Morgan's study would be *American Freedom, American Slavery*. With this title, Morgan could proceed from freedom and move toward explaining slavery as what it was: the attempt to destroy freedom. This attempt showed its failure in two very big ways during the age of slavery in the American mainland setting. First, at its independence from Great Britain in 1776; and again in 1866, during its own Civil War fought to end slavery, in order to make the new nation whole and complete. The question I start with is this: why was slavery created? Was it not freedom that slavery tried to destroy or to circumvent? Why were ideologies of suppression, domination, and extreme subjugation, such as racism and church discipline and indoctrination, rationalized and organized and brought into the effort to start and support slavery, if slavery was not an imposition or essentially the destabilization of freedom? Regrettably, the institution of slavery is presented by scholars such as Patterson and Morgan as the loss of freedom, and the death of slavery as the big and noble gesture that freedom was finally made, or a little more generously, was finally regained.

For me, the start of this offensive against freedom is, ironically, Western Enlightenment (1650–1800). The whole basis of this Enlightenment was the supposed promotion of human freedom. However, thinkers such as Montesquieu, Locke, Rousseau, and Paine were all complicit, in one way or another, in the re/conceptualization of freedom as destructible, creatable, and worse, as limited to certain groups of deserving people. Montesquieu had intervened with the idea of the separation of powers in government. There was to be, according to Montesquieu, an independent executive, a legislature, and a judiciary, and their purpose, both separately and together, was the preservation of civil liberties or the preservation of freedom. However, the point at which the separation started was also the starting point of freedom. Similarly, Locke's *Two Treatises of Government* positioned the English Parliament as the great defender of freedom in England and then all of Great Britain, but at the same time, this same body also authorized and profited from the brutal enslavement of Africans and their descendants in the Americas. Parliament assumed that it had the power to give freedom to some, while also taking this away from others. As the defender of freedom, Parliament was also its creator, its disseminator, and its destroyer. Slavery was seen as legitimate and lawful as long as it had Parliament's approval. Government in general was only for those few deserving (British) people, who truly deserved this. In Locke's view of the world, Africans did not deserve freedom, however much they might have shown that they desired to also live free from all the kinds of unnatural bondage around them.[7]

Rousseau started from the correct assumption that "Man is born free," but then he proceeded to this profound contradiction, "and everywhere he is in chains." Although Rousseau admitted that "no justification" could be found "for depriving" any people of their freedom, this assumed that deprivation was also real. Freedom could be lost, and regaining it was a matter that was entirely dependent on "the social order" and its "conventions." There was no such thing as "natural rights," or no such thing as rights that "come from nature." In 1776, the American pamphleteer, Thomas Paine, in his *Common Sense* pamphlet, called on the American colonists to end British tyranny on the mainland. However, Paine's disillusionment was also based on the assumption that only those who had shown the willingness to fight and to die for American freedom should receive it.[8] This view was factored into the continuation of African-American enslavement and the disintegration of Native American freedom, even following the end of British tyranny on the mainland. Freedom was not a right, but a privilege, and soon, even skin color and ethnicity became factors that gave one the privilege to live in freedom or not. The point is that conditions were attached to freedom because of the attempts by Enlightenment thinkers to associate freedom with a range of external criteria. These included governments with separated powers, Parliaments with bills of rights, participation in the fights against tyranny, and ultimately one's skin color and ethnicity or culture. While I will agree that protecting freedom takes hard work, I disagree with the assumption that the absence of this work should also signal or validate the absence of freedom. In reality, there is no such state as slavery, and slavery can never be lawful or valid or legitimate. There is, however, enslavement, which is an unnatural condition imposed on people, and vindicated by external criteria, including some of the propositions, presuppositions, and assumptions of Enlightenment scholarship.

Fortunately, studies by James C. Scott and Obika Gray have been showing that seeing freedom as destructible is an exercise in nonsense. These scholars have argued that even when freedom is hidden, this does not and should not signal that freedom has dissipated or disappeared. Resistance is the permanent and powerful reminder that freedom persists, the symbolic representation of freedom's permanency, empowerment, and raw power, all of which are viewable even in the instances where horrific suppression and oppression are actively taking place. As Gray has put the matter succinctly, the "demeaned" are never really disempowered, or as Scott has added, freedom is still visible even when resistance is designed to remain hidden.[9] For some time now, history-writing on the early modern Atlantic world has also been moving toward acknowledging the survival of freedom in spite of slavery. This can be interpreted as a move in the direction of slave freedom. Recently, we have seen Vincent Brown's seminal analysis of even death as one of the symbolic acts of resistance of enslaved people. Brown had shown that death played a central role in the survival of slave freedom among enslaved Africans and their descendants in the Americas. Christian J. Koot has explored the imperfections of empire, which we can interpret as partly the consequence of slave freedom. This made Anglo-colonization and Anglo-Dutch trade severely problematical, and the reality was that empire remained a project or a goal. Long ago, Eugene D. Genovese presented evidence of *The World the Slaves Made*, which was a sign of the persistence of slave freedom and of its counteractions of slavery. Ann Stoler, despite questioning "the historic turn," has left us with the impression that this project to turn history toward the dispossessed and oppressed was indeed a worthwhile pursuit, but one that we now need to deepen, if our goal is to make it even realer. We need to recognize, for instance, as Stoler suggests, the limitations of colonial archives. Evidence of this turn was E.P. Thompson's famous essay on the "moral economy" of the English poor in the eighteenth century, which asserted the presence of conceptions and genuine ideologies among the poor, which challenged the cultures of domination in late early modern England. Applied to the enslaved, the "moral economy" was their agency and resistance, and, in broader terms, their consistent disavowal of slavery as the death knell of their freedom.[10]

History-writing on the Caribbean has not been left behind, to which the studies of B.W. Higman, Hilary Beckles, Gad Heuman, Michael Craton, Roderick McDonald, Trevor Burnard, and Diana Paton can readily testify. These historians have examined the resistance of enslaved people either directly or indirectly. Higman, for instance, has shown the existence of slave families in spite of slavery, arguing that Patterson's "social death" analysis provided an inaccurate and grim picture that portrayed the world that enslaved people created as almost nonexistent and certainly insignificant. McDonald's reconstruction of enslaved people's economic activities showed a thriving economy that was largely independent of slaveholders. Enslaved people created and recreated the world in which they lived, and they did this even while contending with massive suppression and extreme acts of brutality. Burnard and Paton have examined the issue by exploring the culture of slaveholders. Burnard's case study of Thomas Thistlewood, the Scottish slaveholder in Jamaica, leaves us with no doubt about the terrorism that shaped slaveholding in eighteenth-century British Jamaica. However, enslaved people's responses, both concealed and overt—such as subtle acts of disobedience, sabotage, and cultural retentions, and on the other side, suicide, infanticide, running away, and Tacky's famous revolt in 1760—all revealed that even brutality at the predatory level of a Thomas Thistlewood could not extinguish the determination of the enslaved to show that they were free. Paton's work on the Jamaican prison system exposes the powerlessness of slaveholding, which had to resort to the spectacle of incarceration at the state level in order to control the uncontrollable black masses, the majority of whom were supposed to behave as prescribed, or like slaves. Now is the moment that we need to take the analysis further. We need to depart from the view espoused recently by Rebecca J. Scott that the resistance and agency of the enslaved, and even the formerly enslaved, constituted merely *Degrees of Freedom*. This is seeing the trees, but not the forest.[11]

If Michel-Rolph Trouillot has told us nothing else that is valuable, the one worthwhile thing of which he has made us more aware is that history is not neutral. It is a production of power, and if we continue to underestimate the enslaved, we are rehearsing Western ideologies of power, which were also used in former times for the suppression of enslaved people. These ideologies of power have continued to shape some of the history-writing on the age of slavery in the Americas, and are resonant in the studies on West Indian slavery by J.R. Ward and Robert E. Luster, for example. Ward and Luster have examined the internal transformations of slavery, known as amelioration, but from perspectives associated with the dominators of the enslaved.[12] In their work, Ward and Luster show almost no regard for the agency of enslaved people, or the centrality of the contributions that they made to ameliorating or shifting the conditions of enslavement toward abolition. On the matter of education or instruction for enslaved people, for example, Luster states frankly that "success" was achieved, "both by the missionaries and secular teachers," who gave the "slaves religious instruction" and "were able to inculcate Western moral values, which became part of the local culture."[13] I use in this present study two entire chapters to reexamine instruction or education during slavery, but I shift the emphasis toward the recipients, the enslaved, in order to reevaluate the goals and achievements of the instructional system. Because of this focus, my conclusions are very different from Luster's. Instruction or education of schooling was indeed successful, but because enslaved people themselves accepted the chances to become literate. As we know, literacy is the start of social power, so to be enslaved and in school at the same time was a practical and wise decision. As for the inculcation of Western values, how is this really measured? How do we know that enslaved people took what they were taught seriously? In my chapters on instruction or education, I show that the schools were contested terrains, and no teaching actually took place unless the enslaved really wanted it.

The main point I am making here is that there was a centrality that was visible in the activities of the enslaved. Even when we examine the attempts to dominate them, we are examining the slaveholders' concerns about the potency of enslaved people's resistance and agency. We are getting a glimpse of slave freedom, in other words, which was not a side show, but as I like to call it, *the* show during the age of slavery. When slaveholders made their choices to shift the productions and relations of power in colonial settings, these choices were made because of or with due consideration made of enslaved people's choices. The people at the bottom were the shaping factors in the decision-making of the people who we generally assumed sat at the top. The bottom was all the time subverting the top in these subtle ways, and this is the vital consideration that I make in this work. Slave freedom was agency, but it was also much more than that; it was the central consideration in the major decisions made to shape and reshape the age of slavery, to create and recreate the colonial environments of the Atlantic world. In his two-volume study, *Slaves Who Abolished Slavery*, published from in the mid-1980s, Richard Hart tried to suggest that we should make the shift toward examining enslaved people much more closely. Hart was convinced, as I am also, that the enslaved ended the system of slavery, rather than British politicians, abolitionists, or slaveholders who could no longer turn a handsome profit. Slavery ended because of people power, not because of politics, or because of economics. However, Hart was too limited in his view of resistance. He could see resistance only as resistance, and ultimately, he did not accomplish his goal to show in a convincing way that enslaved people made the seminal contribution to the abolition process, which made freedom the central trope of Western culture during and post-Enlightenment. Hart could see the forest, but showed us only the trees.[14]

My goal in this work is to use slave freedom to suggest another start. We need to go back to resistance and view these not as actions taken against slavery, but as assertions of the freedom that enslaved people knew that they still had. We need to shift from seeing resistance as the pursuit of freedom, and instead view these as the accommodations that the enslaved needed to make in order to assert their right to be acknowledged as free. We need to move away from treating resistance in narrow terms, so that we can see its importance during the age of slavery. We need to see resistance in the actions of the enslaved, but also as the motivating factors in the decisions of their enslavers. Once this is done, we shall begin to see that resistance was the central narrative that shaped the age of slavery, a narrative that had a goal bigger than itself, a narrative that was crucially a discourse about the presence, permanency, and power of freedom.

And I begin with Marc Bloch's important advice that history-writing must not be mathematical or too positivist because human beings, of whom history is essentially about, were generally not mathematical in thought or action. If we are too positivistic, we will miss the creative expressions of power through resistance, and we will not see the unseen, such as slave freedom. We will "only" be "doing," as Bloch warns, "exactly what the writers" of the past "expected us to do," meaning, in this case, the enslavers.[15] Slave freedom was not overt in most cases, it was designed to remain hidden from slaveholders, this was part of its wisdom and subversion, part of how it survived and became an annoyance, part of the reason it could force changes upon slaveholding, and part of why historians need to literally look through pin holes in the records to see it. It requires rereading documents generated by dominators, or reading which is against the grain. Most, if not all, of the archival sources I use in this study were not created by enslaved people, at least not in any direct sense. However, I view these records also as the records of the enslaved, since they do tell a great deal about enslaved people, albeit in indirect ways. The most important ones I use are the parliamentary papers of the British House of Commons, the records of the House of Lords, the correspondence of Anglican clergymen now at Lambeth Palace Library, London, and the online minefield known as the Eighteenth Century Collections Online, which contain legislation, published and unpublished primary sources, all written by supporters and critics of the enslaved and enslavement.

The Chapters

The chapters in this study are arranged thematically rather than chronologically. This introduction is listed as chapter 1 because it provides a definition and explanation of the idea of slave freedom. The study thus really commences in chapter 2, which is an examination of slave freedom close to the abolition of slavery in 1834. The assessment is of a spectacle on the plantations owned by the absentee sugar planter, Matthew "Monk" Lewis. Lewis' decision to label the enslaved people that he encountered as "perverse" is used in the chapter's title. He could find no other way, at least initially, to describe the enslaved on his estates. Fresh from England, where there was no slavery, as soon as he arrived in Jamaica, Lewis was confronted by people facing the daily vulgarities of slavery and who had decided to use the presence of the estates' owner as part of their resistance. Lewis' experience introduces slave freedom in the way that this manifested on his estates in Jamaica.

Chapter 3 examines an unexplored type of runaway slave who used the courts to resist the legality of slavery after they had been captured. Choosing to run away was always in some fashion about questioning slavery. However, those enslaved persons who were caught and then used this to petition for their freedom added a new dimension to the resistance inherent in running away. The point that these petitioners made was that they completely rejected the label of running away, whether or not they were illegally taken into slavery after the abolition of the British slave trade in 1807. In other words, they never lost sight of their freedom and rejected enslavement because of this. The chapter analyzes their successes and failures in order to illustrate their determination, but also to make the point that this determination was not to win freedom, but to assert it. The pressure that they placed on the colonial judiciary also took place closer to the end of slavery. Of course, no enslaved person at that point could have known that slavery would be abolished in 1834. This is important to remember when assessing the empowerment that was shown by the petitioners. Though they benefited from the abolition of the slave trade, it took a great deal of courage and confidence to petition the courts for their freedom. Many of them did this even while knowing that they were not legally free. These unsuccessful petitioners were sent back into slavery when the courts concluded their investigations.

Chapter 4 begins the evaluation of instructing or schooling the enslaved that constituted an early system of education in Jamaica. The chapter makes two connected points. First, it challenges the idea that no real education system predated the abolition of slavery in the British-colonized Caribbean, and secondly, the chapter argues that the construction of this system was an indication of the power of slave freedom, which continued to appear in the schools that were started. At the very least an attempt was made to fashion a system of education or schooling in spite of its limitations, one designed to indoctrinate the enslaved using Christian knowledge. The purpose was to ensure that they were pacified to maintain slavery and the plantations. This fledgling school system, like any such provision, was part of preserving the social order. The problem was that this social order was based on slavery. The church of state, the Anglican Church, was brought in to construct and run the schools, and through this church, rather than the Protestant missionary churches, systematic provisions were put in place for what was thought of as educational purposes. This education was far from ideal, but the limitations themselves do not negate the fact that an attempt was made to build a system that served the society as it existed. Acknowledging the existence of this early schooling project provides an avenue into assessing how much enslaved people had to endure in their resistance to the domination of the slaveholders.

Chapter 5 continues the discussion about the early system of instruction, as it was called, but turns this assessment toward the enslaved people. This is important partly because close evaluation of the activities of the enslaved in the schools is missing from the history of education in the British Caribbean, and partly because these activities provide evidence of slave freedom and which are more important because of the setting in which these acts of resistance occurred. The schools were not formed for the enslaved. They were formed to serve the slaveholders and to maintain the social order, but enslaved people attempted to influence how they were taught and by whom, and reshaped the instruction that they received in a number of ways. The first sign of this influence was in fact the heavy investment in instruction, and the question answered in the chapter is why was this investment seen as necessary? It signaled fear, one of the consistent features of slaveholding.

Chapter 6 examines the mandate of the church of state, issued by the British crown after the 1660 Restoration, to ensure that enslaved people conformed to the domination of enslavement. This mandate was connected to slave freedom because it was also an investment in the attempts to build and maintain slavery. The chapter focuses on the foundational period of British colonization of Jamaica and draws upon the work by Edmund Hickeringill, an Anglican cleric, to show how the mandate was envisaged and why it was seen as necessary. In this work, *Jamaica Viewed*, Hickeringill wrote about the island and its future as a valuable British colony, but one that needed a stable system of slavery to make it profitable and important. In the chapter, the preexisting ideology of racial difference is discussed as part of the model used for enslavement and how this kind of enslavement was seen as possible with the assistance of the church. Hickeringill's emphasis on indoctrination is also used to show the presence of hegemony, which existed in England as part of the Restoration of the monarchy, and which Hickeringill used as a means through which to materialize the conformity of enslaved people.

Chapter 7 proceeds to the discussion about the reaction of the enslaved to church membership, and examines this through mass baptism in the church after the 1797 decision of the slaveholders to promote the conversion of enslaved people in this church. The chapter shows that though mass baptism was an attempt to use church domination to control the enslaved, the people who were baptized became agents of change within the church. Baptism provides a way to assess slave freedom as this appeared in the church of state. That this was the most powerful ecclesiastical body in Jamaica during slavery also increases the importance of the agency displayed by enslaved people in their interactions with this church. They saw advantages in the church that were not advertised by the clergymen, and these motivated the enslaved to embrace church membership. However, the documents available permit only an assessment of the colonization of the church by enslaved people. The advantages that they saw in the church were not outlined in the documents in any specific fashion. Nevertheless, some of these can be ascertained by inference, and the chapter makes an attempt where possible to discuss what these advantages might have been. The colonization of the church by the enslaved took place within the framework of resistance demonstrated by the decisions the enslaved made to gain access to the church on their own terms, to pay the baptism fees with their own money, or to make the slaveholders pay.

Chapter 8 uses the slave laws and amelioration to examine the perilousness of slavery as a result of slave freedom. These laws were enacted in anticipation of resistance or in response to it. Amelioration was also an attempt to modify slavery largely because of the resistance of the enslaved. The chapter thus examines slave freedom using the activities of the slaveholders, namely the fear which the agency of the enslaved created and which resulted in the reshaping of slavery, first to make it more brutal and suppressive, and then to replace these extreme measures with the hegemonic controls embedded in amelioration. None of these measures succeeded. Enslaved people continued to resist slavery in both violent and nonviolent ways. The chapter discusses two forms of nonviolent resistance: marriage and manumission. Both are presented in the chapter as evidence of the agency of enslaved people. Marriage was previously restricted to free people and the marriages of the enslaved sent a powerful message to slaveholders about the erosion of their exclusionary rights to institutions signaling freedom, social status, and upward social mobility. Manumission was the acquisition of legal freedom and, as the chapter discusses, this resulted from the activities of the enslaved people themselves.

Chapter 9 closes the study with an assessment of amelioration, the last rebellion of the enslaved in Jamaica, and the apprenticeship system which was introduced along with the act abolishing slavery. The purpose of the chapter is to show the survival of slave freedom to the very end of enslavement, and its continuation during apprenticeship since this was viewed by the former enslaved people as another system of domination and an attempt to delay full freedom. The chapter argues that apprenticeship ended prematurely because of the dissatisfaction of the former enslaved people with this system. The problems which arose during apprenticeship were due largely to the apprentices, as they were known, who refused to succumb to the attempts of former masters to treat them the same as during slavery. Some apprentices, as the chapter also shows, removed themselves from apprenticeship through self-purchase, which is presented as a continuation of the manumissions that had occurred during slavery. Overall, the chapter shows that the former enslaved people maintained their objective to live as people who were fully free.

Notes

1. R.F. Stalley, "Plato's Doctrine of Freedom," *Proceedings of the Aristotelian Society* 98 (1998), 145.

2. Stephen Taylor Holmes, "Aristippus in and out of Athens," in *Aristotle's Politics: Critical Essays*, Richard Kraut and Steven Skultety, eds. (Lanham, MD: Rowman & Littlefield Publishers, 2005), 9.

3. Dogan Baris Kilinc, "Labor, Leisure, and Freedom in the Philosophies of Aristotle, Karl Marx, and Herbert Marcuse," MA Thesis, Department of Philosophy, Middle East Technical University, Ankara, 2006, 36.

4. Francis Fukuyama, *The End of History and the Last Man* (New York: Free Press, 1992), see the introduction entitled "By Way of an Introduction."

5. Orlando Patterson, *Freedom in the Making of Western Culture*, Volume 1 (London: I.B. Tauris & Co. Ltd., 1991), 3.

6. Edmund S. Morgan, *American Slavery, American Freedom: The Ordeal of Colonial Virginia* (New York: W.W. Norton and Co., 2003), see especially 293–388.

7. See Baron de Montesquieu (Charles de Secondat), *The Spirit of the Laws*, 2 Vols. (London: G. Bell & Sons, Ltd., 1914 [1748]); and John Locke, *Two Treatises of Government: In the Former, The False Principles and Foundation of Sir Robert Filmer, And His Followers, are Detected and Overthrown. The Latter is an Essay concerning The True Original, Extent, and End of Civil-Government* (London: Printed for Awnsham Churchill, 1690 [1689]). Also see Jeremy Waldron, *God, Locke, and Equality* (Cambridge, UK: Cambridge University Press, 2002).

8. Jean-Jacques Rousseau, *The Social Contract or Principles of Political Right*, H.J. Tozer, trans. (Hertfordshire, England: Wordsworth Editions, 1998), 5. Also see Thomas Paine, *Common Sense* (Philadelphia: Independence Hall Association, 1995 [1776]).

9. See James C. Scott, *Weapons of the Weak: Everyday Forms of Peasant Resistance* (New Haven, CT: Yale University Press, 1985); and Obika Gray, *Demeaned but Empowered: The Social Power of the Urban Poor in Jamaica* (Kingston: University of the West Indies Press, 2004). The titles of these books illustrate the point that suppression does not extinguish people's belief in their ability to exercise their freedom and this freedom is shown in their resistance.

10. See Vincent Brown, *The Reaper's Garden: Death and Power in the World of Atlantic Slavery* (Cambridge, MA: Harvard University Press, 2008); Christian J. Koot, *Empire at the Periphery: British Colonists, Anglo-Dutch Trade, and the Development of the British Atlantic, 1621–1713* (New York: New York University Press, 2011); Eugene D. Genovese, *Roll, Jordan, Roll: The World the Slaves Made* (New York: Vintage, 1976); Ann Laura Stoler, "Colonial Archives and the Arts of Governance," *Archival Science* 2 (2002): 87–109, she starts the discussion of "the historic turn" on 88; and E.P. Thompson, "The Moral Economy of the English Crowd in the Eighteenth Century," *Past and Present* 50:1 (1971): 76–136.

11. See, for instance, B.W. Higman, *Slave Population and Economy in Jamaica, 1807–1834* (Kingston: The Press, University of the West Indies, 1995); Hilary McD.

Beckles, *A History of Barbados: From Amerindian Settlement to Nation-State* (Cambridge, UK: Cambridge University Press, 1990); Gad Heuman, "The Free Coloreds in Jamaican Slave Society," in *The Slavery Reader*, Gad Heuman and James Walvin, eds. (London: Routledge, 2003), 664–667, and Gad Heuman, ed., *Out of the House of Bondage: Runaways, Resistance, and Marronage in Africa and the New World* (London: Frank Cass, 1986); Michael Craton, *Empire, Enslavement, and Freedom in the Caribbean* (Kingston: Ian Randle, James Curry, and Marcus Wiener, 1997), and Michael Craton, *Testing the Chains: Resistance to Slavery in the British West Indies* (London: Cornell University Press, 1982); Roderick A. McDonald, *The Economy and Material Culture of Slaves: Goods and Chattels on the Sugar Plantations of Jamaica and Louisiana* (Baton Rouge: Louisiana State University Press, 1993); Trevor Burnard, *Mastery, Tyranny, and Desire: Thomas Thistlewood and His Slaves in the Anglo-Jamaican World* (Chapel Hill: The University of North Carolina Press, 2004); and Diana Paton, *No Bond but the Law: Punishment, Race, and Gender in Jamaican State Formation, 1780–1870* (Durham, NC: Duke University Press, 2004); Rebecca J. Scott, *Degrees of Freedom: Louisiana and Cuba after Slavery* (Cambridge, MA: Belknap Press of Harvard University, 2008).

12. See J.R. Ward, *British West Indian Slavery, 1750–1834: The Process of Amelioration* (Oxford, UK: Clarendon Press, 1988); and Robert E. Luster, *The Amelioration of the Slaves in the British Empire, 1790–1833* (New York: Peter Lang, 1995).

13. Luster, *The Amelioration of the Slaves*, 162.

14. See, especially, Richard Hart, *Slaves Who Abolished Slavery, Volume 2: Blacks in Rebellion* (Kingston: Institute for Social and Economic Research, University of the West Indies, 1985).

15. Marc Bloch, *The Historian's Craft: Reflections on the Nature and Uses of History and the Techniques and Methods of Those Who Write It* (Manchester, UK: Manchester University Press, 1992), 16, 50.

CHAPTER TWO

~

Those "Perverse" Slaves

This chapter examines events during the final two decades of slavery in Jamaica. It starts almost at the end of slavery rather than at the beginning, or uses a format that is different from the one normally used in the writing of Anglo-Caribbean history. The future contained a set of more clear-cut evidence of slave freedom and its outcomes, and the purpose of this chapter is to highlight one of these through an examination of a specific act of resistance. This showed that the enslaved people not only obtained the objectives that they hoped for, but that they also exposed in some vivid ways aspects of the central role that slave power or slave agency had continued to play in the decisions that were taken by both slaveholders and colonial administrators. In other words, slave freedom was the driving force behind the evolution of the age of slavery.

A Troublesome Inheritance

The famous English Gothic novelist, Matthew "Monk" Lewis, was the inheritor of two large sugar plantations in Jamaica upon the death of his father in 1812. Lewis had never been to the Caribbean before then, and knew exactly nothing about the slave system in an island-colony such as Jamaica. After inheriting the properties, Cornwall and Hordley in the parishes of Westmoreland and St. Thomas-in-the-East, respectively—one in western Jamaica and the other one in the far eastern section of the island—Lewis traveled to Jamaica to see his inheritance with his own eyes. What he saw, however, was not only two large sugar estates, but the enslaved Africans and people of African descent whom his father had left under his control, and hopefully his care; and more importantly, the great extent to which the survival of the two estates was dependent on the labor power that was provided by these enslaved people.

This dependency would convince Lewis of the great need for a "new code of laws" for the estates, which he wrote during his first visit in 1816.[1] He visited once more in 1818, spending about the same three months, as he did before. However, he died of yellow fever, either on May 14 or May 16, 1818, while on the return journey to England, and was buried at sea.

Lewis wrote about his experiences on his Jamaican properties in a journal that was published posthumously in 1834, and entitled the *Journal of a West India Proprietor*. The changes contained in the "new code of laws" that Lewis introduced on his estates would be viewed as evidence of the planters' sense of patriarchy and paternalism by the famous Brazilian scholar of slavery, Gilberto Freyre.[2] And although Freyre's work was published as early as the 1960s, the same view that he took has been maintained in some of the scholarship on slaves and planters in fairly recent years. Richard J. Follett applies the perspective in his assessment of the slave/planter relationship in the cane world of southern colonists in Louisiana.[3] J.R. Ward's perspective on the amelioration of slavery in the British West Indies is very much the same point of view.[4]

However, Mary Turner has addressed the insufficiency of this view that the planters who introduced ameliorative measures on their estates were operating out of benevolence for the slaves, which was tied to the expectation that this would pacify the slaves and result in greater productivity. Turner argues that these planters did not act out of a paternalistic patriarchy, but because they had material hopes. However, Turner's critique has indeed examined mainly the material-side of the impetus for the decisions taken by the planters.[5] Matthew Lewis' interaction with the enslaved on his estates indicates that there was another aspect of the stimulus that planters felt when adopting measures to improve conditions on the estates, even with the hope of raising the productivity of the enslaved. Lewis had realized that his slaves had been promoting a greater sense of morality, from which some of the decisions of the planters emanated. This was seen, for instance, in the slaves' disapprovals of the conduct of the white managers and overseers on Lewis' estates.

On his properties, Lewis encountered enslaved people who had embraced an enlightenment of their own, one that was not limited to whites or to free people of any color, but an enlightenment that extended to all human beings in the colony. The fundamental difference between this discovery and the argument that Turner, for instance, provided, is its nonmaterial aspect. Lewis had discovered the promotion of an attitudinal change, which had a more far reaching potential and practical importance than decisions taken under material considerations to improve production on any one or any group of sugar estates. A social change was visibly underway; one enveloping Jamaica as a whole and by the time that Lewis visited the island, this change had matured to the point that he, as one of the observant sugar planters, could not possibly ignore it.

Later in the 1820s, the Baptist missionary, James Murcell Phillippo, would join forces with the enslaved in the moralizing mission that was challenging slaveholders' notions as to how the world around them should really work. Phillippo advised (or rather warned) the planters in particular, but also the colonial administration, that the "unblushing licentiousness" that was visible "from the Governor downwards through all the intermediate ranks of society," and which was carried on "in the broad light of day," were "notorious" and ill-advised relics of the past.[6] These practices needed to disappear without delay, and this change must start from above. The frightening fact for Phillippo, however, was the presence of clear signs of this change from the very bottom of the society, meaning the enslaved. The emphasis Phillippo placed on the social ills of Jamaica was not only a sign of the Baptists' views about the hierarchies of culture, class, and race. Patrick Bryan correctly states that Baptist missionaries in Jamaica, and possibly elsewhere in the Anglo-Caribbean, "shared with the planters a belief in hierarchy, a belief in the cultural superiority of Europe, and to a large extent they accepted the hierarchy of race and gender."[7] However, this was not the full story.

The focus of Phillippo was also due to the frightful reality that the group deemed the most insignificant, meaning the enslaved, were already underway with a virtual social revolution. This, as Phillippo well knew, had the potential to explode into a disaster for the slaveholders and colonial government; quite possibly in the same way that the colonial/slave society suddenly went up into flames in French St. Domingue in 1791. Enslaved people in that colony took control of the entire society in due course. If the slaveholders continued to neglect what the enslaved were doing, if they maintained their "violent opposition" to the preaching done by the missionaries, Phillippo warned that they would surely not have a future as members of the Jamaican society. This explains the trepidation that Phillippo felt when he witnessed the obstacles faced by missionaries who wanted only to preach the Christian gospel in the colony. It was regrettable, but also dangerous, Phillippo suggested, to force these preachers to leave "their flock" unattended and therefore "scattered." To have them out in the world "like sheep without a shepherd" was shortsighted thinking.[8] This particular flock that Phillippo was referring to was, of course, mainly the enslaved people. He felt that they had to be led, but not because they were incapable of leading themselves. It was a dangerous policy to simply leave them up to their own leadership and their own devices.

Heeding these warning signs, long before Phillippo's indictment, Lewis himself made it unlawful for the white employees on his estates to maintain sexual relationships with the slaves; relationships that the enslaved themselves considered as highly inappropriate, immoral, and flatly exploitative. These sexual relations were never consensual, given the nature of slavery. They were sources of disrespect and distress, reminders to the enslaved that they were very much in slavery, while each of those slaves also wanted to preserve the sense of freedom that they had and in spite of the bondage that they knew they were also in. The idea on which Lewis based his decision to deny his white male employees sexual contact with especially enslaved females was the anger that was expressed by especially enslaved males over these contacts. White males were creating a more dangerous environment for themselves, forcing enslaved males into active resistance mode, encouraging insurrection which, as Lewis knew, was never quite absent from the enslaved community on the estates.[9]

No slaveholder, based on Lewis' decision, could simply pretend as if this information about slaves as agents of sudden and violent change through unrest, if necessary, was not present. One such outburst erupted all of a sudden on March 16, 1816, on a property that was always otherwise calm: Martin's Pen in St. Elizabeth, which was owned by Lord Balcarres. Slaves at this property, Lewis also noted, were treated better than many other slaves in the parish, and even the island. Yet, the enslaved people had been busy planning a revolt for about a month, and while the overseer, described by Lewis as "an old man of the mildest character," who treated the enslaved people "with peculiar indulgence," was completely oblivious to these plans. Interestingly, the slaves had also made a song for the revolt, "Song of the King of the Eboes," as they named it. The slave who led the revolt was called by this name, "King of the Eboes," and even after he was caught and confined for trial, the other enslaved people continued to sing the song to praise him. They did not view the "King" or the revolt that he led as defeated, though, on the surface, it appeared as though it was to the slaveholding people. Besides, the King's two captains had "escaped to the woods," and most importantly for the enslaved people, the freedom which they used the song to enunciate was still theirs and still there.[10]

The story of this freedom is itself interesting. The song in which the slaves sang about it contained a reference to William Wilberforce. By then, everyone knew who Wilberforce was: the man who had orchestrated the parliamentary decision to abolish the British trans-Atlantic slave trade in 1807. However, what was not known by everyone was that Wilberforce was not a liberator. Instead, he was the messenger, the person that the slaves saw as one of only a handful who knew about their freedom. The slaves sang about Wilberforce for this reason only. This was not Wilberforce's song. He did not make them free. His role was to make the knowledge of slave freedom known to more people, to spread the message to especially the slaveholders of Jamaica; who, strangely and regrettably, as far as the slaves were concerned, were still denying that this freedom was real. The song was a declaration of war because of this denial. Slaveholders had taken this decision to their own detriment. And the sense in which the slaves saw themselves as free from birth was expressed in the many references to "God Almighty." The song thus said:

> Oh me friend, Mr. Wilberforce, make we free!
> God Almighty thank ye! God Almighty thank ye!
> God Almighty, make we free!
> Buckra in this country no make we free:
> What Negro for to do? What Negro for to do?
> Take force by force! Take force by force![11]

It is still mentioned in the scholarship that the slave revolts in Jamaica and the wider Anglo-Caribbean in 1816 were "triggered" by the "attitude of the plantocracy." The usual argument offered is that the slaves revolted in response to actions taken by slaveholders, as well as personalities in Britain. For example, it is almost the norm to state that, "coupled with the belief held by the slaves that emancipation had been granted by the King [of England] but was being withheld by their owners," the slaves were stimulated into action, and revolted. All kinds of elaborate arguments are then attached to this. One of the most longstanding and annoying is that, while "the humanitarian campaign" in Britain "gathered momentum, and as the planters displayed an almost inflexible reluctance," the enslaved people "became increasingly impatient and resorted to further types of action."[12]

Why are we still assuming that slave freedom was not always there? Enslaved people revolted before and after 1816, before and after decisions to abolish the slave trade, for example, to introduce Slave Registration in 1817 and the British amelioration policies in 1823; and they resorted to both hidden and visible forms of resistance throughout the course of enslavement. Tying slave freedom to actions taken in Britain or by planters in the colonies is to continue the narrative of the colonial regime. Enslaved people could think about freedom on their own, and they always knew that they had this freedom. Furthermore, if we take the example of the revolt at Martin's Pen, Jamaica, where the overseer was an old, accommodating, ameliorative type of man, the slaves on this property then had no reason to plan and execute a revolt. Yet, they did, in spite of the "kindheartedness" of the overseer, if we wish to put it in this way.

The slaves were delivering the information about their freedom in all kinds of ways. Lewis realized this and decided to act. He made a noticeable break from the intransigence of most slaveholders in Jamaica and elsewhere in the Caribbean. As an outsider, he was probably seeing things a bit clearer. However, he did not fundamentally change the terms under which enslaved people gave their labor power to the estates. Lewis did not abolish slavery on either of his properties. Instead, he tried to make insensitive slavery sensitive, a contradiction which, of course, backfired. The enslaved people knew that Lewis' biggest mistake was to think that they would settle for an amelioration of slavery. This was not acknowledging slave freedom, and Lewis paid for his own denial.

Changing Slavery to Appease the Enslaved

Enslaved people knew that they were shouldering too much of the planters' burdens. They knew that they were doing too much of the work that the planters needed to support their often lavish lives and those of their family and relatives. There was no reason for enslaved people to compromise when they knew that everything depended so much on the work that they did for sugar planters, especially. They knew that they should have rights, and they demanded these rights the same as anybody else did, and the same rights as the people who were not in slavery.

One of these, which Lewis came face to face with, was the right to choose their sexual partners, and to do this without harassment or reprisal from slaveholders. A female slave having sex with a white male on an estate, or in any other scenario, knew that she was not getting an advantage. Sexual relations of this nature placed severe strains on the female slaves, and the entire slave community for that matter. Slave families were affected in arguably some of the worst ways. We now know, based on research done by Higman and published from the early 1980s, that the slave family did exist, even while these enslaved people were not privy to the marriage contract solemnized by either Anglican clergymen or other duly appointed officials of state.[13] And the survival of these families in situations where they were not encouraged, as well as suppressed, was further indication of the work that enslaved people put into forming and maintaining family bonds. The family was one of their most cherished institutions, one that they practically fought for, and then fought to preserve. Cecilia Green has uncovered that the slave family was a very problematical issue that manifested in the fight over slave marriage, a struggle that Green investigates using the example of British Bahamas during the second decade of the nineteenth century.[14] Interrupting these slave family bonds, or denying the enslaved people the potential to form these bonds, due to any malfeasance, was unacceptable to enslaved people. Especially aggravating was when the females were inveigled into sexual relations with white males.

Further considerations of the slaves' complaints had led to Lewis' inclusion of stringent clauses to ensure that they were receiving everything that they asked for, such as adequate and regular medical attention. These were, in fact, among the most frequent of the complaints. Thus, they were among the most vital parts of Lewis' "new code of laws." He made preparations for the construction of a new hospital on one of the estates, and stipulated that the care of pregnant enslaved women should be the hospital's top priority. Of course, this can also be interpreted as an investment on Lewis' part. Slaveholders right across Jamaica and the wider Anglo-Caribbean were now in need of slaves with the capacity to generate more slaves. This became a fact of life because of the abolition of the slave trade.

However, as Higman has also shown, there was also no significant decline in Jamaica's slave population after the ending of the slave trade. Because of this, there was also no great need even to import large numbers of illegally captured or illegally purchased slaves in contravention of the act abolishing the slave trade.[15] And Higman is right. The busiest port in Jamaica, the one in Kingston, reported a mere twelve illegally enslaved seizures in 1816–1817. There was no apparent increase after this. Even the number of legal importations declined. Jamaica had no need to replenish its slave stock, no need for the slaveholders to be worried about pregnant female slaves not giving birth successfully, and no reason to encourage them with payments for successful births. Even the authorized or legal importations dropped dramatically from 16,261 in 1807 to a mere 3,364 in 1808. Furthermore, 9 percent of these imports in 1808 were shipped to other destinations. Jamaica was not the final port of call.[16]

Therefore, slave owners who might have seen an investment in promoting the health of pregnant female slaves, and even paying these females and the midwives who cared for them for each successful birth, were making these payments based on observations of what was actually taking place in the enslaved community. Enslaved people were having babies; they were replenishing their numbers without the help or encouragement of slaveholders. Every newborn slave was a new sign of hope for enslaved people, a new encouragement that enslaved people created on their own and for themselves. For while the parents of these newborns might not live to see slavery toppled, they would still live through their children. Promoting good health, especially among female slaves who were pregnant, was for slave owners protecting these females as well. The children that these women then had were indeed considerable bonuses that the slaveholders no doubt accepted and thought of in advantageous terms. But these were dangerous bonuses, too. They replenished slave freedom itself, and, in any case, any prospective future advantage that the slave owners hoped for from these births was never a guarantee. Lewis discovered this in time.

The 1816 slave code, passed by the Jamaica House of Assembly, its legislature, later in the same year that Lewis introduced his own "new code of laws," had also stipulated that payments should be made to slave women for each successful birth, along with half of these sums paid to the midwives who cared for these women.[17] All of this was based on the belief among planters in general that the island stood to benefit from what the enslaved people were doing. In other words, the generation of new slaves was not the slaveholders' doing; and besides, pregnancy became a source of income for enslaved women, money with which they and family members could then use to do a range of other things. The real implication of the decision to strengthen the stipulation that payments could be made for successful births was a sign of the nervous anticipation of the slaveholding people. Fewer slaves meant a loss of profits earned previously. However, a larger number of enslaved people also meant a growth in the demographic predominance of the enslaved. Slaveholders were investing in the potential for their own destruction, and enslaved women were earning money from this in the meantime.

Slave laws were designed to immobilize and control the enslaved. This same conception was rehashed in the 1816 slave code. The slaveholders, ironically, considered this new slave code the most forward-thinking legislation enacted for enslaved people in Jamaica up to that point. They were probably right, but not for the reasons that they had in mind. This new slave code, like all of the previous ones, represented a new realization of the fears of the slaveholders, their inability to dominate, demobilize, and control enslaved people. A slave code was necessary because slave owners knew that on their own, they could not control enslaved people. They needed the support that the law could give to their attempts to fashion a perfect system of slavery, one in which domination was not a goal, but a reality. Nevertheless, the legislation, when enacted, also rehashed all of the old trepidations of slave masters, and they never gave thought to the fact that many enslaved people could not read and write, the laws were of little, if any, real consequence to them. These laws were always about slaveholders and their choices, the need for self-assurance, the need to feel that they were in control.

The slave laws enacted after Tacky's revolt in 1760 are very informative. The 1816 slave code was literally trivial in comparison to this one in terms of the fears of the slaveholding people that the previous laws enunciated. Signified by the 1760 laws was the profoundness of the transition that had been quite literally forced upon the slaveholders. Those laws were passed in direct response to Tacky's attempted revolution. Slave masters thought that they had to act fast, and they did. They used the new laws passed at that time to execute an immobilization of every enslaved person on the island. The fears were indeed widespread. No liberties granted previously could continue. All slaves, in one way or another, had to be made to see that what Tacky did was reprehensible, and there would always be consequences. Thus, the laws had revitalized the stipulation that slaves could only leave estates if they were issued tickets by overseers or by some other white person in charge. Further bans were imposed warning slaves not to assemble for any reason, especially after sunset, not to blow shells or horns, interpreted by slave masters as ways the slaves used to communicate with other enslaved people from far away. Even free blacks and coloreds faced new restrictions. They now had to wear blue crosses on the right shoulder of their clothing as marks of identification. Otherwise, it was assumed that they were slaves, who were likely attempting to run away.[18]

Lewis' experiences on his estates were not unique. Every slaveholder was forced to reckon with the power of slave freedom, and the slave codes enacted at various points during the age of slavery represented parts of this reckoning. For Lewis, the matter of slave punishment was one of the thorniest issues he himself faced. He had to contend with this however unwillingly. Enslaved people complained about the use of the cart whip to punish them, but also other forms of chastisement. Stating the cruelty which went into these myriad forms of punishments, they assured Lewis that if these practices continued, the estates would become more dangerous places for every one of his white employees. The enslaved people stated explicitly that whippings using the cart whip, in particular, were always unfair and unjust. These punishments were administered in response to acts which the enslaved themselves did not view as acts of resistance. Instead, they advised Lewis that these were assertions of their conviction that they were human beings who deserved better and fair treatment. After hearing many of these complaints, Lewis decided to completely abolish the use of the cart whip for any reason whatsoever. He also decided to prohibit all other forms of punishments until after twenty-four hours had passed. As Lewis said, he did this so that nothing would be done "in the heat of passion," which, of course, would further aggravate the enslaved people.[19]

In spite of all the good work that he has done, Higman has unfortunately contributed to the opposite view that "the choices made by slave-owning people" mattered more than the choices made by the enslaved. In his more recent work, where this view appears, Higman himself seems to have gone backward instead of forward. The view he has expressed here is not supported by the conditions in which the slave laws, for example, were passed, or the reports from Lewis, tendered upon visiting his Jamaican sugar estates. For Higman, the choices of slaveholders were *the* markers of the "mature slave society" that Jamaica had become by 1800, a society in which, as Higman adds, "slavery dominated social relations, with nine of every ten people enslaved."[20] This seems to be intended as a general description of the fact that Jamaica indeed had a slave system and one that had undergone significant change. However, the view Higman expressed does very little to explicate the contentious relations between enslaved people and slave-owning people that did not disappear even as slavery in Jamaica, to use Higman's term, reached maturity. Neither does Higman's perspective give us any good understanding of the impact that these changes toward maturity had on the choices that the slave-owning people made.

Choices are never made in isolation—this is the point. They are made from both convictions and interactions, though convictions are always more powerful than interactions in any scenario. Convictions drive interactions and their outcomes, and are themselves oftentimes the sources of the interactions in the first place. Slaveholders, for instance, believed that they were in charge of the slave society in Jamaica; however, when making decisions, they also reacted to what the enslaved people did. This is the central realization that runs through Lewis' journal. He came to the conclusion that even though he was a slave owner, his ownership was dependent on the feelings of the enslaved people toward the whole business of owning them. And they did not accept that they were owned, and expressed this to Lewis by informing him of the many objectionable horrors on his estates, and by forcing Lewis to implement the many changes that they wanted to see.

For Lewis' enslaved people, however, there were only modicums of fairness and justice in the stipulations in his "new code of laws." These were not satisfactory to the enslaved people; they did not relieve them of much, in their estimation. However, a start was made. Punishments, for example, would continue, but only after tempers were calmed and hopefully so that the punishments might now better match the infractions. What this signified, more than anything else, was that enslaved people completely rejected as old-fashioned the practices of disciplining and punishing them. This was not a way for Jamaican society to go forward into its future. Diana Paton's work on the prison complex in Jamaica has shown us that this view was far ahead of the view held by even the colonial government in the island. The state adopted the conservative stance: it had expanded the prison system to make discipline and punishment into spectacles of power, rather than even to rehabilitate inmates for re-entry into the society. Civil disobedience was interpreted in the most illiberal way possible, and was factored into the organization and rearrangements through expansion of the island's prison complex.[21]

Enslaved people, in the meantime, were introducing the idea that civil disobedience occurred for valid reasons. These were activities aimed at eradicating injustices. Even rehabilitation was therefore only necessary for the people committing acts of violence because they were of the view that they were slaveholders, that they could own other human beings. Challenging this impression, enslaved people showed a certain level of enlightenment, and exposed that this was occurring in Jamaica, that the slave society was really maturing, but in the sense that the enslaved people were the ones rejecting old practices, and that the changes which they were suggesting were in fact emanating from their choices, not those of the slave-owning people. The community that was assumed to be the very bottom rung of the society was showing that it really was not. This community was actively challenging the hierarchical structuring of the society, showing through their defiance that the light that was emanating from the bottom was the light that everyone should look toward. In other words, they were showing that the bottom was actually where the society's foundation was, and this bottom was where everyone should look for social advancements.

There was an actual instance when Lewis confronted this reality that the bottom of the society was where social improvement had begun; and that these improvements were taking place while slaveholders were trying to find ever more creative ways to conserve the unjust slavery system. When Lewis visited the parish and town of Port Royal in 1816, he was given more evidence of the slaves' code of morality: the ways in which enslaved people were seriously thinking through the problems of enslavement, and working out models for the society's complete and permanent redemption. Lewis was told, while conversing with a black coxswain in Port Royal, that "flogging would never succeed," and "kindness was the only way to make good Negroes." Planters, the coxswain added, should be made to understand that blacks "can think, and hear, and see, as well as white people" can, and that they "are wiser...than they were, and will soon be still wiser."[22] Lewis immediately felt a sense of optimism. He felt that he had made the right decision by crafting a new set of rules for his estates. However, the directive that the coxswain passed on to Lewis contained much more than indicators about the advisability of introducing rules designed to prolong the slave system. Actually, the coxswain spoke about the prospect of a free Jamaica in the near future. He added that this redemption of the society was already happening, slave freedom was real. The slave-owning people could either try to prevent it and fail, or they could accede to the slaves' wishes. Taking the latter option might give slaveholders the chance to protect their investments in the plantations and any other venture heavily dependent on the labor that the enslaved people had been providing.

Of course, none of this made it into Lewis' journal in any explicit way. He was still a planter despite his many pronouncements that he had taken a different stance on slavery. He was still very aware of his status as a white man as well, still conscious of the race, class, and gender hierarchies. Lewis was not yet at the point of completely diverting from any of those assumptions in response to the militant disavowals of these notions of superiority by the enslaved population. However, the manner in which Lewis articulated the story about his conversation with the coxswain was one of visible relief. He felt that at least he had started the necessary preparations for the future that the coxswain spoke about. Lewis realized that he would have to continue along the path of gradually conceding more concessions to the slaves, because the process that was underway would not end until slavery itself had disappeared.

Furthering Change: The Response of the Enslaved

There was also, in the final analysis, the matter of the slaves' response to Lewis' first visit. Despite the gratitude expressed by the slaves that they were "perfectly happy" and "well treated" because of Lewis' arrival, none of this, in the end, produced an increase in per capita production. Lewis expected this to follow his concessions to the enslaved people. He was their liberator, and he felt justified in expecting a reward. However, the enslaved people showed him quite the opposite. On March 25, 1816, five days before he left, Lewis checked the books and realized that sugar production on the estates had declined instead of increased. Reporting on this, Lewis stated that prior to arriving per capita productivity stood at thirty-three hogsheads per week. After his arrival, this "dwindled to twenty-three, and then to thirteen."[23] At first, Lewis was in total shock. However, afterward, he went through a rapid series of conflicting emotions: disappointment, rage, denial, and discovery.

Overall, what confused Lewis were all of the kind sentiments that the enslaved people had expressed in reaction to his arrival. These gave Lewis a great deal of confidence. They made him feel as if he was indeed the slaves' liberator. One slave at Cornwall had expressed his gratitude in this way: "So long since none come see we, Massa; good Massa, come at last." Later, Lewis visited another slave named Charles, an elderly man who had been hospitalized because his leg had been badly burnt. The conversation Lewis and Charles had in the hospital was long and amicable. Lewis felt that he had made a new friend in Charles. And Charles, for his part, took the opportunity to remind Lewis about his long service to the estate. Charles said that he knew Lewis' "grandfather, and his young massa, and the young missies, [and] his sisters." The conversation lasted for an hour. Lewis was even convinced that, as Charles chattered away, "he totally forgot the pain of his burnt leg." Previous to this, Lewis had expressed awareness of the slaves' knack for saying one thing, but doing another. One other slave named Nicholas, for example, who ran away repeatedly, had said this to Lewis: "It is not that I wish to go away, sir; it is only for the name and honor of being free, but I would always stay here and be your servant; and, I had rather be an under-workman on Cornwall, than a head carpenter any where [sic] else." After hearing this, Lewis wrote that it was "all palaver (in which the negroes are great dealers)."[24]

However, even this awareness did not prepare Lewis to predict that these same enslaved people for whom he had ameliorated conditions on the estates would repay him the favor with lowering their productivity. The first three phases of Lewis' emotional rollercoaster, upon seeing what transpired, were vocalized in the indictment that he issued when he called the slaves "perverse beings." However, he added one more vital piece of information and this was given during his discovery phase. Lewis wrote that he knew the slaves loved him "very well," but also that "they love themselves a great deal better."[25]

Lewis had written mainly about his experiences with the enslaved people on his estates. However, throughout, he reflected on conditions on other estates and in the society in general. In other words, Lewis did not have reason to believe that what he had seen on his properties were unique occurrences. The complaint from an enslaved woman named Nelly, who was at Friendship estate in the parish of Westmoreland, was one of the many other examples of similar acts of defiance that Lewis also gave. These all suggested that the slaves in general felt empowered even in situations where they were demeaned. Furthermore, as Nelly showed in her case, empower-ment was there even when punishment and other acts of brutality and sup-pression were absent. Enslaved people did not need anything external to resist enslavement; kindness or punishment did not matter. Nelly had gone straight to the magistrates in the parish capital of Savanna-la-Mar because she felt slighted. To her, this was more than a good reason for her to register her complaint. Nelly protested that she was mistreated, but the hurt that she felt was because the overseer had turned his back on her while she told him that she was ill.[26]

Most enslaved people positioned themselves to extract any advantages that they could from the slave world that they were in. Lewis indicated that enslaved people made choices of their own that slave masters could only hope to predict and contain. Commenting on one of these instances, Lewis expressed doubt as to whether any preacher of the Christian religion could actually convert the slaves on his properties, given the slaves' demonstrated inclination to make their own decisions. There was a great rush afoot at that moment to convert and baptized the entire enslaved population in the island, and the church of the state, the Anglican Church, had been lead-ing the charge in this endeavor. However, this gave Lewis no comfort; no conviction that Christian conversion would ever be possible if the slaves continued to refuse it. Lewis did not expect the Anglican clergyman, Rev. Edmund Pope, to do any better than the missionaries had done; and he had seen the abject failure of the missionaries with his own eyes when he visited Mesopotamia estate, where Moravians had been invited by the proprietors from since the mid-eighteenth century. Writing of his own estates, Lewis stated that he still thought "it right to give the Church of England clergymen full room for a trial of their intended visitations." If they succeeded he would be happy, but he was not hopeful. But the one thing he was not prepared to do was to waste any time inviting "the Methodists." He knew for sure that these particular missionaries would never succeed.[27]

Christianizing the enslaved was now state policy. For many years, the planters resisted this, but now the new dispensation was that conversion, especially in the state church, would produce indoctrinated and therefore passive slaves. This entire campaign was based on the belief of slavehold-ers that the enslaved were "stupid beings."[28] Writing about St. Vincent and Trinidad, Mrs. A.C. Carmichael warned that viewing the enslaved in this way was a really shortsighted undertaking. Nothing could be more wrong, based upon what she herself had seen in her two little corners of the British colonial world in the Eastern Caribbean. Her entire two-volume study was a sociological examination of the values and norms of enslaved people, in addition to similar reflections upon free blacks, free coloreds, and whites. Carmichael gave the work a title that would show this: *Domestic Manners and Social Condition of the White, Coloured and Negro Population of the West Indies*. It was first published in 1833, during slavery.

Among Carmichael's most valuable discoveries were the preparations for the ending of slavery that she observed among especially enslaved women. It is not surprising that she found enslaved women the fascinating subject. Aside from being a woman herself, enslaved woman demonstrated slave freedom in some of the most talented ways because of their capacity for keeping these activities hidden. Even when they did these in open the real intentions remained veiled. Enslaved women were simply artful in expressing slave freedom and this artistry was present in the clandestine character of these acts. One example given by Carmichael reveal that black women used every chance that they could to express familiarity with the latest fashions in Europe. They articulated a clear perspective on how free women should dress, but they would express this by either complimenting or criticizing what white women wore. In other cases they expressed interest in learning how to make similar dresses. None of this performance was ever shown as insolence or resistance in any way. Rather, white women were led to believe that these enslaved women envied them. However, it was clear to Carmichael that this was the wrong interpretation. She noted, for example, how she "was very much amused by observing what connoisseurs the negro women are of dress." But her amusement was not about joy. For as she added, "standing near me, at one time, I heard them criticize every thing [*sic*] I wore, both in the materials and make."[29]

Other enslaved women used kindness as a sort of backhanded slap. They brought food from their provision grounds to white people, usually masters who had fallen on hard times. In this way, these enslaved women showed that even as enslaved people, they had not lost their human compassion. Some of the plantations were indeed not doing well, as Carmichael indicated. The usual pomp and pageantry galas were events of another era. Enslaved women also used the expressions of kindness as an investment. It reminded these whites of their own humanity and that they should never lose this because of slavery. These acts reminded the whites that they were "kind benevolent owners of negroes," as Carmichael stated.[30] It was a powerful cue, the use of humane acts to reinvigorate humaneness, which was in complete opposition to the practice of slavery. What could come from these acts was potentially revolutionary. It could deteriorate slavery from within. It could erode the boundaries established on the basis of color and class. It could create a sense of oneness in societies whose divisiveness was a pillar of their slave systems.

Attitudinal change was the foundation of abolition. This is what Carmi-chael was observing. Lewis observed the same thing during his flagship visit to Jamaica's slave society. Social transformation was underway through this attitudinal change, and according to Lewis, enslaved people were the ones instigating the revolution. This transformation manifested when he himself introduced a "new code of laws" on his properties, banning old practices, encouraging humane interactions on the properties in light of the complaints submitted by the people who were supposed to be merely slaves. They were more than merely slaves, if Lewis is to be believed. They were people who had a sense of fairness, justice, and equity that no slaveholder had adequately expressed that he or she had up to that point. Ameliorating slavery was not justice, as Lewis discovered to his own dismay. It was only the beginning of a movement toward justice, and enslaved people had their own agenda as to where this movement should go in the future. They wanted unfettered improvement. Slave freedom was already a reality and only the slave-owning people were left to admit it.

Conclusion

Mary Turner discovered some of the same revelations in Lewis' journal in the correspondence of the proprietors and plantation records for Papine es-tate in the parish of St. Andrew, Low Ground and Salt Savannah estates in Clarendon, and Amity Hall estate in St. James.[31] Slaveholders who decided to change their approach to slavery based these decisions on interactions with enslaved people. For the most part, however, the changes that Turner brought to light were material adjustments that fell almost exclusively within the realms of working conditions. Lewis had revealed more. His journal contained qualitative discoveries about enslaved people's attitudes, values, beliefs, and norms. Carmichael came the closest to Lewis and in some cases even superseded him in terms of what she herself was able to see and analyze, based on her own sociological enquires into the lived experiences of the enslaved.

Together, however, these three studies show an abiding reality during the period after the abolition of the slave trade. This was that enslaved people were busy transforming the society to accommodate their awareness of their condition, to ensure the society adjusted to the widespread feeling amongst enslaved people that they were free people who regrettably were enslaved. The fact that Lewis was an absentee proprietor is also important because it showed that not all absentees were useless productions of the age of slavery in Jamaica and perhaps elsewhere in the Anglo-Caribbean. As one example of absenteeism, Lewis was, however, quite a valuable asset to enslaved people. He listened keenly to what enslaved people were telling him, and came to only one consistent conclusion: he needed to change how he went about the business of enslavement.

Slavery was undergoing deterioration within Jamaica. Assessing this erosion, however, requires the kind of close and sensitive analysis that Edward Brathwaite and other scholars since have been appealing for. These are the scholars who have placed a good deal of emphasis on what is now called the creole society model of the age of slavery. Creole society, as Brathwaite's famous book indicated, was under construction from before the nineteenth century. We must now see creole society as a manifestation of slave freedom, as the slaves' creation of a social model which went further than adaptations to a "new environment."[32] Slave freedom provided an alternative to the slave society of the slaveholders. Slave freedom was moralizing and therefore changing the face of enslavement. Studies on the creole society phenomenon have appeared in work done beyond the Caribbean. This only shows the presence of slave freedom in areas right across the enslaved world. Megan Vaughan's work on Mauritius is one of the more recent of these studies.[33]

Notes

1. Matthew Lewis, *Journal of a West India Proprietor*, Judith Terry, ed. (Oxford, UK: Oxford University Press, 1999 [1833]), 145–146.

2. Gilberto Freyre, *The Mansions and the Shanties: The Making of Modern Brazil* (Berkeley: University of California Press, 1963). See, especially, pages 3–25 and 26–56.

3. Richard J. Follett, *The Sugar Masters: Planters and Slaves in Louisiana's Cane World, 1820–1860* (Baton Rouge: Louisiana State University Press, 2005), 151–155.

4. Ward, *British West Indian Slavery, 1750–1834*, 194–195, 198–199, 272.

5. Mary Turner, "Planters Profits and Slave Rewards: Amelioration Reconsidered," in *West Indies Accounts: Essays on the History of the British Caribbean and the Atlantic Economy in Honour of Richard Sheridan*, Richard B. Sheridan and Roderick A. McDonald, eds. (Kingston: The Press, University of the West Indies, 1996), 249.

6. James Murcell Phillippo, *Jamaica, Its Past and Present State* (London: John Snow, 1843), 124–125.

7. Patrick Bryan, "Aiding Imperialism: White Baptists in Nineteenth-Century Jamaica," *Small Axe* 14 (2003), 140.

8. Phillippo, *Jamaica, Its Past and Present State*, 280.

9. Lewis, *Journal of a West India Proprietor*, 146. However, see, again, 145–146 for the full story.

10. Ibid., 139.

11. Ibid.

12. Bernard Marshall, *Slavery, Law, and Society in the British Windward Islands, 1763–1823: A Comparative Study* (Kingston: Arawak Publications, 2007), 224, 223.

13. Higman, *Slave Population and Economy in Jamaica*, 159, 172, 173. Also see B.W. Higman, "The Slave Family and Household in the British West Indies, 1800–1834," *Journal of Interdisciplinary History* 6:2 (1975), 261–287.

14. See Cecilia A. Green, "'A Civil Inconvenience?' The Vexed Question of Slave Marriage in the British West Indies," *Law and History Review* 25:1 (2007): 1–59.

15. Higman, *Slave Population and Economy in Jamaica*, 47, 181.

16. HCPP 1821 (61), VI.—Jamaica. Dated 2d September 1816. A List of Negroes Received from on Board the Transport Brailsford from Honduras, and Seized by David Macdowall Grant, Esq. Collector for the Port of Kingston, Jamaica, the 2d Sept. 1817, Jamaica, *Negroes. Copies of the Several Returns Annually Made by the Collector of the Customs in the Several West Indian Islands*, 19 February 1821, 80–81; Roderick A. McDonald, "Measuring the British Slave Trade to Jamaica, 1789–1808: A Comment," *The Economic History Review* 33:2 (1980), 254.

17. HCPP 1818 (433), An Act for the Subsistence, Clothing, and the Better Regulation and Government of Slaves; for Enlarging the Powers of the Council of Protection; for Preventing the Improper Transfer of Slaves, and for Other Purposes. December 19, 1816, *Jamaica, Further Papers Relating to the Treatment of Slaves in the Colonies*, 10 June 1818, 54.

18. G.W. Bridges, *The Annals of Jamaica*, Vol. 2 (London: Frank Cass and Co. Ltd., 1968 [1828]), 100.

19. Lewis, *Journal of a West India Proprietor*, 146.

20. B.W. Higman, *Plantation Jamaica, 1750–1850: Capital and Control in a Colonial Economy* (Kingston: University of the West Indies Press, 2005), 3.

21. Paton, *No Bond but the Law*.

22. Lewis, *Journal of a West India Proprietor*, 102–103.

23. Ibid., 141.

24. Ibid., 42, 58, 51.

25. Ibid., 141.

26. Ibid., 111–112.

27. Ibid., 113–114.

28. A.C. Carmichael, *Domestic Manners and Social Condition of the White, Coloured and Negro Population of the West Indies*, Vol. 2 (London: Whittaker and Co., 1834 [1833]), 66.

29. Ibid., 46.

30. Ibid., 66.

31. Turner, "Planters Profits and Slave Rewards: Amelioration Reconsidered," 232–252.

32. Edward Brathwaite, *The Development of Creole Society in Jamaica, 1770–1820* (Oxford and New York: Clarendon Press and Oxford University Press, 1978), vii, 306, 307.

33. Megan Vaughan, *Creating the Creole Island: Slavery in Eighteenth-Century Mauritius* (Durham, NC: Duke University Press, 2005), see 2 and 268.

CHAPTER THREE

~

Questioning Running Away

For a long time during the age of slavery in Jamaica, any black or colored person who could not prove that she or he was a free person was automatically assumed to be a slave. The 140 inmates shown on the list produced by the colonial government of Jamaica, and submitted to the Colonial Office, London, and British Parliament in 1823, flatly rejected the notion that black and colored people should have to prove their status as free people. They did not accept that they were enslaved, whether or not this was the actual case in terms of the legal definition of who was a slave. Furthermore, they outrightly questioned and rejected their classification as running away. This is the group that this chapter will examine.

However, there is no mention of this category of blacks and coloreds anywhere in the scholarship on slavery and/or resistance in Anglo-Jamaica, and perhaps neither the wider Caribbean nor the Atlantic world as a whole. Instead, there is the rigid acceptance by scholars of the categorization of "runaway slaves," and the further division of this into "temporary" and "permanent" runaways. These are shown by the research which has been done by Higman, Gad Heuman, Hilary Beckles, Kenneth Morgan, and many other historians.[1] In 1985, for example, the famous journal, *Slavery & Abolition*, published a special issue on runaway slaves entitled, "Out of the House of Bondage: Runaways, Resistance, and Marronage in Africa and the New World." Every one of the articles in this issue stands as a representation of the still current thinking on runaways from slavery in the Atlantic world. The interpretations that runaways were temporary or permanent and nothing else seem to be what everyone wants to accept about the slave. Each slave is depicted as viewing enslavement as the realest and most powerful fact of their lives, and the marronage that the slave embarked upon showed only an attempt to escape from this life either temporarily or permanently. The journal's special issue was even republished in the following year as a book for general trade to ensure that the interpretations went viral. It is probably worth noting that the original title was kept, *Out of the House of Bondage*.[2]

Since then, the wildfire has spread further afield. Everyone now accepts that the slaves viewed running away in the limited terms set by their enslavement. The 2005 publication, *Slavery and Resistance in Africa and Asia*, shows the application of this perspective to further places in Africa and even on to Asia. Worse, this book was published simultanuosly in Britain, America, and Canada.[3] In even more recent times, Kenneth Morgan's 2007 work regurgitates the views from 1985. In his own work, *Slavery and the British Empire: From Africa to America*, Morgan presents what is viewed by one famous professor of history, Stanley Engerman, as "An excellent introduction," which means it is an updated, comprehensive work, introducing historical thinking on a range of issues in the lives of slaves, including the famous running away.[4] However, running away is still measured using the institution of slavery, not the slaves' belief that they were really free people.

The most unfortunate problem is the generalization. The view that running away represents the enslaved people's "attempts to escape bondage through stealing away from masters," which exemplifies the generalization well enough.[5] This view depends far too much on the thinking of the slaveholders, or on the idea that marronage was an illegal stealing away from slavery on the slaves' part, and nothing more or nothing else. This is why one slave master in Virginia, Robert Carter, could even believe that he had the power to "cure many a negro of running away."[6] This was seen as possible only because running away was viewed exclusively as resistance to enslavement.

Running away by enslaved people has to be re-envisaged in the way that the slaves themselves saw it: as expressions of slave freedom, if we are to understand its importance to the enslaved people themselves. This is the only way that we can widen this demonstration of slave agency to include previously unknown categories, such as those enslaved or alledged enslaved people who completely rejected the categories of slave and running away. We now have a chance to make a new beginning, with seeing running away not in slavery terms, but in freedom terms. Running away was not done in response to slavery, whether these runaways were actually enslaved or not. It was not about coming *Out of the House of Bondage*, but about the assertion of the freedom that enslaved people always knew that they had, even in cases where they were truly enslaved. It was an illustration of their freedom using mobility, not the pursuit of freedom. Running away is how the enslaved saw themselves. It showed their actions had meaning, that their views were the ones that mattered to them.

A Problematical List

Even the updated and comprehensive slave code passed by the Jamaica Assembly as late as 1816, the one that was seen as the most ameliorative up to that point, chose to adopt the longstanding view of the slaveholders that running away was to be divided into "habitual" and "permanent" running away. However, this division itself was important. It was also a reflection of the slaveholders' fears about the powerful message that enslaved people sent whenever they resorted to either of the two types of running away. The slaveholders chose to identify these because of the trouble that these demonstrations of slave freedom caused for the entire system of slavery. The powerful message resonated in both, but the first of the two categories, it can be argued, had the most visible and troublesome of these displays for the slaveholders.

For example, the former category, the habitual runaways, was quite impressive in the strain that they placed on the planters, and even magistrates. Both had to contend with these enslaved people, who themselves wanted to temporarily but continuously remind slaveholders and everyone else that they were free people. They could do as they pleased, and they did do as they pleased by running away, and through each time that they ran away. Habitual running away was not a temporary reprieve from enslavement. Instead, it was the incessant illustration of slave freedom, delivered in such a way that it would also unceasingly remind slaveholders of its existence and starkness.

More than the permanent runaways could ever do, the habitual runaways were truly an annoyance to the slave-owning people. In other words, it was a constant way to remind slaveholders that enslavement was really artificial and really weak. It could be cast off, even overthrown, at any moment's notice. It was not the effective demobilization of enslaved people that slaveholders thought it was. The slave code of 1816 acknowledged this, too. It had to stipulate that for these habitual runaways, time spent in prison was a necessity. Anyone of them could be made to serve time in prison for up to "six months," or they could be transported off the island "for life." If they persisted with running away, this intentional assertion of freedom through mobility was too dangerous for the slaveholding establishment to ever ignore.[7]

The permanent runaways, on the other hand, were written off by slave-holders. They were permanently lost. Their freedom was real in the realest of possible ways. This loss was determined on the basis of the number of days that these runaways had been absent from the estates, for example. If they could not be returned to enslavement within "five days," they were consid-ered as lost. Since catching these runaways was also interpreted as a major triumph by the slaveholders, their confinement in the prisons, whether workhouses or gaols, could be shorter, up to a maximum of "three months."[8] Nevertheless, the need to use incarceration to discipline and punish even this category of runaways was a sign that they also spelled trouble for the slaveholding system. No form of running away was ever less than serious. Each was an annoying reality for the slaveholders to contend with in its own way.

The category that questioned the entire business of running away and enslavement was a completely different problematical feature of the age of slavery. Their protests also arose from the conviction that they were free people, but this particular demonstration of slave agency, or slave freedom, had absolutely no precedent. This is why it was never considered for inclu-sion in the slave codes. Planters and other slaveholders could not imagine that this was even possible, that people that they viewed only as slaves could ever challenge and even reject the very categorization that they were slaves. On top of this, they asserted that accusing them of running away was a flat out lie. This was an interpretation that required the compilation of a spe-cial list, and one that took time to check and process, putting the colonial government and its judicial system under duress, putting them to work on the enslaved people's behalf. These questioning runaways were attacking slavery from within, but also from new and a variety of special angles. This made dealing with them uniquely problematical for the slaveholders, as well as the colonial government. This was the kind of challenge that could not be ignored.

Already uniquely difficult, it was more aggravating to the social order be-cause it was also fundamentally a legal dispute. It turned what made slavery lawful against the system that these same laws supported. The law became the enslaved people's weapon of choice, since this was also one of the biggest weapons that the slaveholders themselves had. The courts' and magistrates' attention were commanded and were received. This was a judicial system created not to deal with slave freedom claims, but to enact suppression, especially when dealing with nonwhite people, who were generally and automatically assumed to be slaves. Even if these people who put such a tremendous and unprecedented strain on the legal system did not get what they wanted in the end, they were still victorious. Their conviction that they were free people was heard, discussed, and weighed. This was something that was worth celebrating.

When the Duke of Manchester (William Montagu), governor of Jamaica, submitted the list in 1823, although the number of persons on it was small in comparison to the overwhelming one-quarter million slaves in the island at that time, he was nonetheless motivated. This came from Manchester's belief that this list was symbolic of an important development.[9] It was connected to the amelioration of slavery, but it was also more than that. The British government had been proposing further measures for the amelioration of slavery in that same year. Colonies like Jamaica, with elected Assemblies, rejected the British proposals as impositions on their right to make their own laws. Colonies without Assemblies, such as Trinidad, had no choice but to accept the proposals, which were implemented as Orders in Council. Manchester was also keen on reforms, and especially interested in amelioration as a way to reduce the harshness of slavery. However, he shared the perspective of the Jamaica Assembly that amelioration was already underway in the colony. Little help was therefore needed from Britain. Furthermore, the slaves themselves were also ameliorating their condition, and the list which Manchester was eager to submit in 1823 was one piece of evidence of the slaves' amelioration endeavor, which the British authorities would benefit from knowing.

This is why Manchester was never silent about any act of violence against enslaved people that was brought to his attention. These represented the kind of intransigence that gave the wrong impression about Jamaica. As far as Manchester was concerned, every group in the island had now fully embraced the principle of amelioration. Among them were slaveholders and slaves alike. Slave owners such as Thomas Ludford were really just distractions from the norm, departures that needed to be censured as soon as these were detected. Ludford had murdered his slave named Cuffee in 1818. Not surprisingly, Manchester described this murder as "one of singular atrocity," and sent word to London that a summons had been issued under the hand of the attorney general of Jamaica for Ludford to be arrested immediately and tried for the murder of his slave.[10] Even the very idea that a slave could be murdered by a master was a sign of the new dispensation that Manchester supported. This was not the same Jamaica of the eighteenth century.

Manchester's list avoided altogether the use of the term "slave." The people on the list rejected the appellation, and out of acknowledgement of this, so did the governor's list. In any case, it was this same refusal not to accept the castigation as slaves which had prompted the creation of the list in the first place. The people named on the list simply did not accept that they were enslaved, even if it was later established that they were. So, instead of using the term "slave," the list identified the people as claimants or petitions who had communicated to the magistrates in several parishes that they were illegally captured and confined because of the even more illegal ascription to enslavement. This, the petitioners proposed, was an embarrassment not only to them, but for the colony as a whole. Steps therefore needed to be taken immediately to return them to their rightful condition as free people.

The neutral identifications used in the list also did not make any assumptions that these claimants were wrong or that they were lying. Instead, it was assumed that they had a legitimate case, especially in light of the abolition of the slave trade in 1807, which made it highly likely that illegally enslaved people were being imported into the island. This, on its own, was another declaration of the claimants that they had knowledge of the law and the rights which the law provided people who believed that they were free people, even if this was also not true in stringently legal terms. In the end, all of this complication had to be embraced in the compilation of the list, and the list was therefore given the following neutral but informative title: "Persons Committed to Gaols and Workhouses as Runaways, but Who Declared Themselves to Be Free."[11]

There is also no reason to speculate on whether this title was given careful thought. What was decided on came out of nothing but considerable discussion about the matter. When submitting the list, Manchester stated in his letter to Lord Bathurst, the colonial secretary in London, that he was now "unwilling" to allow "any further delay." The list had already caused them too much trouble, it had undergone enough deliberation, and it was time that the people in London knew about it. They had to see what was really going on in Jamaica.[12]

Revelations and Evaluations

On the list, there were some further revelations. As shown in the table below, this was not a matter that was occurring in every parish in the island. Nevertheless, it was interpreted by the colonial government of Jamaica as one that concerned the island as a whole. This is very important. Most of the parishes in Jamaica at the time had no records or had not submitted any records showing that the petitioners existed inside of their borders. Yet, the list was deemed important by the government. It was of sufficient importance to be deliberated by the executive in the island's capital of Spanish Town, and with a view to dispatching the information received to London. In addition, it was seen by the executive of the government of Jamaica as having a connection with the biggest legislative hurdle that was crossed in recent memory: the act abolishing the British slave trade. What the claimants on the list had done was simply phenomenal, and the executive branch of the colonial government expressed this quite well.

Since January 1, 1808, the claimants had been raising doubts about the effectiveness of the abolition of the slave trade. Any confidence that was expressed in the disappearance of this trade, either in Jamaica or London, was put into doubt by the claimants. The view that the act was a benefit to enslaved people was a British view. However, the question raised by the claimants was that if the abolition was so good, why was it that they were put into slavery? Ending the slave trade was supposed to end slavery for at the very least a proportion of the people who would otherwise be assigned to the category of slave. This was not goodness, only a move in that direction. Furthermore, as the claimants showed, it was a clandestine measure to continue enslavement and while giving the impression that something good and beneficial had been done. These claimants were protesting the very basis of British Enlightenment with respect to abolitionism. To them, abolitionism did not exist. If its existence was real, they would not be now castigated to enslavement.

The celebration of the abolition of the British slave trade was not an African celebration. African people and their descendants were still feeling the

Table 3.1. Persons in Jamaica Committed to Gaols and Workhouses as Runaways, but Who Declared Themselves to Be Free, since January 1, 1808 (submitted in 1823)

Parish	SU	UNS	UND	Total
Portland	5	1	2	8
St. George	29	23	10	62
St. Mary	2	1	0	3
St. Elizabeth	1	1	5	7
St. James	28	4	2	34
Westmoreland	0	12	0	12
St. David & St. Thomas-in-the-East	4	8	2	14
Total	**69**	**50**	**21**	**140**

Missing Parishes: Kingston, St. Catherine, Hanover, St. Dorothy, St. Andrew, Manchester, Trelawny, St. John, St. David, Clarendon, St. Ann, Vere, St. Thomas-in-the-Vale.

Legend: SU (successful petitioners who established that they were free); UNS (unsuccessful petitioners who could not establish that they were free); UND (undecided or the petitioners whose cases were still occupying the time of the courts when the list was dispatched to London)

effects of this false claim that the slave trade had disappeared, and that the effort to disestablish it had produced any vital step toward freedom. Freedom was already there in the form of slave freedom. The real problem enslaved people now faced came in the form of the effort to continue to undermine their freedom with legislation massaging British egos and doing nothing truly great. Nevertheless, all was not yet lost. There was still time to make the so-called abolition of the slave trade something that was worth celebrating. The claimants showed this and demonstrated how it could also be done.

It required a consensus on the matter of slave freedom. British authorities, those in Jamaica, as well as slaveholders, had to come to an agreement stating that enslaved people were free people, and the former were the ones frustrating the demonstration of this freedom. The real abolitionism that was needed was the abolition of the British and Jamaican social orders from the backwardness of viewing enslavement as a reality and one that was necessary. Enslaved people were far ahead in this respect. They already had a sense of the capital in morality. In this sense, the subjects of Christopher Leslie Brown's *Moral Capital: Foundations of British Abolitionism* should have been enslaved people, who alone were already at the stage where they saw that morality was also capital and worthy of humanity's investment in both tangible and intangible ways.[13]

Importantly, the claimants sent the Assembly scrambling to prove its adherence to the act abolishing the slave trade. In the same year that the list was dispatched to London, another list was quickly prepared and sent off to show "the Number of Slaves Imported under License, or Otherwise, since the 1st of January 1808."[14] And this list, after its arrival in London, was then placed as the first exhibit, or "(No. 1)," submitted to Parliament to show the happenings in Jamaica. Perhaps for the first time in a very long time, the Colonial Office was on the side of the Jamaicans. However, they, too, wanted to show that the claimants were not giving correct information about the island in terms of depicting it's adherence to the abolition of the slave trade. This was a serious undertaking for the Colonial Office. Any impression of abrogation of the abolition of the Slave Trade was also a poor reflection on the Colonial Office, under whose direction and management the colonies fell.

The list of importations, exhibit "(No. 1)," gave quite a detailed breakdown of the imported African people and their descendants to establish that most of these were not slaves illicitly captured and sent to the island in contravention of the abolition. The point was made that any illegal importation was known, and the figure for these was not great. It stood at a mere 1,028 between 1808 and 1811, for instance.[15] The existing scholarship on this matter has, in fact, confirmed these figures as representative of a serious commitment by Jamaican slaveholders not to import illegally enslaved people. Quite a good deal of work was put into producing these accurate figures, which would leave no doubt in anyone's mind that they were anything but accurate. Examining this issue, Higman has shown that no large-scale importation of illegally enslaved people was apparent during the post-slave trade period using figures that he could get from the Returns of Registrations of Slaves, which started in 1817.[16]

Even if the figures submitted in the first exhibit were not a true reflection of reality, the petitioners who were at the time in the gaols and workhouses should not have been the ones to make this known. This was the point that the Jamaican regime wanted to make without having to state it. Stating it was self-deprecation, but it still needed to be stated inexplicitly. The presence of the other list showing the claimants was already an embarrassment in itself, an embarrassment for the Jamaican government and slaveholding people. It showed that they were intransigent and lawbreakers. Adding to this embarrassment would simply be foolish.

It is however true that neither the Jamaican government nor the island's slaveholders could mask what some of the African and African descended people were doing to challenge notions upholding enslavement in the colony. The government took the stance of self-defense. Aided by the slaveholders in the Assembly, the government submitted other pieces of evidence reassuring British authorities that even the island's busiest port, Kingston harbor, had only twelve reported illegal importations of Africans and African descendants between 1816 and 1817. This was undoubted proof that the island, meaning the government and slaveholders, was hard at work with trying to live up to the ban placed on the slave trade. Yet another submission stated that there were as many as 16,261 legal importations in 1807 alone. The implication of this was that there was no necessity to import people illegally. Furthermore, new importations declined after 1807. In the following year, the number had dropped significantly to 3,364. Importantly, it was also added that 9 percent of these imports did not remain in Jamaica, but were reshipped to other destinations. Jamaica's need for newly imported slaves was dropping in any event.[17]

Strategies and Outcomes

Only two of the claimants on the list had recanted their petitions by the time that this list was prepared and sent to London. Most of the people listed remained committed to the task of showing the government that they were free people. One of the two who withdrew, James Williams, had "died a few days after."[18] Because of this, Williams' reason for recanting is suspicious. It is possible he gave up because he knew that he was dying, and at that point, nothing else mattered. Another plausible explanation is that Williams knew that he was enslaved under the terms set out by the laws of the slaveholders. This is not the same as saying that Williams admitted he was a slave; rather, Williams might have just accepted that the discovery that he was asserting his freedom in spite of what the law said would bring him more trouble than he was prepared to endure anymore. There was always another way to show that he was a free man. The one thing that is clear is that neither Williams nor any of the other claimants accepted slavery.

Thomas Nicol also withdrew his petition. In his case, it was either that Nicol was a *raconteur* as well, meaning that he made a skillful decision to lie to obtain acknowledgment of his freedom, or he was aware of conditions in the parish he was in, St. James in northwestern Jamaica. If by 1819, when Nicol submitted his retraction, his freedom was not already acknowledged, based on the parish trend, obtaining this acknowledgement might never materialize. However, it was not that the challenge facing Nicol was difficult; rather, it was easy. St. James had one of the two largest numbers of claimants on the list, and the second largest number of successful outcomes. Along with St. George, which had the highest number overall, these two parishes accounted for ninety-six out of the 140 claimants, and fifty-seven of these were successful. Nicol's time had clearly passed, a fact that he would have known. His lack of success by 1819 meant that it was more likely he would never see this success and would have to join the other four unsuccessful petitioners in the parish. Also, St. James was now quite used to handling these claims, and surely the level of scrutiny there was one of the greatest.[19]

The claimants who did succeed in any parish were described as having their freedoms "established."[20] On its own, this is an important word, which indicated that despite what the slave laws stated, the petitions submitted by these claimants were treated as serious enough to postpone any rash decision that they were really enslaved people. The word also showed that work had to be put into checking to see if these claims were false or true. In fact, it was the truth rather than the falsity that was checked. Ironically, the claimants had accomplished the unaccomplishable for most enslaved people. They were beneficiaries of the presumption of innocence until proven guilty. The burden of proof rested on the people who were calling them slaves. This slave freedom was eroding traditional treatments of enslaved people as always wrong, and therefore always having to prove their innocence, rather than the other way around. This demonstration of slave freedom represented a significant change in its challenge to this fundamental tenet of the slave system.

The fact that there were nineteen more successful outcomes than unsuccessful ones is equally significant. The general trend was toward success rather than failure. In this regard, also important is that the successes outnumbered by far the undecided cases. Among those undecided, twelve escaped confinement before decisions could be made. This suggests that they either felt that the court process was too slow or they were lying to have the courts establish their freedom. Either way, it shows the adoption of more than one strategy to obtain the acknowledgement of their freedom. This acknowledgement could also come from running away, and some of the claimants chose this route after testing the court system.

To use the jargon of the existing scholarship, if they were permanent runaways, then having the courts intervene further was now unnecessary. This appeared to have been the last resort of the claimants in general. Those who took this choice to run away permanently exposed the ineffectiveness of confinement. Even unsuccessful runaways made this known. Confinement did not kill their desire to have their freedom recognized. Running away was more than about *Testing the Chains*.[21] The chains were already broken even with just the thought of running away as an option, with each time that anyone ran away, and shown to be forever broken in the case of successful permanent runaways.

The Infamous Writ

There was one very intriguing case among the claimants. This involved four of them, John Turner, William Clark, Harry Royal, and Burnett Green. They submitted a joint petition under the writ of *homine replegiando* to have their freedoms "established."[22] This writ is today more frequently referred to as *habeas corpus*, and this is described as "The most celebrated writ in English law." The question is: how did the four claimants know this? By what means did they come to the knowledge of this "celebrated" English legal device, or who among them was the learned man?[23]

We have to assume that they had no lawyer. No reference was made to any of the claimants having legal representation. This would have been an important piece of information that Manchester would have wanted to communicate to London. It showed that the colony was doing something to assist enslaved people who had grouses with the system of enslavement. It was a way for the colony to expose its own effort to ameliorate conditions for the slaves. However, if a lawyer was defending the four petitioners, this would still not close the discussion. The question could still be asked: why this writ? Lawyer or not, the use of the writ shows a commitment on the claimants' part that cannot be understated.

However, I am more inclined to believe that they had no lawyer defending them. It was not usual for enslaved people tried in slave courts, as these came to be called around the mid-eighteenth century, to have lawyers representing them. Furthermore, the case of the four claimants, along with all of the others, were such unlikely cases that a lawyer was more likely procured by the slaveholders, on whom the burden of proof now rested. So the question still stands: how did the claimants know about the writ, and how did they know that it was applicable to their case? Somehow, they had acquired the knowledge, and possibly because one or more of them could read. Of course, we know that literacy can bring social power, and if present in this case, it did show this power in a very visible way. But also important, with respect to the use of literacy, is the follow up: the defense of the writ before the magistrate. This exchange, if indeed it happened, would add substance to the determination shown by the writ itself. Regrettably, the information just is not there. Perhaps it is, but for the discovery of another researcher.

However, the little information that is there can still be used to make an assessment based on a comparison with another case. There is certainly a good deal more knowledge about this other case. This is the famous Somerset case of 1772, which took place in England, not Jamaica. Nevertheless, James Somerset, an enslaved man, was equally convinced that his enslavement was illegal, was equally committed to gaining acknowledgement of his freedom. Somerset's case involved the use of *habeas corpus*, which the court accepted as a way to protect Somerset from further aggression and punishment by his alleged owner. The writ also placed the burden of proof on the slaveholder. Somerset benefitted from the fact that slavery was not practiced in England. He was freed on that basis, but the writ was the first step. The writ showed his conviction that the slaveholder had no power to punish or control his person. At its most basic, this writ was applied for and issued so that the person of Somerset could be produced in court and placed under the court's protection until the case was resolved. The writ gave the case a good deal of its importance, in addition to making sure that Somerset remained safe and alive for the resolution.[24]

The application the four claimants in Jamaica made for their own writ provided them with the same protection for as long as the case remained in court. It necessitated an actual trial, and we can assume this trial was done by a senior magistrate, as in the case of James Somerset, whose case was tried in the highest court in England, the King's Bench.[25] Of course, this also made the case a greater gamble for the claimants. It ensured careful scrutiny of their claim. But also, it gave the court system a good deal of work. Even if the case was resolved in favor of the slaveholders, there was still a small victory for the claimants. They had brought slavery to court, a real court at that, one normally reserved for cases involving free people, not persons assumed to be enslaved. Agency is best demonstrated whenever the stakes are at their highest.

The claim of the four petitioners is also interesting. Each of them claimed having "descended from an Indian."[26] This alone raised the stakes even higher. There was no Jamaican statute for this. However, the Jamaica Assembly, since it had jurisdiction over British Honduras (modern-day Belize), where Indians or Amerindians were, had passed a law from as early as 1741 protecting Amerindians from enslavement.[27] This law stated that no Amerindian could be enslaved after its enactment. The law originated not from abolitionism, but from the need to protect British interest in the logwood trade especially on the Mosquito Shore. Tensions over slavery, between Amerindians and British colonists, were endangering this trade. The law was revised once in 1776, with a further proclamation by the then governor of Jamaica, Basil Keith, that infringers would be dealt a more serious blow. The amended act increased the fine from £50 to £500 for any person who had enslaved Amerindians who were not born into slavery. Incarceration was added to the punishment, and for a period decided on by the magistrates, which meant it could be any amount of time.[28]

The presence of this law did not, however, make it any easier for people claiming freedom under the law to get the resolutions that they wanted. In Honduras, Samuel Potts had to wait until 1822, about thirty-five years, for a decision in his case. In the end, Potts' freedom was acknowledged, but not until he was "upwards forty years of age." It was established that his mother was indeed an Amerindian, which, of course, gave Potts Amerindian descent.[29] In Jamaica, it was even harder for claimants using Amerindian descent, since it was assumed that no such nonwhite persons were present in Jamaica. The risk taken by the four claimants was thus higher. However, the fact that the matter was taken seriously by the court indicates some amount of respect for the claimants' effort. Again, the question that needs to be asked is: how did the claimants know? How did they know about the law passed from 1741 and revised once in 1776? If indeed they were using this law, which the evidence indicates that they were since they claimed they were free because of Amerindian descent, which was not a Jamaican law, so, if indeed they were using this law, where did the knowledge come from? Again, the evidence just is not there to make a solid assessment. However, what is there indicates awareness and understanding that the law could apply to them as well. Enslaved people, operating from the principle that they were free people and enslavement was illegal, drew upon even legal devices to make this principle known and acknowledged by the social order.

Another case in Honduras, involving an enslaved woman, Bess Meighan, showed another dimension of the difficulty which was also very applicable to Jamaica. In 1822, Meighan petitioned for the recognition of her freedom on the basis that her "possessor" (another interesting word), Clarissa Paslow, had given orders for her, Meighan, to be "severely and cruelly beat[en]" and "confined in irons during the night." Paslow was summoned to court to defend actions. Her rebuttal was that Meighan was insolent and disobedient, accusations which Meighan herself did not deny. However, Meighan made the point that the punishment did not match the infraction, and on this basis, she should have her freedom established. Meighan's point was that cruelty disqualified slaveholders from possession of enslaved people. Furthermore, Meighan feared the reprisal now that she had brought Paslow to face the embarrassment of a court trial.[30] Any alleged enslaved person who did this, faced the same risk.

The slaveholders in Jamaica, however, had a special legacy of brutality toward enslaved people. The risk of reprisal was especially high in Jamaica. We need only reference Thomas Ludford, who murdered his slave Cuffee, and then made a hasty retreat from Jamaica to escape trial in 1819. Of course, there is also the infamous Thomas Thistlewood in Jamaica between 1750 and 1786. His brutality was especially pronounced, and included the rampant sexual exploitation of enslaved females.[31] Meighan's counterpart in Jamaica was Kitty Hilton. Hilton's case showed that enslaved people knew that they were not born in chains, and that there was so much and no more that they were willing to tolerate. Hilton's case is interesting too because she accused a clergyman of the state church, Rev. George Wilson Bridges, of ordering another enslaved person to beat her, during which Bridges even administered his own blows. Afterward, Hilton was locked up without medical attention. This matter came before the magistrates in St. Ann's parish in 1828, after Hilton escaped and walked an entire night to show the magistrates the gashes on her body.[32] At this point, her body was her site of resistance. She situated her resistance in the brutal effects of enslavement on her body. Her body was colonized, but then again, it was not. The "colonization of her body," to use David Arnold's celebrated idea, was used against the colonizer to expose the brutality that enslavement was.[33]

The special writ submitted by the four claimants showed a similar turn of events. The same system of laws used to support the system of enslavement was turned into a means of resistance in the hands of the enslaved. Nothing could show more clearly the absence of "social death." The idea that slavery was "social death" is Orlando Patterson's celebrated thesis about enslavement. However, Patterson was fixated on slavery; he was not examining closely enough the enslaved people themselves; and because of this, he also situated the appearance of freedom as a production of slavery, while the enslaved had been showing the existence of freedom even while they were enslaved.[34] Unfortunately, the case of the four claimants was unresolved when the list was prepared. Despite my searches, I could not find anything more on the case after that. Nevertheless, there is Hilton, whose challenge had some concrete effects, which manifested in visible ways the power of slave freedom. Rev. Bridges was relieved of his appointment as a justice of the peace in Jamaica.

Afterward, Bridges also fell into a more vicious cycle of recalcitrant brutality. In short, he became much worse. He made Hilton into a virtual saint, while Bridges himself, even while still a priest, became a literal monstrosity. His evil multiplied and was revitalized when he joined the Colonial Church Union (CCU) in 1832, as that organization's "Rev. 'Trooper'." This was the power of slave freedom displayed in the grossness that it forced upon some of the slaveholding people; the effect of slave freedom at the most intimate of possible levels. One newspaper made the point clearer by reminding its readers that Bridges was supposed to be one of the "servants of the Most High God."[35]

The CCU victimized Baptist and Methodist missionaries, whom the organization suspected of helping the slaves who had revolted in Sam Sharpe's rebellion of 1831–1832. The CCU threatened to "tar and feather" at least one missionary, and destroyed several churches and missionary meeting places across the island. There was a branch of the CCU in almost every parish. The violence was an epidemic, which had spread quickly like a wildfire. The British crown, all the way in England, had to issue a Royal Proclamation outlawing the CCU in 1833. However, during just a year of existence, the estimated cost of its destruction was reported by the missionaries to have reached £20,000.[36] The British Parliament, however, undermined both the damaged caused by the CCU and the influence that slave freedom had in stimulating this intransigence by revising the estimate of the missionaries to the much lower figure of £12,750.[37]

Conclusion

Both Richard Hart and Michael Craton have stressed the important point that enslaved people were victimized but they were not victims. In other words, enslavement did not diminish their belief in their freedom.[38] Enslavement did not shape the enslaved; it did not make them think of their condition as permanent and hopeless. If nothing else, being in slavery was viewed by enslaved people as a reason to ensure that everyone knew about their inalienable and indestructible freedom. This was the philosophical basis on which the claimants for freedom made their claims. Herbert Aptheker, examining slave freedom in the form of revolts in the American context, made a similar point from the early 1940s: slavery did not make the enslaved.[39]

The inheritors of this philosophical perspective were the claimants who used the system of justice in Jamaica to petition for the acknowledgement of their freedom. This was not resistance in the traditional limited sense of the term. These claimants did not acknowledge slavery and then resisted it. Instead, they flatly rejected the classification of slave and showed by running away, even after they were confined, their rejection, and their refusal to ever admit that slavery was authentic and could describe who they were. This view was not limited to just the 140 claimants examined in this chapter. It was seen in the conduct of Kitty Hilton, in Bess Meighan and Samuel Potts in Honduras, and in Cuffee, whose life was taken from him because of his refusal to act like a slave. Other enslaved people used schooling to expose their freedom and to make the point that they could take advantage of even systems designed for their indoctrination, and could transform these into the means to have their freedom recognized and sufficiently acknowledged. Slave schooling is the subject of the next two chapters.

Notes

1. Higman, *Slave Population and Economy in Jamaica*, 178–179; Gad Heuman, "Runaway Slaves in Nineteenth-Century Barbados," *Slavery & Abolition* 6:3 (1985): 95–111; Hilary Beckles, "From Land to Sea: Runaway Barbados Slaves and Servants, 1630–1700," *Slavery & Abolition* 6:3 (1985): 76–94; Kenneth Morgan, *Slavery and the British Empire: From Africa to America* (Oxford, UK: Oxford University Press, 2007), 129–130.

2. See Heuman, ed., *Out of the House of Bondage*.

3. See Edward Alpers, Gwyn Campbell, and Michael Salman, eds., *Slavery and Resistance in Africa and Asia* (Oxon, England: Routledge, 2005).

4. Morgan, *Slavery and the British Empire*, see back cover.

5. Ibid., 129.

6. Ibid. Robert Carter is quoted by Morgan.

7. HCPP 1818 (433), An Act for the Subsistence, Clothing, and the Better Regulation and Government of Slaves; for Enlarging the Powers of the Council of Protection; for Preventing the Improper Transfer of Slaves, and for Other Purposes. 19 December 1816, 65.

8. Ibid.

9. HCPP 1823 (347), (No. 5.) – List of Persons Committed to Gaols and Work-houses as Runaways, but Who Declared Themselves to Be Free, since the 1st of January 1808; with an Account of the Final Disposal of Such Persons, Jamaica, *Slave Population. Further Papers and Returns, presented pursuant to address, Relating to Slave Population of Jamaica, St. Christopher's, and the Bahamas,* 14 May 1823, 131–133.

10. HCPP 1818 (433), Copy of a Letter from His Grace, the Duke of Manches-ter to Earl Bathurst; with Two Enclosures. King's House, Jamaica, 21st June 1817, Jamaica, 259; and Copy of a Letter from the Earl Bathurst to His Grace the Duke of Manchester. Downing Street, 11th August 1817, 267.

11. The full title was this, as shown earlier in note nine (9) above: HCPP 1823 (347), (No. 5.) - List of Persons Committed to Gaols and Workhouses as Runaways, but Who Declared Themselves to Be Free, since the 1st of January 1808; with an Account of the Final Disposal of Such Persons, Jamaica.

12. HCPP 1823 (347), Extract of a Letter from His Grace the Duke of Manchester to the Earl Bathurst, Dated King's House, Jamaica, the 17th of March 1823, Jamaica, 14 May 1823, 5.

13. See Christopher Leslie Brown, *Moral Capital: Foundations of British Abolition-ism* (Chapel Hill: University of North Carolina Press, 2006).

14. HCPP 1823 (347), (No. 1.) – a Return of the Number of Slaves Imported under Licences, or Otherwise, since the 1st of January 1808; Distinguishing Each Year, and the Sex of the Slaves So Imported, Together with the Places from Which They Were Brought, Jamaica, 6.

15. Ibid.

16. Higman, *Slave Population and Economy in Jamaica,* 47, 181.

17. HCPP 1821 (61), VI. – Jamaica, Dated 2d September 1816. A List of Negroes Received from on Board the Transport Brailsford from Honduras, and Seized by David Macdowall Grant, Esq. Collector for the Port of Kingston, Jamaica, the 2d Sept. 1817, 80–81; McDonald, "Measuring the British Slave Trade to Jamaica," 254.

18. HCPP 1823 (347), (No. 5.) – List of Persons Committed to Gaols and Work-houses as Runaways, but Who Declared Themselves to Be Free, since the 1st of January 1808; with an Account of the Final Disposal of Such Persons, Jamaica, 133.

19. Ibid.

20. Ibid., 131–133.

21. I am referring here to Craton's *Testing the Chains.*

22. HCPP 1823 (347), (No. 5.) – List of Persons Committed to Gaols and Work-houses as Runaways, but Who Declared Themselves to Be Free, since the 1st of January 1808; with an Account of the Final Disposal of Such Persons, Jamaica, 133.

23. E.R. Hardy Ivamy, *Mozley and Whiteley's Law Dictionary* (London: Butter-worth and Co., 1988), 211.

24. TNA 548, The Case of James Somerset, a Negro, on a Habeas Corpus, King's Bench: 12 George III, A.D. 1771–72, *Howell's State Trials, Vol. 20,* Cols. 1–6, 1771–72, 82.

25. William Bohun, *The English Lawyer: Shewing the Nature and Forms of Original Writs, Processes and Mandates, of the Courts at Westminster* (London: E. Nutt, R. Nutt and R. Gosling, 1732), 295.

26. HCPP 1823 (347), (No. 5.) – List of Persons Committed to Gaols and Workhouses as Runaways, but Who Declared Themselves to Be Free, since the 1st of January 1808; with an Account of the Final Disposal of Such Persons, Jamaica, 133.

27. HCPP 1823 (457), Appendix No. 2, Copy of an Act of the Legislature of Jamaica, Dated 1741, Anno Decimo Quarto Georgii II, C. VI, An Act for Recovering and Extending the Trade with the Indian Settlement in America; and Preventing for the Future Some Evil Practices Formerly Committed in That Trade, Jamaica, *Slaves at Honduras, Correspondence Relative to the Condition and Treatment of Slaves at Honduras: 1820–1823*, 16 June 1823, 52.

28. HCPP 1823 (457), Appendix No. 3, Copy of Sir Basil Keith's Proclamation, Dated 29th December 1775, Jamaica, 52; Appendix No. 4, Copy of an Act of the Legislature of Jamaica, 1776, Anno Decimo Septimo Georgii III, C. XXIII, An Act to Explain and Amend an Act, Intituled an Act for Recovering and Extending the Trade with the Indian Settlement in America, and Preventing for the Future Some Evil Practices Formerly Committed in That Trade, Jamaica, 53.

29. HCPP 1823 (457), Appendix, No. 7, Proceedings of the Board of Commissioners of Indian Claims, with the Correspondence and Documents Appertaining to the Same, Honduras, Jamaica, 59.

30. Ibid., 69.

31. The best works on Thomas Thistlewood are: Burnard, *Mastery, Tyranny, and Desire*; and Douglas Hall, *In Miserable Slavery: Thomas Thistlewood in Jamaica, 1750–86* (Kingston: The University of the West Indies Press, 1999).

32. HCPP 1830–31 (231), No. 1, Copy of a Dispatch from Sir George Murray to the Earl of Belmore, Downing-Street, 23rd October 1829, Enclosures 2, 3, 4, Great Britain, Jamaica, *Copy of any information which may have been relieved from Jamaica respecting an Inquiry into the TREATMENT of a FEMALE SLAVE, by the Reverend Mr. Bridges, Rector of St. Ann's, in that Island; with the MINUTES of EVIDENCE taken by the MAGISTRATES on that occasion, and the result of the Inquiry*, 10 March 1830, 3, 4, 5.

33. See David Arnold, *Colonizing the Body: State Medicine and Epidemic Disease in Nineteenth-Century India* (Berkeley: University of California Press, 1993).

34. Orlando Patterson, *Slavery and Social Death: A Comparative Study* (Cambridge, MA: Harvard University Press, 1982), see especially pages 8 and 38–45.

35. *The Watchman and the Jamaica Free Press*, 28 March 1832, 8; *The Kingston Chronicle and City Advertiser*, 21 January 1833, page number unstated.

36. HCPP 1833 (540), Return to an address of the Honorable the House of Commons, dated 25th July 1832;—for, memorial and statement of the Baptist missionaries in Jamaica, *Baptist Missionaries, Jamaica*, dated 19 April 1833, 3, 4, 5.

37. HCPP 1834 (476), Estimate of the sum required to enable His Majesty to make a grant to the Baptist Missionary Society, and to the Wesleyan Missionary

Society, on account of expenses incurred in the erection of certain chapels destroyed in the island of Jamaica, *Jamaica Chapels*, 10 July 1834, 451.

38. Craton, *Testing the Chains*, 208, 209, 210. See also Hart, *Slaves Who Abolished Slavery*, Volume 2.

39. See Herbert Aptheker, *American Slave Revolts* (New York: Columbia University Press, 1943).

CHAPTER FOUR

~

Instructing the Enslaved

In this chapter, I challenge the longstanding view that no real system of education predated the 1834 abolition of slavery in Jamaica and other British colonies in the Caribbean. A number of scholars have expressed and retained this view. Perhaps the person who started it all was the historian, Shirley C. Gordon.[1] The revision is necessary to show that enslaved people had a formidable system of education, schooling, or "instruction," to use the term of the period, through which to work as they continued to demonstrate their freedom. The use of the term "instruction" appears in most of the primary or archival manuscript documents from the pre-abolition period in Jamaica. It indicates that education was defined in a limited way.

When contemporaries spoke of education, they were really referring to schooling for indoctrination. Today, we might see education as learning to foster progress individually and collectively, but we cannot use present-day definitions to determine what took place in the past. Progress itself was defined with reference to the continuation of slavery, and this was the purpose of schooling enslaved people. The use of the term "instruction" was deliberate. It was to indicate the way that education was perceived. It was seen as a way to promote domination under slavery, rather than as a route to liberation and social power. And this was the phenomenal obstacle that enslaved people were up against, which makes it more important to show the existence of the system. The presence of a system of instruction or education gave slave freedom greater importance in this arena. It is in this sense that I view the continuation of the claim of an absent system as a serious undermining of enslaved people's attempts to overcome and even overpower the effort to dominate them and make them truly into slaves. The next chapter examines the other part of this phenomenon of the importance of slave education to slave freedom: the agency shown by enslaved people who were actually inside of the school system.

Education can be a site of liberation, or it can be the source of a more efficient way to exercise the collective domination of any group of people. Classical education scholarship by scholars such as Paulo Freire have shown the existence of a *Pedagogy of the Oppressed*, for example, which presents itself as the route to social power but in effect condemns the poor of society to submissiveness, subservience, and flat-out ignorance.[2] Professor of education, Norrel A. London, was clear that this was the purpose of education systems in British West Indian colonies even up to the last days of colonial rule. These systems were constructed, London argues, to "teach students those values, attitudes, and beliefs which were to make them hard working and responsible hewers of wood and drawers of water," and I might add, nothing more.[3] Recently, Caribbean educationalists, Benita P. Thompson, S. Joel Warrican, and Coreen J. Leacock, have reexamined the continuation of the colonial legacies in Caribbean education, which they call "the pervasive influence of the past," seen most clearly in modern-day practices such as "the hierarchical structure of secondary schools," examinations still in use that function mainly to support this hierarchy, and the equally prejudicial exercise of "streaming" within schools.[4]

Education in this respect serves only the social order and does so by propping up the status quo and by diminishing the critical thinking skills of the masses inside of the school system. This chapter is about the early attempt to create just such a system of education in colonial Jamaica. Its appearance during the age of slavery was the first sign of the realization that education was viewed as a form of domination. Handing the system over to the churches, especially the notorious Anglican Church, which was traditionally viewed by slaveholders as the church of the planters, also made sure that the agenda of the education system was domination and mainly through the use of Christian knowledge and indoctrination. In other words, it was designed to keep enslaved people in slavery, never to liberate them in mind or in body.

M.K. Bacchus argues that the slaves were trained to become obedient, passive, and dutiful Christians; in other words, the kind of people who would work for their slave owners no matter what.[5] This opinion of education was attractive for obvious reasons. First of all, any kind of education gave the impression of ameliorating slavery, making the system better for the slaves. But secondly, this same education could be used to strengthen the slave system. It was, in other words, a win-win situation for slaveholders. The problem that they would soon encounter was that they never gave thought to what enslaved people might do to and within the education system. Enslaved people benefited from the planters' view that they were, as Carmichael so ably expressed, "stupid beings."[6]

Also worth bearing in mind, as you read this chapter, is the turn in Freire's scholarship in the later years. He begins to assess the students in the schools in a more serious and substantial way, in, for example, *Pedagogy of Hope: Reviving Pedagogy of the Oppressed*, and *Education for Critical Consciousness*.[7] These revised works take the perspective, among others, that the world around you is under your control even as this world might be attempting to control you. Classical sociological thinking provides some direction where this is concerned. Herbert Blumer, for instance, whose perspective has been labeled as "symbolic interactionism," notes that social institutions can, to some extent, determine behavior in the classical structuralized interpretation of things. However, people react to the symbols put out by these institutions, and reactions are the result of interpretive behavior. In other words, a "process" involving exchanges is always afoot, one in which "symbols" become sites of resistance even while their intention is also control.[8]

There is now quite a good deal of scholarship interrogating the so-called proceedings of domination to show the reactions of the dominated. None of this scholarship assumes that dominated people are ever truly dominated. James C. Scott's work is quite famous, *Weapons of the Weak*, in particular, in which Scott gives details about the underhanded and silent ways in which people protest against and resist domination, and how effective this resistance can actually become. Scott has fully adopted the view of E.P. Thompson, whose contribution to "the historic turn" in 1971 led to one of the most enduring conceptualizations of modern history-writing: the "Moral Economy" of the oppressed. This, in short, proposes, or rather shows, how poor people understood and responded to the institutions that made them poor, and through openly violent and nonviolent resistance, made changes to these institutions. Jamaican scholar, Obika Gray, has employed both the moral economy concept and the notion of hidden resistance to argue that even in present-day Jamaica, its poor people might be demeaned, but they are never actually disempowered.[9]

How Do We Teach These Slaves?

The Anglican Church made the religious teaching of the enslaved its main focus in the amelioration period in Jamaica, which began around the 1780s. However, the effort to "instruct" the enslaved, as it was called, really got fully underway after the abolition of the slave trade in 1807. Planters and other slaveholders had realized and accepted that instruction was one way to ensure the enslaved people remained in slavery and produced for them future dutiful slaves. With abolition enacted, this became a more urgent necessity. Nevertheless, as with all systems, time was needed for the endeavor to show the success that was intended. In other words, the system of instruction that was under construction from before began to bear fruit, as far as the slaveholding observers were concerned, in the 1820s. One of its advocates, and the person who has left us some of the most vital information about the system, is the Anglican bishop of Jamaica, Christopher Lipscomb.

Lipscomb was Jamaica's first local bishop in the sense that he came to live in Jamaica. Before this, the bishopric of London had imperial control over the Anglican Church in Jamaica and in other British colonies in the Americas, a situation that had existed in the Caribbean diocese since 1681. However, with the appointment of a local or resident bishop, all of the initiatives of the church in the colony of Jamaica received a boost. The bishop became the resident monitor of the educational enterprise, for example. His reports were based on firsthand observations and reports received from the various clergymen in the parishes, from planters, and from church curates as well as catechists of the Church Missionary Society (CMS). We will get to the curates and catechists later on.

Lipscomb arrived in 1825, and immediately took a keen interest in the matter of slave instruction in Jamaica and other colonies within the Jamaican diocese: British Honduras, Cayman, and Bahamas. By 1831, looking back at what was accomplished in Jamaica, Lipscomb had no reservations about using these keywords to describe what he had seen, and knew to be true: "sound" and "system."[10] For Lipscomb, British culture was incredibly superior and too far up on the scale of "civilization" for him to ever assume that enslaved people would, or even could, resist the instruction in Anglican doctrine and principles that they were being offered. Furthermore, the mere fact that the enslaved were now privy to instruction marked a significant turn in the system of slavery itself. In other words, enslaved people now had fewer reasons to complain about slavery being a harsh and brutal system. Slaveholding people were now almost completely on board with the educational system. And why not? Lipscomb asked, already knowing the answer.

The system of instruction that Lipscomb had seen was essentially fixated on transitioning enslaved people into hegemonized individuals. In other words, the work that they did as slaves would now be seen by them as *their* lot in this life. Hegemonic control, as the scholarship has told us, depends on the victims' acceptance that the control that they are under is right, just, and beneficial to them. (The discussion on hegemony is voluminous, and I will deal with some of it in greater detail in chapter six, where it applies more.)[11] They—the hegemonized—never see hegemony as a mechanism designed to undermine their potential, nor to control them in any way. They are too simpleminded for these kinds of complicated thoughts. All that they can see is the interest in making them literate and thus better. This was classical slaveholder thinking; reformed, of course, to suit the new dispensation that instruction, mainly in Christian knowledge, was not incompatible with chattel enslavement.

Lipscomb arrived with the baggage of the British Enlightenment inside of his head. This Enlightenment advertised itself as the best way forward for humanity, but not all of humanity, only those who were white. Lipscomb was, because of this, a cultural imperialist in every respect. He felt that the Anglican Church was the best church, and the only church that could truly benefit enslaved people, and for that matter, the whole of colonial Jamaican society. Lipscomb also had a hierarchical structure well established in his mind. In this structure, enslaved Africans, and their descendants, colored, or not so "privileged," were at the very bottom of the social pecking order. But all was not lost for them. As a religious man, deeply religious I suspect, Lipscomb had a clear view as to how enslaved people could redeem themselves. Protestant Christianity offered them this light toward self-redemption. Protestantism was their route to betterment, but they would have to still accept enslavement while on this earth, and they would get their redemption as a reward in heaven. I could find no reference in Lipscomb's letters about instruction relieving the enslaved of slavery. This, if ever this could happen, it had to be done by enslaved people themselves out of their own longstanding conviction that they were free people, and slavery was the monstrosity that they were up against.

In terms of his commitment to Protestantism, Lipscomb was no different from all of the other British preachers who had arrived in Jamaica, starting from the mid-1700s. Even while speaking against the conditions of slavery, as some did, they remained more focused on improving public morality than on eradicating enslavement. This was the Baptist missionary James Phillippo's stance. In his 1843 *Jamaica, Its Past and Present State*, Phillippo describes Jamaica as a rampantly immoral place, but he did not go so far as to advocate emancipation. The Moravians never did either, and even owned "thirty to forty slaves" at one point.[12] Not until slavery was already abolished and Phillippo, for his part, could see no benefit in the apprenticeship system which replaced it, did he mention emancipation as the proper alternative. At no time before or after this did Phillippo see slave freedom as a reality or even as a prospect. He viewed apprenticeship, the imposed transition period in 1834–1838, as a stupid compromise because it "was only a *modification of slavery*—a substitution of half measures for the whole (his italics)."[13] This was not an antislavery stance. It was anti-apprenticeship.

Lipscomb was also not motivated by thoughts about slave freedom or emancipation. His motivation for supporting the effort to give the slaves instruction came from his professed belief in the beneficial effects of exposure to English culture. Lipscomb was keen to always point out that instruction was succeeding because of the combined effort put into the endeavor by the clergymen, curates, catechists, and slaveholders. Addressing this concerted indoctrination, Lipscomb noted that, on one occasion, he could see very clearly that the enslaved had acquired the necessary "quiet and civilized manners" that were taught to them. Of course, as Lipscomb added, this was "highly creditable to both the proprietors and the teachers." The teachers, meaning catechists, were particular instrumental, particularly useful, because of their own decisions to use a "kind, humane and enlightened method of instruction" when teaching the slaves.[14] There was no room in this kind of view for any admission of the enslaved people's points of view or capacities. As far as Lipscomb was concerned, any progress made in slave instruction was due to the teachers, and to the support that they received from slaveholders, the Anglican Church, and the church's associate, the CMS. The enslaved were indeed too stupid, as Lipscomb's fixation on the teachers implied, to do anything for themselves while interacting with the effort to build an education system during slavery.

Sensitivity to enslaved people was not one of Lipscomb's noticeable qualities. He wrote favorably about enslaved people in the schools, but always to make the point that the church had undertaken a massive enterprise in the form of slave instruction. One important point that came out of Lipscomb's observations is the rudimentary character of this undertaking. This did not, however, as Lipscomb indicated, make the effort any less like a system or any less systematic. Lipscomb was expressing the same view that even educators in the present-day know to be true: there is no such thing as a perfect education system. However, this does not disqualify whatever is in place from being classified as a system. As late as 1984, Jamaica's education system was criticized because its "existing science curricula, although laudable in their intention and in their carefully formulated aims and objectives, when put into operation in the schools falls far short of conveying to the pupils the real nature of the scientific enterprise."[15] All educators know that education will forever have challenges, and indeed should always be under construction. However, this is not a disqualification in any way. Rather, it shows acknowledgement that the system can and should indeed get better. Lipscomb delivered this same message when he highlighted the work that was already done. The problem with Lipscomb was his imperial perspective on education in the colonial environment. He was there to promote British cultural superiority, and he did not appeal for the immediate emancipation of the enslaved.

The 1816 slave code had stipulations for the establishment of formal instruction of the enslaved in Jamaica "in the principles of the Christian religion."[16] Most noticeable here is the promotion of Christianity through instructional indoctrination. However, linking instruction to the church—in this case, the church of the state—signaled that instruction was seen as important and was therefore prioritized. The church was always one of the significant arms of colonial governance. Even while the sugar planters rallied against the clergymen who promoted slave instruction from as early as the late seventeenth century, this did not mean that they also objected to the church's presence. This opposition came about because of the planters' wish to control the church, and this struggle appeared most often at the parish level, where the clergymen were appointed as members of the vestries. These were the bodies which administered the public affairs of the parishes. In fact, it was stipulated that none of these vestries could hold a meeting without the presence of the clergyman.[17] Tying instruction to the church was done as a safety measure consistent with the thinking that instruction should become part of the overall governmental administration of the colony. The immediate administrator of the instructional system would be the bishop, but the supreme headship was at the governor's office in Spanish Town. Regulating the entire system were the laws passed by the legislature, the House of Assembly. These started with the slave code, where all matters pertaining to enslaved people were relegated.

A brand new legislation also passed in 1816 took notice of the inadequacies of teaching. A new group was added to form the first set of regular teachers of the enslaved. These were known as curates. A curacy did exist from 1813, but their mandate was different. At that time, they were mainly the clergymen's assistants, there to aid in the Christian conversion and baptism of enslaved people.[18] They provided some amount of instruction to the enslaved to prepare them for conversion and baptism. However, with the 1816 legislation, a special new group of curates was created. These were to provide instruction prior to conversion, but also afterward. The aim was to continue the indoctrination of even converted enslaved people. It was assumed that this was needed in order for the indoctrination to become successful. Much importance was attributed to the work of these curates. Prior to this, curates were paid a salary of £100 annually. The new curates appointed under the

1816 act were paid £136 per year. The salary increase was intentional. The goal was to indicate that the government, and the church, viewed the services of the new curates as important and indeed crucial. Adding to this pressure was the stipulation that only "unavoidable" events should occasion any curate's nonperformance, and these were listed: illness, old age, or death.[19]

In the meantime, no nonconformist church—Baptist, Methodist, Moravian, for example—received any similar encouragement from the government. State support was reserved for the state church and its workforce: the clergymen and curates. State support for slave instruction was present, but not for every church group offering this instruction. The state's intention was to ensure that the state church held a monopoly over the education that was provided to the majority, the enslaved. Instruction was viewed as too serious an undertaking for the social order to give official support, or even acknowledgement, to church bodies that did not conform to the principles and doctrine of the Anglican Church, the church of state.

In fact, the reverse was still happening. Nonconformist churches were still facing suppression in Jamaica, both from individual slaveholders, who distrusted them as abolitionists, and the vestries and other parish bodies, which had enacted suppressive ordinances. A report submitted to Parliament in 1815, for example, referred to this presence of one of these ordinances, which had been passed by the Common Council for Kingston from 1807. Only the name of this ordinance is needed to show its intention: "an Ordinance for Preventing the Profanation of Religious Rights and False Worshipping of God, under the Pretence of Preaching and Teaching, by Illiterate, Ignorant, and Ill-Disposed Persons, and of the Mischiefs Consequent Thereupon." A £100 fine was imposed on preachers or teachers who did not have a license to preach or teach in the city and parish of Kingston. In addition, they could be jailed.[20]

In 1817, the Governor of Manchester stated with all confidence that the Anglican Church was well ahead with providing the enslaved with regular instruction in the teachings of the church and Protestant knowledge. Manchester was understandably happy to submit this report since it was a good reflection on his administration. It showed that the colony was undergoing change, which in Manchester's view was change for the better. The education of the enslaved was seen as part of the amelioration of slavery, and Manchester, reporting on the change, also credited the clergymen whose "pious labors," he noted, were "indefatigably exerted to the conversion of the slaves to Christianity."[21]

In his 1823 A View of the Past and Present State of the Island of Jamaica, John Stewart reported that the colonial government of Jamaica had set aside

£10,500 per annum for slave education.[22] Each of the twenty-one parishes by then had at least one curate assigned to providing instruction to enslaved people on a regular basis, at least once a week and ususally on Sunday after church. Of course, only those enslaved people who were attending church regularly would receive this instruction. But two considerations must be made where this is concerned. Firstly, the provision of instruction was a separate issue from school attendance, and secondly, nonattendance or irregular attendance showed in many cases that enslaved people themselves were making decisions about their presence at church for schooling. This was symptomatic of their agency. However, it had nothing to do with the instructional provisions which were actually in place.

The Assembly saw the two issues as separate. It did not express any concern about attendance. Its focus remained on the money it now had to spend on what was clearly a public education system. This was a new venture for assemblymen. Worse, the money that was being spent was escalating. Education was expanding and so was the cost of funding it. By 1825, a report indicates that the curates, who were at one time paid £136, were now getting a whopping £500 annually.[23] Adding to the aggravation this created among assemblymen was the realization that the govenrment was also spending the same to pay the clergymen and sometimes more in individual cases. This was a frightening reality. It suggested the worst of the assemblymen's fears: that the church was positioning itself to take over the colony, at least in terms of the budgetary allocation to this body and its associates.

Frightening, too, was that slave instruction was responsible for a good portion of this expenditure. Enslaved people, even though the goal was their indocrination, were now costing the colony. The whole idea of enslavement was to make money through the slaves, not for the slaves to then take back a good proportion of this money and because of an initiative that might very well make them independent of the slaveholding people. By 1831, it was clear that slave instruction was now a major budgetary allocation of the Jamaican government. In that year, the salaries of the curates accounted for £8,000 of government spending, while clergymen were receiving £11,718 for their own incomes. Together, this was £19,718.[24]

This was not cause to be frightened, according to John Stewart. Rather, these showed the "positive enactments" that had led to the creation of the curacy, for example. Furthermore, the money spent was only part of what was taking place. A whole host of encouragements were in place to motivate the teachers, namely the curates. Many took their teaching seriously because of "the prospect of being promoted in time to vacant rectories."[25] In this way, the church was promoting its own initiative, but it was also moving toward creating a more proficient and hopefully professional body of teachers. It was making teaching more attractive to candidates, whose performance, if acceptable, could lead to their appointments as clergymen.

Missionaries, English Movements, Jamaican Realities

I have stated before that the nonconformist missionaries received none of the governmental encouragement reserved for the Anglican Church in Jamaica. The missionaries were basically on their own, a situation worsened by the fact that they were in a hostile colony. But, the real importance of the comparison is the fact that it shows how far ahead the Anglican Church and its associates were with respect to what we can call "public education" prior to the abolition of slavery. While the Anglican Church was being funded by the Jamaican government, Moravian and Methodist missionaries, for example, were paid by their churches, sums supplemented by tithes received from congregations whose growth became significant only in 1823. Phillippo could not even find figures before this date for his church, the Baptist Church. He estimates that this growth from 1823 was 1,350 new congregants annually; he did not specify how many of this number were enslaved people.[26] However, from 1815–1817, the Anglican Church was already recording an annual growth rate of 16,818 new congregants, and these were only the newly converted and baptized slaves.[27]

Stewart reported that the money the Moravians and Methodists were getting in terms of income in 1823 averaged £149 annually for each missionary. Even Anglican curates, who were not preaching, received more than this sum. According to Stewart, the money that a missionary got was "hardly sufficient to support him with as much comfort, in Jamaica, as a third part of the amount would in England."[28] The point Stewart makes is that Jamaica was already an expensive place to live in, and a small income only made matters worse. Furthermore, in 1831, the Anglican Church had fifty-two clergymen in Jamaica, while the Baptists and Methodists had sixteen each, the Moravians had eight, the Presbyterians four (Table 4.1).[29] Sheer manpower alone gave the Anglican Church the upper hand in the business of pre-abolition education.

Since 1780, English education had been changing. Jamaica benefitted from this in an indirect way. English views on education now accepted the principle of "mass education" as a worthy objective. The provisions made for this, however, were designed "to protect the social order," and the state church was called upon to widen access to education in England, and to view this as part of its "traditional Christian roles."[30] Almost the same viewpoint

Table 4.1.   Church Manpower (Priests and Pastors) in Jamaica, 1805, 1831, 1841

Church	1805	1831	1841
Anglican	—	52	74
Baptist	31	16	27
Native Baptist	14	—	—
Wesleyan Methodist	31	16	29
Moravian	12	8	12
Presbyterian	12	4	13
London Missionaries	11	—	—
US Congregationalists	5	—	—
Total	**116**	**96**	**155**

Source: Phillippo, Jamaica, Its Past and Present State, 289–90.

was embraced in Jamaica after over a century-long struggle between Anglican clergymen and slaveholders in the island. In the 1780s as well, the latter finally began to relent from its traditional stance that instruction, even if in Christian knowledge, could give enslaved people ideas about emancipation; it could make them more insolent, since education in any form was literacy, and slaveholders themselves accepted that literacy was a form of social power. When change came to Jamaica, the slaveholders had the English example and its justifications to verify that taking the same route in Jamaica could shore up the social order, rather than destroy it.

An important feature of the events in England was the leadership of the elite in the decision to widen access to education. T.L. Jarman writes that the English elite combined "zeal and apprehension" to reach their "united" stance on the changes that were made under the new concept known as "public education." The elite saw that "their influence on these experiments" was needed to help the system cultivate "meekness, Christian fortitude and resignation" among England's poor. Dr. Thomas Pole, for instance, played one of these prominent roles and in 1816, he encouraged other members of England's high society to lend their "benevolence and charity" to the new dispensation in England's outlook on education. Other members of the elite in leadership roles, such as Henry Brougham, told fellow members of the House of Commons that education "never promoted either turbulence or unbelief."[31]

The Jamaican initiative also had its elite supporters. Most prominent among them were the sugar planters, who donated land and money for the construction of church schools on or near the sugar estates. Some gave money to the church to widen its existing buildings to accommodate schools where enslaved people were taught. Money from planters also supplemented the surplus fees of clergymen, and the incomes of curates and catechists. Without this support, it was unlikely that the church would have made any headway in the creation of systematic education for enslaved people in Jamaica. One Anglican clergyman, Rev. J.M.C. Trew in Manchester, challenged the planters to increase their support even further. Trew took the matter of slave instruction quite seriously, advising that he found it "Strange" that any planter who professed to be a Christian would continue to oppose Christianizing enslaved people, and through this, exposing them to Christian knowledge. However, in 1821, Trew had to admit that things had changed quite significantly, and the turnaround was seen most clearly in the notion that planters now had that slave instruction "embraces alike the spiritual comfort of the slave, with the security of the master." Adding that "the work of instruction has made some progress," Trew showed that he was expecting the access to schooling to continue to widen. In his view, this was security for the Jamaican slaveholding elite.[32]

The Governor of Manchester was one the most avid promoters of slave instruction from the beginning of his tenure as governor of Jamaica in 1808 until he demitted office in 1827. Manchester was one of the island's longest serving governors during slavery, and this proved a valuable asset for the widening of public education island wide. But Manchester's intention was always to promote Jamaica as a forward thinking colony. He did not see slavery as contradictory to this perspective. Manchester was one of Jamaica's Enlightenment idealists, who could accept that slavery could be transformed into a humane system. This policy of giving a human face to slavery was known as amelioration, and Manchester, as indicated earlier, was an advocate of Jamaica's policy for the amelioration of slavery.

In this regard, Manchester was really not different from proslavery writers, such as James Macqueen, who also saw amelioration as a virtuous policy that could aid the slaves, but not produce emancipation until much later. And Macqueen's amelioration, like Manchester's, was best produced locally in Jamaica, rather than in Britain. Proslavery writers saw value in what Macqueen himself called the "diffusion of true knowledge" to enslaved people, meaning Christian knowledge from the state church, but to delay emancipation, rather than produce it. Macqueen had no doubt that this knowledge would one day "bring about emancipation," but he wanted this to be done on terms determined by slaveholders in the colonies, such as Jamaica, not the enslaved, and certainly not the abolitionists in Britain, which was far away.[33] There is no indication, based on the documents I have seen, that Manchester viewed the future of the slave world any differently.

Lipscomb, when he arrives in 1825, joined the thinking of the local slaveholding elite, the governor, and the proslavery network on the matter of slave instruction as a form of amelioration. The first Anglican bishop resident in Jamaica made the church into a more prominent and committed partner of the social order. He supported the arrival of the CMS in 1826, which came to Jamaica also to promote slave instruction and Anglican doctrine and teachings among enslaved people. With Lipscomb's advocacy, the CMS created a local branch to serve the island's parishes, known as the Jamaica Auxiliary to the Church Missionary Society (JACMS). Every one of these organizations and individuals showed the immense structure of power that the enslaved were up against, but also highlighted the importance of the agency enslaved people displayed when interacting with this structured and institutionalized exercise of domination.

The Role of the CMS

The CMS began in England in 1799. Initially, it dispatched missionaries, known as catechists, mainly to the African colonies of Britain. In 1804, its missionaries had reached Sierra Leone. Seven years later, the CMS's workforce arrived in the Caribbean, first Antigua and Barbados, and then Jamaica in 1826.[34] The point is this: by the time of its arrival in Jamaica, the CMS had a wealth of experience in promoting Christian knowledge as education. It had worked on the conversion of free black people in Africa, and transferred this knowledge and experience to the instruction of enslaved Africans and their descendants in the Caribbean. This was not the kind of organization that enslaved people could depend on to promote their freedom. Rather, the CMS was an advocate of British cultural imperialism, and would do very little to promote unfettered emancipation in Britain's colonies.

It should be known that William Wilberforce, Britain's most famous abolitionist, was a founding member of the CMS.[35] The CMS was also in support of ending the British slave trade in 1807. After this, it became one of the supporters of slave instruction. In other words, British abolitionism cannot be seen in a separate light from the advocacy of slave indoctrination through the means of Protestant instruction. Even while abolitionists might have viewed immediate emancipation as a better alternative after 1807, they were very aware of the need to put the enslaved in schools to protect the social order, which included mechanisms to prolong the life of the sugar plantation economy and society. Abolitionism was not interested in the complete and far reaching liberation of enslaved people. Instead, the movement wanted to replace slavery with wage labor, replace obvious exploitation with invisible exploitation, and for this, British abolitionism had Adam Smith's economic arguments as inspiration and to show the way. Smith had proposed in 1776 that, since people have to "live by" their "work," they should be paid "wages," which should also be "sufficient to maintain" them.[36]

Work itself was the priority. This was Smith's message. Enslaved people, for their part, were never the really significant factors; neither of the abolitionists nor the CMS; and not the government of Jamaica, slaveholders in the colony, or the Anglican Church there. For the abolitionists and CMS specifically, the main factors were British culture, the concept of British Enlightenment, and the economic reward viewed as attainable and sustainable through the promotion of this culture and the Enlightenment ideals. These were seen as threatened by slavery; but, at the same time, enslaved people and their culture, their views about how the world should work, should not become replacement threats. It was British to advocate emancipation, but the emancipated should not be put in a position to remove Britain from any part of this process, either before or after the emancipation when it came.

There is a good deal of scholarship which ties capitalism and its inequalities to the Enlightenment. Rousseau, himself an Enlightenment thinker, foresaw the pitfalls of creating private property out of Enlightenment ideas in the inequities that this would generate among humans. This would lead to competition, injustice, and exploitation. Rousseau had begun to analyze capitalism as the bastard child of Enlightenment, which promoted the rights of the individual, but at a cost that other humans would have to bear.[37] The more limitless private acquisition became, this multiplied capitalist exploitation, so that "the process that brought us the best of Enlightenment principles" becomes, as Ellen Meiksins Wood points out, "the same process that brought us the capitalist organization of production."[38]

While in Jamaica, the CMS made no attempt to hide its reason for being in the island. It was there to promote slave indoctrination using Anglican doctrine and principles. These were to pave the way for the introduction of Smith's capitalist system of wage labor exploitation. This proposed the manipulation of the human need to work in order to grow private accumulation, but this was a significant underestimation of the capacities of enslaved people to modify the indoctrination for their benefit. The one thing that the CMS could not be faulted on and which is important here is its rejection as "highly preposterous" the notion still held by some slaveholders that enslaved people were "too stupid and barbarous" to learn in school.[39] The CMS felt that it could help to further undermine this perspective by increasing the number of enslaved people exposed to Anglican instruction. In this respect,

Protestant education could "confer an important benefit" above and beyond its indoctrination.[40] It could make the enslaved literate, which would show that they indeed had the capacity to learn in school.

The CMS's presence had another benefit. Even as late as 1826 when the organization arrives in Jamaica, slave instruction was still a debated topic. The CMS joined the local proponents, but a proportion of the slaveholders were still skeptical and doubtful. The CMS literally landed in the middle of one of the most troubling issues in Jamaica in the 1820s, and realizing this, one of its first decisions was localization. It made itself part of the Jamaican social and political landscape by establishing a local subsidiary known as the Jamaica Auxiliary of the CMS (JACMS). This branch was formed with the assistance of sugar planters. Their involvement was expected to help promote the contribution of the JACMS to slave education. One form of help was funding, another was showing that planters could and should support slave instruction. The Auxiliary was modeled on England's Society for the Diffusion of Useful Knowledge and adopted the strategy of disseminating books not normally used in schools for the enslaved before its arrival in Jamaica.[41] However, the Auxiliary went further by distributing these books to the schools for free.

Another contribution was its decision to make sure that enslaved people paid part of the cost of their education. The JACMS saw this personal investment as important because it gave enslaved people a stake in the education that they were receiving. This was seen by the JACMS as a sign of development, meaning that adult enslaved people would hopefully take the instruction that they were getting seriously, attend schools regularly, and ensure that their children did the same. However, the personal investment would also show enslaved people that they could indeed play a role in their schooling, and they received empowerment from knowing that some of their money was used in some fashion in the educational provisions made available to them. The first public library in Spanish Town, the island's capital, was established by the JACMS in 1830, and some of the money for this library was collected from enslaved people from all over the parish of St. Catherine, where Spanish Town was situated. The records show that enslaved people donated £53, to which the JACMS added another £73, and most of this money went into buying books for the public library.[42]

Also important was the role that the Jamaica Auxiliary played in enhancing the notion that slave instruction was popular or public education. This means education accessible to the majority of the population, in this case, the enslaved majority of Jamaica. Through this means, the JACMS aided the growth of the island's early education system. The Auxiliary also supported viewing the provision as a valid system, which was widening based on the decision to end the exclusionary practices of schooling only whites and then only free people in the island. The first schools in Jamaica were known as free schools, such as the Wolmer's Free School established in Kingston in 1729. This school was formed with money from the trust of John Wolmer, a goldsmith, and initially, Wolmer's catered exclusively to whites. A sign of change was seen in 1815 when the first free colored student was admitted into Wolmer's. By 1822, the majority of the students were the sons of free coloreds.[43] For many years, Wolmer's Free School was racially, socially, and gender exclusive. However, after 1822, the racial and social barriers began to give way, and this was complementary to the wider development of popular education, which provided schooling for enslaved people as well—but gender exclusivity persists to this day. There is, however, a separate Wolmer's school for girls. This primary Wolmer's school, now also in existence, has done better. It is a school for girls and boys.

Before the arrival of the CMS, and the formation of its local Auxiliary, the widespread view among whites was that local educational facilities were grossly inferior. Stewart notes that, in accordance with this perspective, "no parent, with the means of giving his son a British education, would think of placing him in these seminaries," meaning even the free schools in Jamaica.[44] However, this view had to change so that enslaved people would also place a value on the instruction that they were receiving. Part of fostering this change was to get local whites to teach even in the schools for enslaved people. The JACMS gave its support to this venture, even while also insisting on a professional teaching staff with the necessary training for the schools with enslaved people. The JACMS put aside the importance of qualified teachers, viewing the change in attitudes toward local educational offerings as a more immediate obstacle that the island needed to overcome. For example, the report from Bishop Lipscomb in 1831 stated that bookkeepers, the "young men" put "in charge of the negroes" but "under the overseer," were performing teaching duties on a regular basis. This was done in schools for enslaved people in the parish of Thomas in the Vale, and when the bishop's report was submitted, the number of these students had increased to 300.[45]

A period of cooperation started with the arrival of the JACMS. Nonconformist missionaries now felt that they could profit from the attention that was now given to educating enslaved people. The formation of the JACMS made it known that instructing the enslaved was now an island wide priority. Moravian missionaries, seeing this development, requested help from another organization associated with the Anglican Church, the British and Foreign Bible Society, London. The help requested was a "supply of New Testaments" which arrived in Jamaica in 1828. They were delivered to the missionary chapels at New Carmel and New Eden. The Moravians responded with gratitude and delight, stating how "truly acceptable" and "so seasonable a gift" the "supply of New Testaments" were.[46]

There were other signs of collaboration and aid that were more directly connected to the work of the JACMS and its teachers. This cooperation, again, signaled the seriousness of the venture and the view that this was a society wide initiative and not one of only the Anglican Church and associated organizations. The JACMS collaborated with the Ladies Society of Kingston to put 2,065 enslaved people in school in Kingston by 1828. This number included both adults and youngsters, male and female. Another 235 enslaved young people on six sugar estates were put into schools with money that came partly from the Ladies Society of Kingston. In addition, schools were also built for the Maroons with help from the JACMS, which provided the teachers or catechists for these schools. About 805 Maroons were attending each of these schools in 1828, a total of about 1,200 from each Maroon community in Jamaica. The JACMS calculated that the schools in which its catechists taught had 75,000 students by that same year.[47]

Sugar planters were among the most important collaborators with the JACMS. The organization acknowledged the fact that assistance from planters, either in the form of material donations or by simply not becoming obstacles, was crucial for the schooling of enslaved people to become a systematic social provision. In the 1820s, one of these planters donated enough land to build a school for 500 enslaved people to be taught in.[48] The Auxiliary provided the teacher for this school. Interestingly, too, this school had both enslaved and free blacks attending. The mixture was evidence of something new.

The education of enslaved people was growing to accommodate free black people as well. This system which had started as part of slavery was now extended to include people who were not enslaved. It was a sign of the urgent need felt to spread Anglican indoctrination. However, the need also created educational opportunities for people who were not directly affected by slavery, or who were no longer in a position to be so affected. If these free blacks had enslaved family members and friends, both could receive exposure to literacy and experience together the social mobility that literacy, on its own, gave to people. There is no telling what kind of additional bonds might be fostered by these two groups while in schools together, bonds that could work against slavery, rather than in support of the institution.

A persistent problem of this early system and one of the challenges faced by the JACMS was providing qualified teachers. All education systems, even in the present day, have to deal with this problem. The JACMS spent a good deal of its funding on paying qualified teachers to teach in schools for enslaved people. The Moravian missionaries put the problem of finding qualified teachers willing to work in schools for the enslaved in this way when they complained about the absence of a "regular teacher," one who could "enforce the necessary discipline" in the school that they had at Fairfield, Manchester parish. Paying such a teacher had cost them £3 10s per week, a sum the missionaries thought was considerable. Nevertheless, it was not enough to attract the kind of teacher that they wanted. The missionaries at another mission station, Chapel Hill, near Hopeton sugar estate, had the same problem and began to wonder if they could acquire a trained teacher "without hiring one."[49] This was very unlikely. Teaching enslaved people was no longer viewed as a pastime, but a serious undertaking for which the teaching staff expected payment in return for services rendered.

Conclusion

The view that systematic education, or real education in the form of an actual system, began only in 1834 when slavery was abolished needs to be totally removed from the scholarship on the history of education in Jamaica. Perhaps the research on other British colonies in the Caribbean will show the same need. The usual reference to the Negro Education Grant, which provided £25,000 sterling annually for the education of former enslaved people and the training of teachers in British Caribbean colonies, as part of the act abolishing slavery, is more appropriately understood as an additional enhancement to the venture that was already in place by the time the allocations were to commence in 1835.[50] There was local government involvement in the venture prior to this, if this is the main marker of the presence of a system, and concerns were even raised about the amount of money that government was spending to educate enslaved people.

Furthermore, concluding that no real system was present before abolition is to also undermine slave agency and completely miss the chance to analyze one of the most important ways in which enslaved people demonstrated slave freedom. It must always be kept in mind that none of this education or instruction given to slaves was intended to liberate them or to give them access to upward social mobility. This was the formidable obstacle that enslaved people in schools were up against. How, and in what forms, they found ways to overcome this challenging situation is the topic of the next chapter.

Notes

1. Shirley C. Gordon, "The Negro Education Grant, 1835–1845: Its Application in Jamaica," *British Journal of Educational Studies* 6:2 (1958), 141, 146; Shirley C. Gordon, "Schools of the Free," in *Before and After 1865: Education, Politics and Regionalism in the Caribbean*, Brian Moore and Swithin Wilmot, eds. (Kingston: Ian Randle Publishers, 1998), 3, 5; Shirley C. Gordon, *A Century of West Indian Education* (London: Longmans, 1963), 18. Also see M.K. Bacchus, *Utilization, Misuse and Development of Human Resources in the Early West Indian Colonies from 1492 to 1845* (Ontario: Wilfred Laurier University Press, 1990), 220, 223; and Howard A. Fergus, *A History of Education in the British Leeward Islands, 1838–1945* (Kingston: The University of the West Indies Press, 2003), 10.

2. See the following works by Paulo Freire, *Pedagogy of the Oppressed*, Myra Bergman Ramos, trans. (New York: Continuum, 1994[1973]); *The Politics of Education: Culture, Power and Liberation*, Donaldo Macedo, trans. (South Hadley: Bergin and Garvey, 1985); and *Pedagogy of Hope: Reviving Pedagogy of the Oppressed*, Robert R. Barr, trans. (New York: Continuum, 1995).

3. Norrel A. London, "Policy and Practice in education in the British West Indies During the late Colonial Period," *History of Education* 24:1 (1995), 99. London is also quoted in the book chapter referenced below this in note four (4).

4. Benita P. Thompson, S. Joel Warrican and Coreen J. Leacock, "Education for the Future: Shaking off the Shackles of Colonial Times," in *Readings in Caribbean History and Culture: Breaking Ground*, D.A. Dunkley, ed. (Lanham, MD: Lexington Books, 2011), 61, 67, 73.

5. M.K. Bacchus, "Education and Society among the Non-Whites in the West Indies Prior to Emancipation," *History of Education* 19:2 (1990), 92.

6. Carmichael, *Domestic Manners and Social Condition*, Vol. 2, 66.

7. The first has been noted before. See also Paulo Freire, *Education for Critical Consciousness* (New York: Continuum, 1993).

8. Herbert Blumer, "Sociological Implications of the Thought of George Herbert Mead," *American Journal of Sociology* 71:5 (1966), 535, 537; *Symbolic Interactionism: Perspective and Method* (Berkeley: University of California Press, 1986), 2–6.

9. See Scott, *Weapons of the Weak*; Thompson, "The Moral Economy"; Gray, *Demeaned but Empowered*.

10. HCPP 1831–32 (481), Letter from the Bishop of Jamaica to Lord Viscount Goderich, Jamaica, 29 August 1831, Archdeaconry of Jamaica, *Jamaica: Religious Instruction. Copy of any Report or Reports from the Bishop of Jamaica, or of any other information in the Possession of the Government, showing the means furnished by the Colony for the Religious Instruction of the Coloured and Slave Population, the number of Churches, Chapels and other places of Worship, and the Rectors, Curates, Catechists and Schools therein*, 24 May 1832, 4.

11. Carl Boggs, *Gramsci's Marxism* (London: Pluto Press, 1976), 39.

12. J.H. Buchner, *The Moravians in Jamaica: History of the Mission of the United Brethren's Church to the Negroes in the Island of Jamaica, from the Year 1754 to 1854* (London: Longman, Brown, & Co., 1854), 22.

13. Phillippo, *Jamaica, Its Past and Present State*, 124, 171.

14. HCPP 1831–32 (481), Letter from the Bishop of Jamaica to Lord Viscount Goderich, Jamaica, 29 August 1831, Archdeaconry of Jamaica, 4.

15. Sheila M. Haggis, *Science and Technology Education in Jamaican Schools* (Paris: UNESCO, 1984), 3.

16. HCPP 1818 (433), An Act for the Subsistence, Clothing, and the Better Regulation and Government of Slaves; for Enlarging the Powers of the Council of Protection; for Preventing the Improper Transfer of Slaves, and for Other Purposes.- December 19, 1816, Jamaica, 52.

17. FP XVII, Jamaica (i) 1661–1739 (93–292), Instructions for our Trusty & well beloved Sir Thomas Lynch, Knight, Our Captain General, & Governor in Chief, in and over our Island of Jamaica—and other the Territories depending thereon, in America.—1681, 95.

18. HCPP 1814–15 (478), No. 14 – Jamaica, Copy of a Letter from Lt. General Morrison to Earl Bathurst; Dated Jamaica, 28th January 1813; with Twenty Enclosures, Jamaica, *Papers Relating to the West Indies*, 12 July 1815, 103; HLRO HL/PO/JO/10/8/302, Stipendiary Curates Bill, Print with MS Amendments, *Lords Journals, Vol. XLIX*, 8 April 1813, 284.

19. HCPP 1818 (433), Copy of Circular Letter from Earl Bathurst to the Governors of West India Colonies. Downing-Street, 7th April 1817, 10 June 1818, 142.

20. HCPP 1814–15 (478), City and Parish of Kingston – an Ordinance for Preventing the Profanation of Religious Rights and False Worshipping of God, under the Pretence of Preaching and Teaching, by Illiterate, Ignorant, and Ill-Disposed Persons, and of the Mischiefs Consequent Thereupon, 12 July 1815, 105.

21. HCPP 1818 (433), Copy of a Letter from His Grace the Duke of Manchester to the Earl Bathurst; with One Enclosure. King's House, Jamaica, 30th May 1817, 170.

22. John Stewart, *A View of the Past and Present State of the Island of Jamaica* (New York: Negro Universities Press, 1969[1823]), 289, 290.

23. HLRO HL/PO/PU/1/1825/6G4n338, An Act to Make Provision for the Salaries of Certain Bishops and Other Ecclesiastical Dignitaries and Ministers, in the Diocese of *Jamaica*, and in the Diocese of *Barbadoes* and the *Leeward Islands*; and to Enable His Majesty to Grant Annuities to Such Bishops Upon the Resignation of Their Offices, 25 July 1825, Great Britain, *Public General Act, 6 George IV, c. 88*, 1825, DIAZO/3489, Reel 211, 837, 838.

24. HLRO HL/PO/JO/10/8/981, An Account of the Estimated Expenditure of the Island of Jamaica, for the Year Ending 30th September 1831, Defrayed by Revenue Raised in That Island, and the Ways and Means for Raising Such Revenue for the Year 1831, Great Britain, *Lords Journals, Vol. LXIV*, 22 June 1832, DIAZO/3490, Reel 212, 313.

25. Stewart, *A View of the Past and Present State of the Island of Jamaica*, 290.

26. Phillippo, *Jamaica, Its Past and Present State*, 297.

27. HCPP 1818 (433), Return of the Number of Slaves Baptised in the under-Mentioned Parishes, for Three Years Preceding the 1st Day of November in the Present Year; Distinguishing the Number Baptised in Each of Those Years, 10 June 1818, 272.

28. Stewart, A View of the Past and Present State of the Island of Jamaica, 291.

29. Phillippo, Jamaica, Its Past and Present State, 290.

30. John Lawson and Harold Silver, A Social History of Education in England (London: Methuen and Co. Ltd., 1978), 226, 228, 231.

31. T.L. Jarman, Landmarks in the History of Education (London: John Murray, 1970), 248–49, 255.

32. Stewart, A View of the Past and Present State of the Island of Jamaica, 292–96.

33. David Lambert, "The Glasgow King of Billingsgate: James Macqueen and an Atlantic Proslavery Network," Slavery & Abolition 29:3 (2008), 391, 395, 396; James M'Queen, The West India Colonies; the Calumnies and Misrepresentations Circulated against Them by the Edinburgh Review, Mr. Clarkson, Mr. Cropper, Etc. (London: Baldwin, Cradock, and Joy, 1824), xi.

34. Church Missionary Society, Register of Missionaries (Clerical, Lay and Female), and Native Clergy from 1804 to 1904, in Two Parts, Part One (London: Published for Private Circulation, 1896), page number missing; Lawson and Silver, A Social History of Education in England, 232.

35. Church Missionary Society, Register of Missionaries.

36. Adam Smith, An Inquiry into the Nature and Causes of the Wealth of Nations, Vol. 2 (Hartford, CT: O.D. Cooke, Lincoln and Gleason Printers, 1804[1776]), 60.

37. See Jean-Jacques Rousseau, Discourse on Inequality, G.D.H. Cole, trans. (Whitefish, MT: Kessinger Publishing, 2004).

38. Ellen Meiksins Wood, The Origin of Capitalism: A Longer View (New York: Verso, 2002), 183.

39. Stewart, A View of the Past and Present State of the Island of Jamaica, 285, 288.

40. Eric Williams, Capitalism and Slavery (London: André Deutsch Ltd., 1993), 7, 29.

41. Jarman, Landmarks in the History of Education, 253, 254.

42. UBA CW/079/8, Rev. John Stainsby to Donald Coates, Mile Gully, Manchester, Jamaica, 10 June 1830, Jamaica, Manuscripts of the Church Missionary Society.

43. Heuman, "The Free Coloreds in Jamaican Slave Society," 662.

44. Stewart, A View of the Past and Present State of the Island of Jamaica, 202–03.

45. HCPP 1831–32 (481), Letter from the Bishop of Jamaica to Lord Viscount Goderich, Jamaica, 29 August 1831, Archdeaconry of Jamaica, 4.

46. Periodical Accounts Relating to the Missions of the Church of the United Brethren, Established among the Heathens, Vol. X (London: W.M. McDowell, for the Brethren's Society for the Furtherance of the Gospel Among the Heathen, 1823), 424.

47. UBA CW/012/5/1, A Few Simple Facts for the Friends of the Negro, Jamaica, 1828, Manuscripts of the Church Missionary Society.

48. Ibid.

49. Periodical Accounts Relating to the Missions of the Church of the United Brethren, Established among the Heathens, Vol. X, 228, 262.

50. Gordon, "The Negro Education Grant," 146.

CHAPTER FIVE

~

Enslaved and in School

At present, there is so much scholarship on slave resistance and agency it seems almost unnecessary to write about the same phenomena among enslaved people who were in schools. However, in this case, truth is indeed stranger than fiction, because there is nothing in the scholarship on resistance and agency in the British Caribbean about enslaved people interacting with the schools. The reason for this is partly the mesmerizing effect of the indoctrination that took place in the entire venture to give enslaved people instruction through Christian knowledge. The histories of education on the region have thus focused quite heavily on the indoctrination, but at the expense of examining what the enslaved did or might have done to benefit themselves and each other.

The other reason is the sheer difficulty involved in discovering these acts of agency in the records that exist about schooling. The vast majority were written by the dominators, the people providing instruction. In this chapter, I will therefore use the technique of reading against the grain, which will show that all is not lost because the evidentiary materials have come from mainly the indoctrinators. This same technique has been successfully used by historians working on other aspects of the lived experiences of enslaved people in the Atlantic world.

Fairly recently, Emma Christopher has reread documents about slave ships crossing the Atlantic to analyze the experiences of black crew members of these ships. The presence of these crew members, both men and women, was quite a revelation itself. Christopher's work has also shown that contrary to our first impression, black crew members were not necessarily providing support for slave trafficking or the institution of slavery because of their role. In fact, she was able to transcend the obvious and flesh out from documentary evidence that the "men, and occasionally women, of African origin among the crews of slavers" participated in resistance aboard these ships. They made the "freedom" that they could materialize as crew members "a prized commodity" or additional inspiration for the enslaved cargoes.[1]

More recently, Walter Hawthorne's work on slave ships en route to Brazil shows the presence of another hidden form of resistance. Hawthorne has called this "social reincarnation," the product of the bonding that took place among the cargoes. This took place in spite of the traumatic experience of the voyage across the Atlantic, which is commonly referred to as the Middle Passage. Hawthorne, using traditional documentary materials, has pointed the way toward a new understanding of the Middle Passage experience. Without denying that some form of "social death" occurred, Hawthorne, however, adds that this is an insufficient assessment of what actually took place. To this view needs to be added the new life that enslaved people created to endure, resist, and overcome enslavement after their arrival in Brazil's port cities, such as the famous Rio de Janeiro.[2]

In this chapter, I make use of similar documentary archival materials that came from slaveholders and their allies to examine some of the ways in which slave freedom manifested among enslaved people in the schools in Jamaica.

The Change to Slave Instruction

The first thing that we need to understand is that slave instruction appeared because of the perceived need for this to suppress resistance and to prolong the life of slavery. The decision to use instruction in church-run schools was part of making the indoctrination provided useful and effective, especially in light of the abolition of the slave trade in 1807. However, slave instruction changed the face of education in Jamaica by making this a government venture supported by the state church as well as slaveholders, who had traditionally opposed granting enslaved people access to any kind of schooling. In other words, the enslaved were always at the center of the venture. They were the main consideration: the targets or recipients. The future of the slave system depended on their presence in the schools, as well as their interactions with the catechists.

When Bishop Lipscomb, for example, looked for signs of the condition of schooling, he always examined how the enslaved responded to their teachers. Though Lipscomb ultimately noted only that the teachers were doing well, and celebrated slaveholders for their support, he was able to note these, as he even admitted in small bursts, because of the attention enslaved people gave to the lessons that they were receiving.[3] Lipscomb knew that instruction was fragile, rudimentary, and uncertain. He knew that how enslaved people viewed schooling was the factor that determined the success or failure of these schools. He was therefore noticeably cautious about intervening in disputes over teaching, or whenever the catechists encountered any kind of trouble that was connected with the teaching that they did.

One such occasion presented itself in 1830, when J.C. Sharpe, a catechist at the Maroon town of Accompong, St. James, complained about interference from the white superintendent in the town, John Hylton. Sharpe's point was that he needed to develop a close bond with the students, and Hylton was an annoyance and an obstacle. Hylton was not liked by the Maroons. Furthermore, he had no knowledge of how to teach. Sharpe had written to him stating this quite plainly, that "our stations are totally different."[4] He also communicated the matter to Lipscomb and asked for his help. However, the bishop took the diplomatic stance. He passed on the matter to the governor and asked him to settle it quietly by writing directly to Hylton. A public display that the Maroons could see had to be avoided. The discordance could affect Sharpe's role. The Maroons might be given the impression that he was more a servant of the colonial regime, and not there to actually promote literacy. The governor's letter, which was signed by his secretary, William Bullock, reprimanded Hylton. This put the matter to rest without further fanfare.

Another situation, which also arose in 1830, involved the catechist Henry C. Taylor. He arrived in Jamaica to teach enslaved people on one of the estates. Shortly after this, Taylor was asked to join the island's militia as a reservist. He rejected the request and argued that his only reason for being in the island was to teach. He was one of the employees of the JACMS, who had travelled from England under the impression that the colony only needed his services as a teacher. However, militia duty was required of all able-bodied white males; such was the fear among whites of internal unrest, especially upheavals started by enslaved people. Either these white males served in the militia on a fulltime basis, or they joined the reserve corps. Taylor took the matter to Lipscomb, but again, the bishop was diplomatic, and expressed only the wish to have the dispute settled quietly. Lipscomb was certainly more aware than was Taylor of the sensitivity of teaching enslaved people. Any evidence of discordance between slaveholders and catechists was potentially hazardous. Enslaved people could interpret the impasse as a suspicious difference of opinion over the kind of teaching that was most valuable for them to receive. The one thing that enslaved people also knew for sure was that slaveholders could not be trusted to empower them through any venture. Taylor did not relent, but he allowed the impasse to die without voicing any further complaint. The government also took the same stance.[5]

Most catechists contracted by the JACMS had never been to Jamaica prior to signing that contract. This gave enslaved people a significant advantage. When the catechists began to teach, they were literally on their own inside of the classrooms with their enslaved pupils. Whatever these catechists decided to teach had to be seen as relevant to the enslaved people, or no teaching could take place. No amount of training on the teachers' part could prevent this from happening. It was one of the most basic and prevalent occurrences in any classroom, whether this was a class of enslaved pupils or free students. Pedagogical training is one thing, but application of this training in the real world situation of each class environment is quite another. Trained teachers in present-day Jamaica still complain about their incapacity to teach anything to students who simply refuse to learn.[6]

However, the JACMS, with assistance from its parent organization, tried their best to reserve teachers that they thought could withstand classrooms with enslaved students. Both organizations were aware of the power play that took place when interacting with the enslaved. Both were aware of the presence among enslaved people of notions connected to their belief that they were free individuals who were duty-bound, for their own benefit, to expose the facts about their freedom to the people who saw themselves as their dominators. Both were also aware of the frailty of any effort to dominate enslaved people. To ward off change from happening in the classrooms, the CMS took the approach it had used in Antigua before coming to Jamaica, which was to rely on a resident supposedly highly knowledgeable of the society to make suggestions as to who might be best suited for the role of catechist and in which of the schools. In Antigua, this local agent of the CMS was William Dawes.[7] In Jamaica, the local agent was replaced with something bigger: a local branch of the CMS, which had slaveholders, clergymen, curates, and other interested whites who were all residents of the island, and supposedly familiar with the social landscape, and especially with enslaved people in varying ways and degrees.

A good deal of thought and cautiousness were put into selecting candidates for the role of catechist in Jamaica. All of the candidates were trained teachers. Some even had prior teaching experience amounting to a number of years. Some had been teaching in London and others in other parts of England, as well as Scotland and Wales. A wide net was cast to capture the best candidates available and willing to teach in the island. The CMS took no chances where these catechists were concerned; selection was done after checking their backgrounds to ensure that they were duly qualified; and all of them appear to have been graduates of the college of the CMS, which was in London.

William Stearn, for example, was from Colchester, Essex, in the southeast of England. He arrived in Jamaica in October 1829, and was a trained catechist, who had graduated from the CMS institution. Stearn had knowledge about teaching, meaning pedagogical training, but he was also trained in the delivery of Anglican doctrine and principles, as well as other subjects, including history, geography, and languages. He would have one of the longest tenures of any of the catechists of the JACMS. He left Jamaica in 1836, two years after slavery was abolished.[8] Lipscomb used Stearn's teaching methods as the basis of a number of his optimistic reports about the state of slave instruction in Jamaica. Among these remarks was the vitality of developing relationships of trust with the enslaved people. Stearn appeared to Lipscomb to be one of the first and lasting success cases where this was concerned. Hence, Stearn became Lipscomb's *sine qua non* on the matter of teaching enslaved people.

Both Henry C. Taylor and Joshua Wood were in their thirties and had a wealth of experience in teaching before coming to Jamaica to teach the enslaved. Their selection as candidates for Jamaica's potentially hostile teaching environment was on the basis of their experience as well as their training and knowledge. Candidates with both training and practical application were the ideal ones. At thirty-eight years of age, Wood was one of the oldest and most experienced. He was also a bachelor, which made him an even more attractive choice. In the gender biased world of British thinking about the colonies, it was assumed that catechists with wives would have a distraction that those without wives would not have. Wood could thus commit himself totally to his teaching, which was seen as a necessity because of the perceived and known challenges with teaching enslaved pupils. Generally, however, the CMS had to hire teachers who were qualified and trained regardless of their marital status.[9] There was not exactly a rush from candidates to take up teaching positions in any of the Caribbean colonies of Britain.

However, an effort was made to offer contracts only to young and still relatively young candidates, men in their twenties and thirties, under the assumption that youthful vigor and enthusiasm were assets needed because teaching in schools for enslaved people was nothing short of taxing and exploratory. The worst situation was if one of these catechists suddenly resigned because he felt overworked, or was sickly, growing too old, or becoming frustrated. All of the work that this catechist had put into developing the teacher-student bond with the enslaved people would be suddenly lost, and there was always an important breaking-in period when new catechists arrived and were introduced for the first time to their students. For some, this period was protracted. Others were lucky to have shorter periods, but only because they made compromises, which we will examine shortly.

Taylor, who was married, confirmed the basis of the gender bias. Immediately after arriving, Taylor had also complained that his accommodation on the estate, Salt Savannah in the parish of Vere, was grossly insufficient. Most aggravating was that he had his wife with him, who had to endure the embarrassment of living in the same house with the overseer. Citing Mrs. Taylor's dissatisfaction, Taylor warned that he would return to England if he was not built a proper house to suit their expectations and in accordance with the contract that he had signed. The overseer, according to Taylor, kept the house like a brothel. He had nightly visits from enslaved females, which made Mrs. Taylor, in particular, very uncomfortable. The main cause of this, as Taylor also pointed out, was that the estate's owner, James B. Wildman, who was said to be very supportive of slave instruction, was not present when the Taylors arrived. Wildman had already returned to England. His presence would have made a big difference. Also aggravating for Taylor was that the schoolhouse was already built, but not their house. This gave both Taylor and his wife the impression that the enslaved people were a bigger priority than they were, and true as this might have been, Taylor felt that it was only fair that the wellbeing of the teacher should also be among the main considerations that were made.[10]

In any case, as Taylor implied, if the teacher was mistreated, this would affect his ability to teach. None of the slaves wanted a teacher who was obviously disadvantaged. Taylor suggested that the enslaved people needed to know that their teacher had some kind of influence in the society, had some kind of social status, one that could help them as students under the tutelage of that same teacher. Henry C. Taylor was most certainly a man who had many grouses, someone who was easily annoyed by almost everything that did not meet his specifications. However, he was also a man with insight. He correctly surmised that enslaved people only responded to catechists perceived by them as having some kind of influence in the society, especially among the slave-owning people. This was the only way the teachers could help them to help themselves. Through these teachers, enslaved people could make their freedom known.

Prioritizing the Enslaved

In Jamaica, the priority was the enslaved, and nothing implied this more than the provisions made for their instruction in Christian knowledge. The catechists were necessary, but secondary to the enslaved people. In any case, no work was there for these catechists unless they had receptive enslaved people to teach. The entire system of this early educational enterprise was predicated on the hope and assumption that enslaved people would cooperate with the catechists. This interest in receiving instruction from the catechists meant that enslaved people had to remain the focus of the venture.

William Manning, one of the catechists who came from England, would discover this quite early after his arrival in 1827. Three years later, Manning tendered his resignation, citing illness as his reason. His physician, Dr. James Macfayden, had in truth diagnosed Manning with liver inflammation, but told the catechist that the cause was his "sedentary" lifestyle as a teacher "for upwards of a year." Macfayden suggested that Manning had been sitting down for too many hours out of each day. His lack of movement had obstructed the proper functioning of his organs, and his liver was the first to show serious signs of deterioration. Macfayden, however, was not the one who suggested resignation. This was Manning's decision. He could not see how he could continue to teach in a classroom with enslaved people without further jeopardizing his health. He knew the toll that it took on him, and he knew that he was replaceable. Any complaint that he might have would not be accommodated as this would be seen as expensive and taxing by his employer, the JACMS. Manning resigned because he was well aware that he was not the organization's top priority.[11]

Welshman Thomas Jones was not nearly as lucky as Manning was; he died in 1827, a mere two years after his arrival in Jamaica to work as a catechist. Jones was only twenty-five years old when he arrived, and twenty-seven the year that he died.[12] The reaction of the JACMS was shock. The loss was sudden and unexpected. However, the concern which the JACMS expressed was not limited to Jones. His death was tragic and the organization made this known, but it also stated that his passing meant the loss of a valuable catechist. Jones had been teaching at the school at Papine estate, St. Andrew, another property that was owned by James B. Wildman. Wildman himself, as Mary Turner has argued, was deeply committed to slave instruction. However, Wildman was influenced by the enslaved people, who had informed him of their dissatisfaction with conditions on the estate.[13] Wildman's main concern was to have an effective catechist expose his enslaved people to Christian knowledge. The loss of Jones was regrettable because he had proven himself as such a catechist. The enslaved people liked him a great deal.

Jones had practically built the school at Papine estate during the short period that he was there. Wildman, it is true, authorized the school's construction, donated the land and the money for the project, and granted Jones access to the enslaved people. However, the rest of the work involved in making the school into a real school was done by Jones. Jones himself, on the other hand, revealed that the enslaved people he taught made the school into a reality, and a story that the JACMS and Wildman could view as a success. The school opened in February 1826, less than a year after Jones arrived. It was one of the phenomenal success stories in slave instruction because of the rapidity with which the enslaved people joined the school. Attendance was regular, based on Jones' reports. But the students came in such large numbers and in such a variety that Jones was soon put under pressure. He was taking on more than he had imagined. In fact, in almost no time, both enslaved people and free blacks were attending the school, and adults as well as youngsters.[14]

They saw something in Jones that they liked. The age of the student body ranged from seven upward to nineteen. Jones felt taxed beyond his capacity, and his health began to suffer as a result. Preparing lessons for the large volume of students and the different groups was one of the most strenuous of his tasks. He had "easy lessons" prepared for the students who were beginners, and separate lessons for the groups he classified as "upper" classes. In total, Jones alone was teaching eighty-one students in the same year that the school began, and within this total, he had groups at different ages and stages. This kind of work could exhaust anyone, even someone who was still in his or her twenties.[15]

Taylor also realized that nothing he did could prevent the enslaved people from determining the outcomes from his teaching. While he was teaching at Salt Savannah, he had to eventually admit that the JACMS was always right: the enslaved people even determined if and how committed he remained to the teaching he had to do. Taylor discovered just how thoroughly frustrating it was to teach enslaved people whom he felt deliberately made themselves less inclined to learn. According to Taylor, he encountered students "who cannot put two syllables together" and this was not simply because of their illiteracy. Much of it was due to their inclinations, their interest, and their willingness to learn what he tried to teach them. Taylor discovered that he could not force enslaved people to learn anything that he taught them, and worse, they all seemed to know this and had decided to use it against him. His decision to divide the school into two groups did not help.[16]

In the end, Taylor had a school with two groups of students that gave him more work to do. His pedagogy began to lean more and more toward rote learning. This experienced teacher basically downgraded his teaching technique to the most basic approach known within teaching circles at the time. Rote learning was learning by repetition only. The repetition itself was the only check on the quality of this teaching. Students learned from the teacher reciting the lessons to them and nothing more. It was a thoroughly uninspired and uninspiring approach to teaching. Taylor had given up and adopted this technique as his last resort. And indeed there were alternative approaches available and well known, such as the techniques developed by the famous Rev. Dr. Andrew Bell and Joseph Lancaster. Both had also developed these based in part on their experiences in teaching in the British colony of India (Madras) and among England's poor people, respectively. Both systems were based on the belief that the better the teaching quality, the better or more effectively the students would learn.

Bell, for instance, insisted on what he called "*perfect instruction*," which meant not passing over any lesson until this was "well and thoroughly learned." The approach relied on teaching "*short and easy lessons*" until these were mastered. Teaching spelling, for example, had to involve some amount of rote learning, such as "first pronouncing the words after the teacher." But then, the students would have to proceed to spelling "the words" independently, first "slowly and deliberately." This approach involved ensuring that the students took ownership of their learning, with the teacher as the introducer of the words to be learned. The teaching of mathematics was very different. Bell's system relied on using the students to teach each other. This was student involved learning, or student interactive learning, and which again depended on the students owning what they were learning or supposed to be learning. As Bell said, "the several pupils set down the respective numbers from the lips of each other, listening to their reasons for these," which was far better than, in Bell's opinion, the "usual solitary mode of studying" the subject of mathematics.[17]

While Taylor resorted to basic rote learning, he did also try to diversify the books he used to teach. The frustration he was facing from trying to make students who were not learning from him learn something, opened Taylor's mind to the use of texts aside from only the Bible. He requested prayer books, for example, which he felt were easier for the students to understand. Taylor hoped that these books would stimulate interest in his lessons and make it harder for the students to hide their reading capabilities, which he knew they had.[18]

Ebenezer Collins, the replacement for Jones at Papine estate, arrived in December 1827 to one of the most difficult situations for any of the catechists. Not only was this school a taxing environment to teach in, it was also where the most visible evidence of teacher-student bonding had taken place. The bond accounted for much of Jones' success, which in the end hastened his early death. Collins had also arrived when Wildman, the estate owner, had left for England. Wildman's absence made Collins' transition into the job even more challenging. The enslaved people and Wildman also had a rapport from which Collins could benefit. It was Wildman who had conceded important changes on the estate based on the pressure he faced from the enslaved people. The enslaved seemed to have developed some amount of respect for Wildman, but only because Wildman's concessions made them feel respected by the estate's owner as well. Collins found himself in a vacuum, one created by Jones' passing, but which had originally come from the reception that enslaved people gave to Jones. Collins could only hope for the same kind of reception from the enslaved in the school.[19]

Three catechists resigned in 1831. All cited being overworked and underappreciated. They had too many students teaching, too many eager to learn. The JACMS was running out of money. By 1830, it was announcing its incapacity to keep up with the enslaved people's demand for schooling. Financial meltdown loomed and became realer in the early 1830s. The three teachers who resigned in 1831 stated that they were not being paid enough for the work that they had to do. Particularly aggravating was the fact that they all had to create multiple classes to teach the enslaved, who were at varying levels in terms of learning. The sheer size of each of these classes was another aggravation.

William Taylor and S. Whiteborne, two of the three who resigned, identified the workload and inadequate compensation as their reasons. Joshua Wood, however, added to his complaint his disappointment because he was not promoted to the clergy. Wood's ambition went beyond teaching, but he was needed more in the classroom. The priority placed on teaching the enslaved took precedence. Wood saw this as unfair; he had taught to the best of his capacity and felt that he deserved consideration for the clergy. However, the position of the JACMS was that Wood was too good a teacher to lose. He would have to put aside his personal aspiration for the greater good, which was teaching in a school for the enslaved.[20]

Henry C. Taylor was eventually asked to resign in 1828. Wildman and Taylor could not get along. Taylor complained constantly. Wildman, writing from England, felt that the estate would be better served with another catechist, but he was thinking mainly about how the enslaved people felt about Taylor. Before he suggested Taylor's resignation, Wildman tried dispatching him to another of his estates for a fresh start with the enslaved people there, Low Ground sugar estate, also in Vere parish. Taylor refused to go and explained to Wildman that his decision was based on his knowledge of his exposure to the enslaved people already under his tutelage. The transfer meant that he would have to indeed start again, and Taylor was well aware of the difficulties making such a start entailed, particularly with respect to getting the students to accept him as their teacher. Also important for Taylor was his belief that enslaved people in the schools made decisions about their learning. Some had the desire to learn, some had less, and some had no desire at all. He opined that those at Low Ground, who had never been exposed to a teacher before, had either no interest or very little interest in learning anything from a catechist. Wildman viewed all of this as additional proof that Taylor was more trouble than he was worth and asked for his removal. The JACMS concurred.[21]

The Auxiliary itself was always quite busy because of the school system. It had meetings several times each month to discuss the issues as they arose. Teaching enslaved people had ongoing as well as new challenges that came up on occasion. It was not a perfect system of education or indoctrination for that matter. The enslaved challenged the system at every turn. Very aggravating under these circumstances was the fact that no member of the JACMS received a salary for the work that each of them did. This was voluntary work. As the workload became greater, the fact that it was voluntary service became a more important issue for the members. In addition, they had to monitor the expansion of the system, which was always expanding. The hiring of new teachers and exercising quality control over the teaching that took place were additional tasks necessitated by the expansion. The work done by the JACMS was a new enterprise for the colony as a whole, and the members of the organization never lost sight of the fact that they were doing all of this novel work because of the enslaved people. It was the militant and nonviolent, but always present agency of the enslaved that instruction was designed to suppress, and there was never a moment when the administrators of the suppression felt that they could rest.

School Politics

After taking over Jones' challenging post at Papine, Collins reported having no doubt that the classroom was a political arena. His transfer to Salt Savannah estate came shortly after his arrival at Papine, after Collins reached the realization that he was making no headway with teaching the enslaved people at the first estate. However, Salt Savannah's enslaved proved to be the same. They, too, were aware that the classroom was a contested terrain, and that they had power inside of the classroom that was real. While at this estate, Collins reported having no smoother transition than at Papine, and that he was confronted by enslaved people who could have been the same set of people that he had been teaching before at the first estate. This impression came to him when

Collins realized that out of the "many" students that he had been teaching, only the very young or those "who are not yet ten years old" had shown him evidence that they could "read well." Furthermore, they showed him this while in church on a Sunday, not in school. Collins wrote that they would "follow the church prayers on the Sunday with a great deal of propriety." They placed more value on church than on schooling, and disseminated respect as they thought fit or as they were told to do by their parents, since these were young enslaved people. In school, according to Collins, the "generality," or adults and youngsters alike, cared "nothing about what is said to them."[22]

Before his suggested resignation, Taylor was of the view that all catechists should be specially trained to teach the enslaved. This was not like any other teaching that they would do. Worse, these enslaved people were nonwhites; they were Africans whom Taylor assumed were far below British white people on the hierarchy of human cultures. Taylor would thus warn the catechists before departing that their main goal should always be "to raise them [enslaved people] up to your standard." Nonetheless, he had also advised each catechist to "Maintain your dignity as teacher," and bond with the enslaved students or "stoop down to your pupils" but "not to be upon a level with them." Taylor's insistence on the teachers maintaining a certain distance was a sign of his view that the enslaved were attracted to dignified conduct and social status. These were part of what would make the teacher respectable in their eyes, and both respectability and status would enhance the teachers' ability to teach them. All in all, Taylor divulged a good deal about the capacities of the enslaved to control the politics inside of the classrooms, even while he wrote disparagingly about the enslaved as being culturally inferior to white British people.[23]

A sign that Taylor viewed the enslaved as having the capacity to learn, but also having the capacity to hide this ability if and when they wanted to do so, was seen in his statement that they can "learn as any other race of people" can. Taylor had seen this himself in his own teaching of the enslaved people. He had reported that he had one class of twenty-one students who had made "the greatest progress," but also within the same general group of students, he had some who were "not quite as forward," nine of them that he could only describe as "rather dull," another ten who were clearly being "indifferent," and one girl who was exceptional because she was cunning enough to convince Taylor that she was "almost an idiot."[24] What Taylor had seen was the use of ignorance as a weapon of resistance by enslaved people. They had realized that they could frustrate the efforts of the teaching fraternity by feigning the incapacity to learn anything. Taylor was already quite intolerant of colonial life in other respects. Facing students who dispatched their ability to learn only on their terms was another source of aggravation for Taylor. His students were making him more of a dislikeable person than even Taylor himself had the capacity to become. In this way, his resignation was due also to the enslaved people, who exposed his irritability and general indisposition toward colonial life to Wildman, the estate's owner, as well as to Taylor's employers, the JACMS.

Books brought in to aid the catechists at Papine estate between 1824 and 1830 were the sort of books that one would expect to find in an English grammar school, a school for the progeny of the elite, not in a school for black and brown enslaved people, where the objective was Christian indoctrination, and nothing else. However, at Papine, as the table below shows, books brought in were on subjects such as history, geography, and languages. Even a book that we could consider as one of Europe's classics made the list, *Caesar's Commentaries*. Two questions need to be asked: what did books on the items that "Belong in a House" or the "Parts of the Body," for instance, have to do with Protestant indoctrination, and who made the use of these books a possibility in the first instance?[25]

The short answer to both questions would be the teachers or catechists, the people who saw the need for these books and brought them in based on what they had seen. They were the ones who submitted the requests for

Table 5.1.   A Snapshot of the Non-Theological Books in Use at the School at Papine Estate, St. Andrew, Jamaica, between 1824 and 1830

Language Category
Latin Grammar
Greek Grammar
Guthrie's Grammar
Ainsworth's Latin Dictionary
French Dictionary and Grammar

Historical/Geographical Category
Ruff's Botanical History
Goldsmith's Greece
Goldsmith's Rome
Goldsmith's Britain
Clark's General Atlas

Classical Category
Caesar's Commentaries

Source: UBA CW/O8D/4, Return No.VI. Books Belonging to the Church Missionary Society at its Station in Papine, Jamaica; for the Year Ending 31 December 1824.

the books, and these were informed decisions based on need or, at the very least, the perception that there was a need. However, the substantial answer would include the enslaved, the people under the catechists' instruction, whose capacity to learn was shown either piecemeal, wholly, or none at all. In other words, when enslaved people exposed their learning capabilities, this was encouragement for the catechists. Seeing the potential of these students exposed the insufficiency of limiting the kind of lessons that they were taught to Christian knowledge alone. One thing that can be said about the catechists is that, for the most part, they were real teachers in the sense of having been trained to teach, and many also came to Jamaica with teaching experience. They knew that teaching any student body changed over the course of time, especially as the students themselves showed that they were changing, as they exposed their capacity for greater knowledge, their eagerness to learn more than the curricula's current offerings. This was another reality of the politics of the classroom. The teacher might be the one in charge, but the students also direct the course of learning that takes place, and decide if any learning takes place in any event.

Some of this politics was seen outside of the classrooms in the decisions made to diversify the educational system to include, for instance, schools which could provide skills training, rather than solely knowledge of the Bible and prayer books. Of course, slaveholders with estates, in particular, saw benefit in some of this diversification, especially the construction of "industrial schools," such as the one that was built in Spanish Town and opened in 1825 for enslaved people described as "Servants & Apprentices," and which was "well attended" by them.[26] Another such school had opened in Kingston in 1826 with a student body of 436 in its opening year. This made the JACMS optimistic beyond words. The organization announced its expectation that the student body would climb to "500 in the course of a very short time."[27]

This optimism was based partly on the fact that coloreds were used as teachers in the school, a practice that was adopted based on observation of the slaves. It was apparent that the enslaved reserved their learning for teachers that they could bond with, and those teachers with whom they shared some sort of ethnic connection were viewed by the education providers as the most likely to get the enslaved people to learn. This idea was adopted elsewhere in the island. In St. Thomas-in-the-East, for example, as of 1826, the JACMS had 2,000 enslaved people in schools where coloreds were among the teaching staff. By the next year, this number increased to 3,000 students.[28] The diversification that was happening in fact took place mostly because of the perception that enslaved people would gravitate to these schools in droves; and the internal diversification, seen in the selection of coloreds to teach in these schools, was another decision taken on the basis of what the school builders felt would appeal most to the enslaved students.

Enslaved people attending the industrial schools stood to benefit from these schools as well. The decision to start these schools might have emanated from the slaveholders and managers of the education system, but the existence of these schools proved an asset to enslaved people who had the desire for skills training. They could learn skills useful in plantation boiling houses, curing houses, and mills, which would doubtlessly benefit the sugar planters. In fact, any kind of technical skill acquired by the enslaved was a potential advantage for sugar planters in particular, but also for the owners of jobbing slaves, or enslaved people who were hired out by slaveholders to work as the replacements of estate slaves on occasion. However, skills training benefits were never limited to the owners of slaves, whoever these might have been. Enslaved people themselves also stood to gain from the acquisition of skills, which were always marketable in the plantation economy, and which enslaved people also used to amass small fortunes while working on their own.

One example was William, an enslaved colored man from the Black River area of St. Elizabeth. William was the slave of a plantation that was in the area, but he was also an independent saddler, shoemaker, barber, fiddler, and horse dealer. William even built a large house for himself with the money that he had made from his diverse skillset, and which he furnished with a sideboard in the dining room, and a Grecian lamp which he hung in the hallway. Almost every enslaved person in his district in the parish knew about William's success. He was an inspiration to other enslaved people. More importantly, he was a source of liquidity for other enslaved people, a source of ready cash needed by others for the purchase of their various consumables. Other people knew that William always had money to purchase a mule, mare, or cow, and any person having these to sell, would normally approach William first.[29]

Rev. John M. McIntyre, an Anglican clergyman in the parish of St. James, did a comparison of slave instruction in Jamaica and Grand Cayman in 1828, and revealed in this some further details about the politics of schooling enslaved people. McIntyre was deeply concerned about the slowness with which the enslaved in Jamaica's neighboring island had been responding to instruction. The number in the schools was still quite small, and those already in school were problematical for the catechists. McIntyre felt that the main cause of these problems was that the educational venture in Grand Cayman did not pay close enough attention to the enslaved themselves. The system was still viewed as a slaveholders' system. In Jamaica, it was clear to McIntyre that the reverse was the case and the reason there was such a larger turn out in Jamaica was because enslaved people knew that they controlled a great deal of what was happening in the school system in the island. To express this without seeming as though he was taking the side of the enslaved people and totally rejecting the slaveholders, McIntyre gave the following advice to the providers of instruction in Grand Cayman, in a letter that he wrote to Bishop Lipscomb on March 24, 1828:

> what they [the enslaved] needed more in the first instance was the presence of a person whom all might respect, who might command attention, awaken in them a better feeling than that which now prevails, convince them of the advantage of education, and incite in them the desire of improving their own condition and that of their children.[30]

McIntyre could have just as easily told the whites of Grand Cayman that they should allow the enslaved people to decide who should teach them and the kind of lessons that they should be taught. However, this was too political an issue for McIntyre to make such a brazen statement. He knew that slaveholders were very sensitive when it came to the matter of their power and status in the colonies. He knew that no slaveholder would ever willingly divulge that he or she was pumping huge sums of money into an education system, for instance, yet had to rely on the responses of the enslaved people for the returns on that investment. This is the reason, the fear of the slaveholders, which accounts for much of the unstated observations about slave instruction in the records that have survived about the system in its early stages. However, coded into each of these records are snippets of information about the events as these were unfolding. The venture that had started out in Jamaica as a top down venture was turned upside down, so that the enslaved people, the prospective victims, were now directing much of the course of the events.

J.C. Sharpe, who complained about interference by the white superintendent at Accompong, did so because he too was well aware of where the real source of power was in the provision of education in the Maroon village. Nicholas Forbes, Sharpe's counterpart at the Maroon's Moore Town community in the Rio Grande Valley of Portland parish, had been reporting the same observation from 1828. However, Forbes was more interested in the number of students attending school. He said that this number was never large, and had continued to decline until 1832, when he decided to change the kind of lessons that he taught and the teaching methods that he used. According to Forbes, once he made these changes (which regrettably he did not specify) he saw a completely different response from the Maroons. Speaking specifically of how his changes were interpreted by those still attending the school in June 1832, Forbes said that he was "glad to find that it stirs them up and puts a little life in them."[31]

William Manning, who was teaching enslaved people in St. Thomas-in-the-East from 1820 and was there during an outbreak of yaws in 1828, said that after the quarantine was lifted on the sixteen suspected victims of the disease, who did not die, none of them returned to school. Others who were not part of the quarantine also stayed away. Manning realized that they blamed him for the outbreak; he had no power to control the school environment, which the enslaved people expected to protect them in almost every imaginable way. Even the combined force of Manning and the Anglican clergyman, who came together to reassure the enslaved people that the school was safe could do nothing to change their perspective. School attendance fell even more after one of the enslaved people was murdered near the school. No one knew who was responsible for the murder, but as far as the students were concerned, the school was clearly an unsafe place for them to be in and even around.[32]

In 1833, William Stearn, arguably the most successful catechist in Jamaica, had admitted that even his situation was "peculiar." Despite the "great preparatory work" that he had done to make sure that each of his students became "an accountable being," he was still faced with resistance. This was partly his doing and partly the doing of the original *modus operandi* of the education system. Stearn admitted that he was circumscribed to teaching about Christianity without having the authority that a clergyman had; furthermore, he was strictly "forbidden to use" the "means" of the clergy, which he felt would attract the enslaved people more. They had a great deal of reverence for religious symbolism, or as Stearn stated, for the "means which the Lord has appointed, and especially blessed to the conversion of sinners."[33]

Teaching with the authority of the Bible appealed to enslaved people more. However, Stearn could only make references to Biblical texts; he could not interpret what the Bible contained, he could give no advice about the message that God had intended for humans. The only thing that Stearn could do was to basically get the enslaved people to recite what was in the Bible. They resisted this as watered down religious instruction, as a disingenuous effort to use Christianity to make them better people, as the worst application of the Christian religion to the transformation of people's lives. The enslaved, according to Stearn, did not oppose Christian knowledge. What they opposed was the limited usage of the Bible to teach them. They wanted the same teaching that whites got; the same teaching, precepts, and principles that they could get from attending church on a Sunday. This was why they accepted Anglican baptism and conversion in any case.

Thomas Jones, who would die while teaching enslaved people in Jamaica, left this piece of advice for others who would undertake the mammoth task of teaching people who knew that they were free, but whose freedom was being challenged by slaveholders; a piece of advice which stated, in no uncertain terms, that the enslaved required a "new manner of communicating knowledge and religious instruction"; and this entailed, Jones added, the "endeavor to gain their attention" and "their affection," if there was any expectation of obtaining "their confidence."[34]

Conclusion

Again, we need to put to rest the old notion that no education system existed in Jamaica prior to the abolition of slavery. Maintaining such a view will only prevent us from analyzing the resistance and agency enslaved people displayed while interacting with the system that did exist. Undermining this system as merely provisions for instruction is also undermining all that enslaved people did to show that they were neither "socially dead," nor did they require "social reincarnation." While I will agree with Hawthorne that "social reincarnation" was evidence of agency, this is still based on the assumption that some kind of "social death" did occur.[35] There is no evidence of social death anywhere throughout the course of the education enterprise established in Jamaica. Instead, what we have seen is the determination by enslaved people to turn this education into something that was their own, into an education that they might use.

Slave freedom itself is maintained by the effort put into establishing controls or, at the very least, influence over systems of domination. Slave instruction was originally designed to try to make dominating the enslaved easier for slaveholders. The use of extreme forms of brutality and punishments were replaced with indoctrination, part and parcel of the thinking of the Enlightenment that domination, if it indeed had to happen, should be done using underhanded and less overtly brutal measures. Slave instruction was part of this new paradigm, part of the Enlightenment model of ensuring that production on sugar estates in Jamaica and other Caribbean colonies of the British continued, but without the objectionable practices of the past. Another term used for this change was "amelioration," which slaveholders adopted in spite of years of resistance. They had finally accepted that it was possibly more effective as a means of dominating enslaved people. Once again, they gave no consideration to slave freedom, no consideration to the agency of the enslaved, or their belief that they were really free people.

Notes

1. Emma Christopher, *Slave Ship Sailors and their Captive Cargoes, 1730–1807* (New York: Cambridge University Press, 2006), 94, 52, 120, 93.

2. Walter Hawthorne, "'Being Now, as It Were, One Family': Shipmate Bonding on the Slave Vessel *Emilia*, in Rio De Janeiro and Throughout the Atlantic World," *Luso-Brazilian Review* 45:1 (2008), 57, 59.

3. HCPP 1831–32 (481), Letter from the Bishop of Jamaica to Lord Viscount Goderich, Jamaica, 29 August 1831, Archdeaconry of Jamaica, 4.

4. UBA CW/03A/8, Mr. J.C. Sharpe to John Hylton, Accompong, 1 March 1830.

5. UBA CW/03A/12, Jamaica Auxiliary Church Missionary Society Proceedings, 26 July 1830; UBA CW/03A/13, Rev. John Stainsby to William Bullock, St. John's, 19 August 1830, On the Subject of Our Catechists Doing Militia Duty, Letter to the Governor's Secretary; UBA CW/083/25, Bishop Christopher to Henry C. Taylor, Liguanea, Jamaica, 8 July 1826.

6. The entire policy direction of the "Education for All" initiative of the Jamaican government since the 1990s is based on the belief that the challenge of making students learn is among the main challenges and one that is surmountable. However, the challenge is still very real. See "Education for All Assessment 2000: Jamaica Country Report," Ministry of Education and Culture, Kingston, Jamaica, September 1999.

7. Church Missionary Society, *Register of Missionaries (Clerical, Lay and Female)*, Part One, 27.

8. Ibid.

9. Ibid., 26, 27.

10. UBA CW/083/2, Salt Savannah, Vere, Henry Clarke Taylor to Rev. E. Bickersteth, London, 26 February 1826; UBA CW/083/15, Henry Taylor to the Secretaries, Church Missionary Society, London, 28 May 1827.

11. UBA CW/056/12, Dr. James Macfayden, Certificate of Mr. Manning's Health, 3 November 1830; Society, *Register of Missionaries (Clerical, Lay and Female)*, Part One, 25.

12. Society, *Register of Missionaries (Clerical, Lay and Female)*, Part One, 21.

13. Turner, "Planters Profits and Slave Rewards: Amelioration Reconsidered," 244–47.

14. UBA CW/04/9/1, Thomas Jones, Return of Papine School, St. Andrew, Jamaica, 1 February 1827.

15. Ibid.

16. UBA CW/083/15, Henry Taylor to the Secretaries, Church Missionary Society, London, 28 May 1827.

17. Rev. N.J. Hollingsworth, *An Address to the Public, in Recommendation of the Madras System of Education, as Invented and Practiced By the Rev. Dr. Bell, F.A.S.S. F.R.S. ED. With a Comparison between His Schools and those of Mr. Joseph Lancaster* (London: Printed by Law and Gilbert, 1812), iv, v, x, ix; For Lancaster's system, also see Joseph Lancaster, *Tracts on Education, 1776–1880* (London: Printed at the Royal Free School Press, 1811), v, iv.

18. UBA CW/083/15, Henry Taylor to the Secretaries, Church Missionary Society, London, 28 May 1827.

19. UBA CW/025/1, Ebenezer Collins to Donald Coates, Church Missionary Society, Salisbury Square, London, 24 December 1827.

20. UBA CW/079/10, Rev. John Stainsby to Donald Coates, Kingston, Jamaica, 10 March 1831; Society, *Register of Missionaries (Clerical, Lay and Female)*, Part One, 26.

21. UBA CW/088/8, Rev. J.M. Trew to Rev. Edward Bickersteth, Church Missionary Society, London, 1 July 1828.

22. UBA CW/025/2, Ebenezer Collins to the Secretaries, Church Missionary Society, Salisbury Square, London, 13 June 1828.

23. UBA CW/083/18, Henry Clarke Taylor to the Secretaries, Church Missionary Society, 20 December 1827.

24. UBA CW/083/9, Salt Savannah, Vere, Henry Clarke Taylor to the Secretaries, Church Missionary Society, Salisbury Square, London, 7 June 1826; UBA CW/083/12, Taylor to the Secretaries, Church Missionary Society, Salisbury Square, London, 11 October 1826.

25. UBA CW/083/14, Henry Clarke Taylor to the Secretaries, Church Missionary Society, 9 February 1827; UBA CW/04/1/7, Lesson Book, Jamaica Auxiliary Church Missionary Society, 1826.

26. UBA CW/02A/1/1, Bishop Christopher, Spanish Town, Jamaica, to Rev. Edward Bickersteth, Church Missionary House, London, 5 December 1826.

27. UBA CW/02A/1/2, Bishop Christopher, Spanish Town, Jamaica, to Rev. Edward Bickersteth, Church Missionary House, London, 4 May 1827.

28. Ibid.

29. Bernard Senior, *Jamaica, As It Was, As It Is, And As It May Be* (London: T. Hurst; Edinburgh: Grant and Son, 1835), 44–45.

30. UBA CW/02A/1/3, Letter from Rev. John M. McIntyre, Rector of St. James, Jamaica, to Bishop Christopher, Montego Bay, 24 March 1828.

31. UBA CW/02A/1/5, Correspondence of Auxiliary Committee with Ecclesiastical Commissioners, Jamaica, March-July 1828; UBA CW/02A/19B, Nicholas Forbes to Rev. R.C. Dallas, Maroon Town, Portland, 23 June 1832.

32. UBA CW/079/1, Rev. John Stainsby to Rev. Josiah Pratt, Church Missionary Society, Salisbury Square, London, 11 December 1820; UBA CW/056/3, Rev. William Manning to Donald Coates, Church Missionary Society, Salisbury Square, London, 19 August 1828; UBA CW/056/4, Rev. William Manning to Donald Coates, Church Missionary Society, Salisbury Square, London, 6 December 1828.

33. UBA CW/080/7, Salt Savannah, William Stearn to Rev. William Jowett, Church Missionary Society, London, October (Received 2 December) 1833.

34. HCPP 1826–27 (009), June 1826, Extract from the Report of Mr. Thomas Jones, of the Church Missionary Society, Transmitted to the Bishop of Jamaica, Relative to His Mode of Instructing the Slave Population at Papine Estate, in the Parish of St. Andrew, Jamaica, *Papers Respecting the Religious Instruction of the Slaves of the West Indies. Diocese of Jamaica and the Bahamas*, 1827, 291.

35. Hawthorne, "'Being Now, as It Were, One Family,'" 57, 59.

CHAPTER SIX

~

The Anglican Mandate

In this chapter, I examine the Anglican mandate. This made sure that the enslaved people in Jamaica became the most important group, especially in the reformulation of the island into a viable British colonial possession. The chapter therefore goes back to the beginning of the colonial enterprise. It examines events in the late seventeenth up to the late eighteenth centuries. This chapter is thus different from the previous chapters in two important ways: (1) the reversal to the start of British colonization; and (2) the examination of slave freedom indirectly. This examination is done through the factors that made certain that slave freedom indeed made the most vital contribution to the making of the British Atlantic. These factors are examined in the chapter using mainly the example of Jamaica.

Two additional considerations need to be made before proceeding. The first is the role of the Anglican Church, which was appointed as the church of the state in Jamaica. The church was viewed as having a central role in establishing Jamaica as a worthwhile colonial enterprise for Britain. The second is the way that the function of the church was envisaged. The church was mandated or granted the authorization by the crown to become the colony's main provider of values. This included moral as well as temporal values. In other words, Jamaica was expected to acquire its own cultural values and norms. However, none of these were expected to clash with the British culture. Jamaica was to become, for better or worse, a valuable British asset that was overseas.

In regards to the latter, the Anglican mandate had to incorporate every inhabitant of the colony. This included, of course, enslaved people. Their inclusion was more vital as it became more obvious that they were demographically the dominant group. In terms of social status, the enslaved were not to be excluded from colonial society. However, they were permanently relegated to a status significantly below the slaveholding people or other free inhabitants. Nevertheless, it was acknowledged that the enslaved were part of the fabric of the society. They made arguably the greatest contribution to the social order. They were, because of this, its greatest potential threat. The sheer strength of their number, as this grew, became a constant reminder of their potential to turn the society upside down. Therefore, it was necessary to indoctrinate enslaved people using the tried and proven means of the day: Anglican doctrine and principles.

As usual, reflection on the scholarship will explain further the significance of this chapter. It has implications for the scholarship on the entire Atlantic world. This is chiefly because of slave freedom itself, which was the main means through which the Atlantic world was made. However, the existing scholarship has not taken on board even the view that the enslaved created the Atlantic world. Their vital contribution has been put aside to accommodate assessments of British abolitionism and the Enlightenment. Part of the reason for the downgrading of the role of the enslaved is the absence of sufficient examination of the Anglican Church. There is no discussion about how this church was put into the position to become the valuable asset that it was. The church was critical to the suppression of the enslaved. This role made the church important, but also gave it another function, which was to aid in establishing the importance of the group that was in slavery.

Scholars have chosen to limit examination of the Anglican Church to its relationship with planters. Evidence of this is seen in this cunning phrase from Arthur Charles Dayfoot that this was the "planters' church."[1] However, this prevents analysis of the church among the enslaved. It prevents us from seeing the church in wider terms. It cannot account for the church's opposition to the planters and their excesses. Other scholars have assessed the enslaved using solely the topic of their suppression. In this scholarship you find details about the harshness and brutality of slavery. You find very little about agency, resistance, and nothing about the belief of enslaved people that they were free. Scholars of suppression often refer to the legislation passed to pacify enslaved people. This is the main feature of the two volumes by Richard Hart, *Slaves Who Abolished Slavery.*[2] Even though Hart makes this bold announcement, his fulfillment of the promise is very limited. His focus is fixed almost exclusively on slave revolts and viewable forms of nonviolent resistance.

He does not seem to know that resistance is still agency when it is unseen. Furthermore, Hart does not broaden his conceptualization to accommodate the view that enslaved people never lost sight or track of their freedom. Resistance was not freedom pursued, but freedom known.

Some of Hart's assessment is evident in today's studies. Gilien Matthews, Claudius Fergus, and David Ryden are among the present luminaries. We can add to this Andrew Jackson O'Shaughnessy.[3] The studies of these scholars have one fundamental error in common. They take the narrowed stance on resistance. The examinations are suppressive themselves. The enslaved would certainly not be pleased. They pay little if any regard to the Anglican Church. Because of this, the suppression is more. Resistance, when it is dealt with, is presented as a side show to a bigger event, British abolitionism. Even American independence is presented as more important than what people in slavery did for themselves. Little mention is made of how the enslaved in American had to adjust to the profoundest contradiction of all time: American slavery side by side with American freedom. Whatever the enslaved did seems never to be good enough. They never started any revolution except for the one in St. Domingue in 1791–1804, which itself is also undermined, if we believe the unbelievable in the studies by Michel-Rolph Trouillot and Susan Buck-Morss.[4]

Without a proper examination of the Anglican Church, there will never be an adequate appreciation of the early effects of slave freedom. This freedom had continuously manifested in the resistance and agency of the enslaved. The factor which mattered in abolitionism was the spectacle that the enslaved gave, the spectacle of slave freedom. Jamaica saw this freedom long before the British struggle to abolish the slave trade or slavery. Before abolitionists were even born, enslaved people were talking back to slaveholders about freedom. It is only just that this is where the scholarly gaze should be. Slave freedom continued the erosion of slavery. Its influence was not ignored even by British abolitionists, who mentioned the atrocities that the enslaved made more atrocious by resisting these and calling upon themselves more excessive suppression inside and outside of the law. Slave freedom spread to aid the British transition into its self-moralizing mission that is now known as abolitionism. But always bear in mind that this had started at a later date, mainly after 1780.

I am by no means arguing that existing scholars have totally ignored slave agency or resistance. Nothing could be falser than such an argument. There is at present the fine study by Trevor Burnard. He is now using the concept of "Powerless Masters" to find another way into assessing how the enslaved were crucial to the downfall of the planters.[5] In addition, Christer Petley has used "Gluttony" and "Excess" to show how planters undermined themselves. The eyes of the people back in Britain were cast upon them. Planter excesses and gluttony were based on exploitation, which is the important point. These were clearer signs of the disregard for the enslaved.[6] However, these studies at best have taken mainly the indirect approach. Slave resistance and agency are looked at through the planters' lenses. Not even the Anglican Church is there to offer a small departure. And there is no conceptualization remotely akin to slave freedom. Slave freedom, to remind you, argues that resistance and agency were signs of freedom maintained. These were not about freedoms won or gained.

The decision to focus the church's indoctrination on the enslaved made the revelation that slave freedom was real. The Anglican Church was the acknowledgement that the enslaved did not and would not accept slavery. They would continue to assert their freedom, forever resisting and undermining slaveholders. This examination of the church's mandate starts with the slave laws of Jamaica. This was where the admission first appeared fully clothed that slave freedom was present and there was a need to address it. One of these laws passed during the late seventeenth century will suffice. All of them basically stated the same things. Through this examination, I intend to show why the church was necessary, why the church aided in the suppression of the enslaved people. These laws were themselves designed to overpower enslaved people. However, these laws had evidence that much more than the law was needed. They contained ideas advocated by early Anglican writers, such as Hickeringill, about the virtues of church indoctrination. Essentially, the laws showed that enslaved people could not be pacified by what the law might have said. They would never work without resistance, even if the law stipulated that they should. Slave laws showed how the church's indoctrination could help. The laws expressed the hope that the church's powers could make the enslaved people put aside their idea that they were free.

The second section of this chapter is about the concept of hegemony. I use this to examine why so much priority was laid at the doorsteps of the church. Why was there so much faith in the church's indoctrination? I argue that hegemony was in use in England. It was part of the Restoration of the English crown in 1660, after Oliver Cromwell's death and the removal of his inept son, Richard. Hegemony was seen as a success in England. It was therefore the type of ideological weaponry deemed vital to the suppression of enslaved people. At the time, Jamaica became Britain's newest colony. The island was acquired just in time for the success of hegemonic rituals in its mother country. The view was that if this worked in England, there was no way that it could fail in Jamaica. This view was part and parcel of the underestimation of enslaved people; a sign of the racist ideology in which enslaved people were seen as inferior and thus incapable of resisting British-bred suppression. Racism, as I point out in the first section, predated slavery, but was applied to make the system work well. The English solution was to develop a hegemonic link between the church and the elite. The same formula was used in Jamaica, through the alliance between the church and slaveholding people, who were the colonial elite.

The final section is an assessment of the church's mandate directly. This draws upon the way the mandate operated. It uses, once more, an early published book about Jamaica, Hickeringill's *Jamaica Viewed*.[7] Hickeringill became an Anglican clergyman, which is important. His connection with the church makes his book vital to the examination of the church's mandate. Hickeringill himself was also of the view that the church should have power in Jamaica. He saw this as the only way to effectively colonize the minds of enslaved people. He was an early advocate of slave conversion and baptism, but not to liberate them, as religion is said to do, but to make them better slaves.[8] Hickeringill believed that perfect slavery was possible. He was an idealist. However, his focus also showed awareness of the difficult position of the slaveholders. They could not destroy slave freedom with their brutish punishment and suppressive atrocities. In fact, as Hickeringill implied, slaveholders only exposed their powerlessness when they resorted to brutalities. Destroying freedom took something more powerful, something clandestine; just as slave freedom itself survived as the clandestine counteraction to slavery. Finally, Hickeringill is useful because of his position of advantage. He saw Jamaica when it was first acquired as a British colony. He was there around four years after the 1655 capture from Spain, and he was motivated to write by what he saw.

The Slave Laws

An early slave law of the Jamaica House of Assembly, its legislature, was passed in 1696. The telling nature of this law is seen in its revelations about the way that slaveholding was envisaged. Importantly, the law was passed at a time when African enslavement in Jamaica was still young. Its necessity was a sign of the slaveholders' need for help. They knew that they would fail to suppress the enslaved if they dared to continue acting alone. Slaveholders realized that enslavement was the attempt to destroy freedom, and it could fail. Enslaved people would never easily give up the idea of being free.

The title given the law was also informative. It also indicates that slaveholders needed help. However, the law's title went further to specify the type of help that was needed. Accordingly, the title stated that the law was to bring about "better Order and Governance of the Slaves."[9] Every slave law passed in Jamaica from 1681 to 1737 was similarly named. In other words, the objectives remained the same. The laws exposed the need for a separate set of rules specifically for enslaved people. They were, in effect, the society's troublesome group. The cause of this was the survival of the belief in their freedom. This contradicted enslavement. The laws are the reminder that enslavement was also real. In addition, they were reassurances for the slaveholding people.

The admission that they needed help was the slaveholders' way of revealing the difficulty that they had with the suppression of the enslaved. This was also a sign of their fear. Slaveholders lived in constant fear of slave agency. Revolts were only one source of this constant fear. The whole barrage of the slaves' strategies of resistance sent a clear message to slaveholders that they were powerless to prevent enslaved people from showing that they had agency. They were in constant resistance mode and could change their situation at any given moment. The discovery of new ways to resist enslavement seemed endless. Some were more and less effective, but they were all seen by slaveholders as symptomatic of slave freedom. The slave laws were about the suppression of this resistance in whichever form it might manifest. For example, enslaved people could "suffer Death, Transportation, Dismembering" for even small offenses such as theft. Even these offenses necessitated the spectacle of a trial, and one that required the services of not one, but "Two Justices and Three Freeholders."[10]

However, also crucial was protecting slaveholding people. They were the ones most at risk. They were the ones that enslaved people saw as their enslavers on a daily basis. The slaveholders were also directly exposed to the daily acts of resistance whenever these happened. It was always only a matter of time before they might be affected in direct ways, physically or psychologically. Resistance took a toll on the minds of slaveholding people, just as it affected their physical security. This only made the law and all other forms of assistance more necessary. Suppression was seen as impossible if the slaveholders could not get this help. Help from the law came in the form of stipulations for reprimands and punishments, some more extreme than others. However, the law also showed the use of underhanded means. These were designed to silently, but with certainty, coerce enslaved people into the conformity that was needed. These underhanded means were signs of indoctrination, and acknowledgement that this was one of the potential sources of domination available to slaveholders. When the slave law of 1696, for example, stipulated that slaveholders had obligations and enslaved people had the right to allocations, this was indoctrination in motion.

All slave owners had to care for their enslaved people. The law stated clearly that while masters had the right to punish the enslaved, they did not have the right to make them suffer from neglect, poor working conditions, or unwarrantable punishments. A sense of justice was to be adopted by each and every slaveholder. This included specifically ensuring enslaved people were fed on a regular basis. If not, plantation lands were to be set aside for them to cultivate their own food crops. They should have access to gardens and provision grounds in these cases. However, the amounts of these allocations were not stated. This was left to the slaveholders themselves. The law's intention was not to totally strip from masters the power to determine how much or how well enslaved people ate, or even how well they clothed themselves.[11] Reserving these decisions for the slaveholders was preserving their ability to show enslaved people that they were their dominators. However, another form that this domination took was seen in the attempt made to give enslaved people the impression that they were important and deserving of proper care. This was an early use of the hegemonic trick.

Connections were made between the slave laws and the relatively recent acquisition of Jamaica as a British colony. These connections highlighted the need for indoctrination going forward into the future. The fortunes that could be made from the exploitation of the island by English settlers were tied to the creation of a viable slave system. However, as a fairly new addition to the British colonization of the Caribbean, the need for Jamaica to have a stable system of enslavement was seen as urgent. Envisioning this stability resulted in arguments in favor of the use of indoctrination, and the Church of England was the institution seen as the only one that could provide this indoctrination on a consistent and therefore effective basis. The idea that the island was a secondary prize, taken after the failure to capture neighboring St. Domingue, was abandoned shortly after Jamaica was acquired by the English in 1655. Though St. Domingue's profitability was doubtless, the idea that Jamaica could become similarly prosperous under British rule was quickly embraced. Once English settlement started, the argument was made that Jamaica's prosperity was also underway. One of the first to make the argument was Hickeringill.

In the pages that he dedicated to assessing Jamaica's prospects in his 1661 *Jamaica Viewed*, Hickeringill advised his English readers that Jamaica had the potential to become England's jewel in the crown. In fact, it could be transformed into the most valuable colony Britain had anywhere overseas. It could supersede St. Domingue, making the loss of this colony not the embarrassment that it was taken as by Cromwell. Jamaica's future, however, depended on the effective domination of the enslaved. There was no doubt

in Hickeringill's mind about the necessity of slavery. He had a clear perspective on the way that the world was structured. In this, nonwhite people were
at the bottom of the hierarchy of racial difference, white people were at the
top. This justified enslavement and made enslavement itself a product of the
racial division of the world into white people versus all other people.[12]

The kind of slavery Hickeringill had in mind relied on indoctrinating the
enslaved to accept their enslavement as ordained. In addition, enslaved people
were to see slavery as the means through which they could be exposed to the
superior culture of English people. In Hickeringill's mind, the people who were
suited for slavery were backward. Enslavement was thus their route to a better life. However, to send this message clearly, the slave system had to adopt
indoctrination and abandon the use of brutality. Hickeringill was well aware
of the double-sided effects of brutality. It could undermine slaveholders themselves. It was a sign of brutishness, which was in opposition to the superiority
that English people were supposed to have. Slavery should not be brutal so that
enslaved people could respect the slave owners, and view them as having the
right to be their masters. In a number of ways, Hickeringill's views appeared in
the slave laws passed after his book was published. There was still resistance to
the Anglican Church. Slaveholders did not give up their belief that exposure
to Christianity might also give the enslaved ideas about freedom. However, the
use of indoctrination as a principle of domination was adopted. The problem
was that this was instituted alongside the survival of brutalities. Hickeringill
would not have seen this as a wise approach. It was one or the other. Using
both would endanger the two. Using both would cancel the effects of each. On
the one hand, brutality would engender in enslaved people more resentment
and hatred for the masters. On the other hand, indoctrination would further
expose brutality and worsen the impression that enslaved people had of those
masters who resorted to using brutal means.

Implementation of the slave laws was tied to Hickeringill's perspective
that the system of slavery was more important than even the slaveholders.
Protecting this system and making it better was supposed to be the colony's
main objective. The slave laws showed this by putting pressure on masters
and enslaved people alike. The pressure was applied to the confinement of
enslavement to the practices stipulated by the laws. Slaveholders were also
required to abide by stipulations such as the provisions made for the subsistence and maintenance of the enslaved. Punishments of various types were
reserved for enslaved people who were insubordinate or resistant in any other
way. The survival of these mandatory clauses was seen in the mid-eighteenth
century, when a new slave law rehashed the tenets of previous laws, but with
severer reprimands and restrictions in response to Tacky's revolt in 1760.

This revolt was interpreted by slaveholders in the widest possible sense. As Burnard has stated, it was a sign of the "undeclared war" between enslaved people and slaveholding people, a war "always likely to erupt," and which did in mid-1760.[13] In its aftermath, as Rev. G.W. Bridges recorded, the slave law that was passed embraced the entire gamut of suppressive measures of prior laws, and made the reprimands severer. Even free blacks and coloreds now had to identify themselves all the time by wearing blue crosses on the right shoulders of their clothing. Bans on the movement of enslaved people were reformulated to include prohibiting them to leave plantations on any day unless they had tickets from masters. No master could issue tickets on a Sunday, except to those enslaved people who sold fresh milk and fish. Enslaved people could not blow horns or assemble for long periods of time.[14] Hickeringill might not have agreed with the extremity of many of these measures. However, he would have found them useful as evidence of the failure to fully embrace the idea of indoctrination, using exposure to the Anglican Church.

On the other hand, even with the extreme measures adopted in 1760, the slave laws were still based on assumptions that Hickeringill also made. The most basic of these was the expectation that resistance was bound to happen. Hickeringill assumed enslaved people would never "go gentle," words penned by Dylan Thomas to capture the human capacity for defiance, but would "rage against the dying of the light."[15] This was the main basis on which Hickeringill proposed indoctrination. He had no way to be sure it would work. However, he felt that this was a safer policy than the other alternative of brutality. Indoctrination would not, in Hickeringill's view, become itself the encouragement of resistance. Brutality could not avoid being this way. Nevertheless, the use of brutality also showed that slaveholders viewed enslavement in problematical terms. Hickeringill's stance on slavery was the same. Spectacular suppression, as Foucault might put it, was therefore necessary, whether this came in the form of extremities or subtle persuasion, whether brutality or indoctrination.[16]

Evidence that slaveholders problematized slavery and therefore anticipated resistance was seen in other areas of the Atlantic world. Long ago, J. Thorsten Sellin wrote that slaveholders in the American South adopted the view that they had to "terrify" enslaved people to make them obedient. They implemented laws to this effect, never for a minute assuming that slavery was the natural state of humankind and therefore free from resistance determined to see the system ended. Slaveholders in the South knew, according to Sellin, that to keep "the slave-labor force intact," they needed all kinds of assistance.[17] The law was brought in to provide one very important aspect of this help. Farther south in Barbados, Britain's first colonial experiment in the Caribbean, a slave law was passed in 1661. This was just in time for the explosion of African enslavement in that island. Hilary Beckles notes, for instance, that Barbados became "perhaps the most attractive colony in the English New World" in the "mid-1640s."[18] As slavery grew, so did the need to suppress the enslaved. The strength of their numbers was a constant reminder of resistance. Slaveholders had created a system that they themselves could not control and were ready to embrace almost any measure that proposed assistance. Richard S. Dunn also observes that the law became an indispensable feature "of forced black labor" in Barbados.[19]

Another clear link with Hickeringill was the racial basis for slavery. Hickeringill, as stated, divided the world into white and nonwhite. Nonwhites were seen as suitable for enslavement. The position of slaveholder was reserved for whites. This division itself was an important statement about the necessity for hegemonic slavery. Dividing the world along the lines of race in order to create slavery was a sign that this hierarchy was needed to validate enslavement. Eric Williams' famous formula that slavery created racism does not quite capture the truth of the dynamic.[20] Slavery did not adopt racism after slavery was created. Race was a factor in the establishment of slavery. Racism predated both slavery and the slave laws, but was pulled into both, with the hope that it could make them work as the slaveholders expected.

In any case, the first slave laws were passed before the system of African enslavement came close to anything we could describe as maturity. This was before the massive importation of Africans between 1678 and 1708, for instance. It was only during this period that Barbados, Jamaica, along with Antigua, imported the whopping 88,108 enslaved Africans.[21] I am sure we can also find evidence of racism in the writings of white adventurers who traveled to nonwhite Africa even prior to Columbus' crossing of the Atlantic. This was prior to the European discovery that other nonwhite people existed over on the real western side of the world. Yet, these were the first people (now referred to as Amerindians) that Europeans would enslave in the New World. That kind of search is regrettably beyond the scope of this chapter. However, there is one book that I know was published in 1623, the year before English settlement of the first English Caribbean colony of Barbados.[22] In this and perhaps others published around that period, nonwhite Africans were depicted in derogatory terms, as the combined force of Carl and Roberta Bridenbaugh has told us. These accounts described black Africans in racist terms, such as having no "code of morals" and no "diffusion of culture" as a result.[23] These racist views were used to justify and maintain the enslavement of both the Africans and the Amerindians before them.

Slaveholders in Jamaica left nothing up to chance. They embraced the Barbadian model for the slave laws when they finally passed theirs. Their preconceptions about nonwhites aided in the building of this system of slavery. Views expressed by early writers, such as Hickeringill, about Jamaica's prospects as a British colony also espoused the virtues of enslavement, in addition to supporting the notion that slavery must be conceptualized in broader terms. It needed indoctrination as part of its machinery of domination. The use of hegemony during the English Restoration exemplified one way in which this indoctrination could be done.

Hegemonic Restoration

According to Carl Boggs, hegemony is an "organizing principle." With this, Boggs is alluding to the engineering of consent.[24] Hegemony is an underhanded way of getting people to consent to their domination. The objective is to prevent resistance. When it works, as it did in ancient Greece, the result is "a relatively consensual form of leadership." There is no need for tyranny. Authoritarian rule is excessive, but exercised with relative ease. At this point, authoritarian rule is seen as the only way to bring about stability, or to manage, shape, and control the society. Hegemony is its own validation.[25] Aristotle saw this clearly. He describes hegemony using the term "legitimate" to indicate how it validates itself. However, Aristotle adds that the legitimization comes about because hegemonic rule attaches itself to "common interests."[26] It is sold on this basis that it provides the kind of rule that people need for their own good. Their interests are shared by the ruler. Even if the ruler has to resort to dictatorial measures on occasion, this too is seen to be done for the good of everyone.

The foundations of hegemony, as Antonio Gramsci has recorded, are its alliances with the elites. Gramsci mentioned the alliance with the "intellectuals" of the society, brought in to function as the virtual "deputies" or "functionaries" of the hegemonic ruler.[27] The success of hegemony in a slave colony would therefore need an alliance of a similar kind. This would have to be with the colonial elite, and these were the slaveholding people, but especially the growing body of wealthy and influential sugar planters.

Hickeringill appealed for the adoption of hegemonic rule in Jamaica which was similar to Restoration hegemony in England. He viewed this as the only way to secure the system of slavery from the resistance of enslaved people. Restoration hegemony applied in England was viewed as a successful venture. The publication of Hickeringill's book on Jamaica occurred only a year after the Restoration became official. Hickeringill embraced the hegemonic rule of the restored king, and proposed that the new colony of Jamaica should adopt the same ideological weaponry to engineer the consent of its enslaved people. Hickeringill made no attempt to differentiate enslaved Amerindians from enslaved Africans. Both were nonwhites and therefore qualified for enslavement. Hickeringill wrote specifically about Amerindians only because they were not yet fully exterminated, and he felt that hegemonic rule could also save them from extinction. It would erase the use of brutality, replacing this with slavery based on consent.[28]

Hegemony was a factor in the Restoration of the English crown. This took place under Charles II, whose father, Charles I, was executed by regicides in 1649. The Restoration occurred on April 4, 1660, but the process really started in 1659, when Richard Cromwell was deposed by the Wallingford House Party. Richard was described as an inept substitute for his father, Oliver Cromwell. At this juncture, England was in desperate need of strong leadership. The history of the monarchy's absolutism gave the impression that it could provide this kind of leadership. The crown was needed to hold the country together. This was in order to avoid another civil war and Interregnum. Restoration was paid for with hegemonic rule.

Under the Declaration of Breda, for example, signed by Charles II, the crown was restored following the king's agreement to certain concessions. However, these concessions were exchanged for the divine right of the king to rule. Charles II acknowledged Parliament and ended religious intolerance throughout the kingdom. He recognized property rights and even paid off the army its arrears, which included servicemen who had fought against the crown. However, according to Thomas Henry Lister, the Breda Declaration was arranged on "ambiguity." Parliament was indeed given the powers that it wanted. However, the most important part of this power was to settle "all difficulties" in which the king did not have to get involved.[29] The powers that had been granted to Parliament had also removed the king from having those same responsibilities.

The readiness with which Charles II had decided to agree to the concessions in the Breda Declaration was also noted by Lister. He states, for example, that "The ambiguity of this declaration must have caused dissatisfaction, if the King had not removed responsibility from himself, and referred all difficulties to the decision of the Parliament." The king had realized, as Lister adds, that "in the absence of kingly rule," for many years in the past, Parliament "had been the sole constitutional source of power."[30] It was therefore from Parliament that the English masses were expecting leadership directly. The king established an alliance with Parliament that also meant the restoration of the crown's popularity among the masses. The crown was reinstituted on the basis of a Gramscian hegemonic alliance with the elected elite.

Following the hegemonic alliance built into the Declaration of Breda, was the use of parochial bodies to restore faith in crown rule throughout England. Steve Hindle has observed that these parochial bodies exercised their control over the parishioners through negotiation.[31] This gave the parishioners the impression of power sharing. They were led to believe that power was no longer centralized, but was diffused. They also had power, but all that time they were doing the bidding of the parochial bodies, which were also working for London. Ordinary parishioners held offices that they would not have held in the past. This was part of spreading the message as widely as possible that the ordinary folk were now ruling themselves. However, real power remained in London, where it was disseminated in a similar fashion to Parliament to do the work that the crown felt was mundane. The king was indeed restored.

Hickeringill saw the Restoration as an opportunity to position himself as the guiding light of Jamaica. He made Jamaica his personal project. On a personal level, this was also of benefit to him. Hickeringill was the kind of person who was always searching for the next big chance to enhance his career and thus his social status. When the first Cromwell assumed the title of lord protector, Hickeringill was one of his supporters. He switched his allegiance to Charles II at the Restoration of the monarchy. Hickeringill's political outlook is best described as opportunistic. He allied himself to whatever appeared to be working politically at any given time. Restoration and its hegemonic pacts gave Hickeringill the impression of a successful political arrangement when this happened.

His opportunism was demonstrated from early in his career as a theologian. He changed sides often after leaving Cambridge University a master of theology in 1652. After this, Hickeringill won a lucrative post as the Baptist pastor for the "congregation in Hexman in Northumberland," Scotland. Hickeringill made himself "their messenger in Scotland."[32] The next year, he gained another assignment as the chaplain of "Robert Lilburne's regiment of horse." This was while Lilburne himself was at the height of his popularity, because he was one of the regicides who had signed the death warrant of Charles I. Over the next few years, Hickeringill secured other positions in church and government. His influence grew as a result. He had a voracious appetite for upward social mobility, seen in the changes that he made. He was a Quaker at one point, and then allegedly an atheist. His Baptist allegiance was known, even his excommunication from Leith when the congregation heard about his atheism. This did not stand in Hickeringill's way. Later, he was redeployed "the lieutenant to Captain Gascoigne in Colonel Daniell's regiment" in Scotland. Small political appointments in Scotland followed. His departure from Scotland in 1657 came when he joined the Foreign Service. At the Restoration, Hickeringill was an Anglican clergyman.[33]

This social climber saw another opportunity when Richard Cromwell was made to leave. Around the same time, Hickeringill wrote that he "made a stay in Jamaica." This was enough to convince him that under English rule, the future of the island was bright. The Restoration was the first step in the direction of this future. Hickeringill also wrote in *Jamaica Viewed* that he was giving his "Description" of the island as his contribution to its bright prospects. He proposed seeing Jamaica as a better prize than even St. Domingue. He wrote that merely describing Jamaica was also "to Praise it." The island was already a "pearl."[34] At this point, Hickeringill was also a "Godly cleric" of the church of state, also a sign that he had "curried favor" with the Restoration king.[35]

Jamaica had its own parliament, the House of Assembly. Concessions made to the Parliament in England could also be made to the one in Jamaica. Hickeringill saw this as a good start for the island. England's control could materialize through Jamaica's parliamentary system. The governor of Jamaica, who was the king's representative, should play the role of the king in the colony. The machinery for a hegemonic diffusion of power was already in place in Jamaica. The Assembly was dominated by the colonial elite, Englishmen who were still Englishmen though they were overseas. They could ensure that power remained where it belonged: diffused to the colonial elite, but still concentrated in the king's representative, the governor. Wherever freedom existed in the colony, it could be made to abide by the guidelines of the Restoration crown. Even the freedom of the enslaved could be controlled in this way, and the Church of England, which was also the church of state in the colony, could be brought in to aid the suppressive manipulation of freedom, wherever this existed.

The Anglican Mandate

There should be no doubt about the wide readership of Hickeringill's *Jamaica Viewed*. It was not seen as "clumsily written" at the time that it was published.[36] Hickeringill wrote the book in the language of poetry because he wrote it for the elite. He was interested only in appealing to this segment of the reading public, who could make a difference to Jamaica. These were people who had money and influence, and were educated enough to see that the island had a bright future. Poetry was a way to also bring out the beauty that Hickeringill thought he saw in Jamaica. The elite could make hegemony work in the colony, comprised as they were of the same people in Parliament who made it work in England.

Surprising to me is that *Jamaica Viewed* has received almost no attention from scholars. Hickeringill's biographers, Justin Champion and J.L.C. McNulty, for example, have paid the book almost no regard. Hickeringill himself knew exactly what he wanted the book to do and wrote it in only forty-five pages, so that it was short enough to be interesting and informative, but not longer to be boring. Readers such as "G.E. Med D." said that the book was timely and praised Hickeringill, stating that "Methinks I love thee for this book the more." Its publisher, Benjamin Bragge of London, took it into a fourth edition many years after its initial publication in 1661. This was during the English "War with Spain" in the early eighteenth century, when the book was still being described by Bragge as "very useful and profitable."[37] This edition, published in 1705, also came out only three years before Hickeringill himself died.

Charles II had either read the book or he was informed of its contents by another party. It was circulated at court, and Hickeringill was presented with a reward as the first "secretary of state for Jamaica." This "post" was said to be lucrative. The salary reached "£1000 a year."[38] Hickeringill turned down the post nonetheless; his mind was made up to return to England. There, he could continue his climb up the social ladder. Leaving Jamaica was not about abandoning the island he claimed that he loved. His contribution to Jamaica was already made; the book was his proof. Furthermore, Hickeringill felt that it had guidelines that any sensible colonial could follow, and the church was already there waiting for instructions to use its powers to fashion the kind of culture that could make the financial prosperity that Hickeringill foresaw. The need now was for the crown to act—to send instructions about the church as the provider of values and norms. These were sent in due course. Governors of Jamaica were told to do as much as they could to promote the church as the church of state. No one should be allowed to stand in the way of the church's mission in the island.

In 1661, Thomas Windsor was governor of Jamaica and was sent the following instructions: "you are to give the best Encouragement you can, to such Conformable & Orthodox Ministers of the Gospel, as now are, or shall come, and be sent unto you, That Christianity, and the Protestant Religion, according to the Doctrine & Discipline of the Church of England, may have a due Reverence & Exercise among you."[39] The same directives were sent to subsequent governors, with additional stipulations to show the decision to foster bonds between church and state, and church and society. There would be no separation of powers at this point. The church might not have a direct role in government, but it was its guide on matters spiritual and temporal. In 1681, the governor, Thomas Lynch, was given this reminder that the

bonds between church, state, and society required his attention and protection. Lynch was told to shield the clergy from imposters that might damage
its reputation and disrupt its important duty and alliances. This instruction
commanded Lynch to make sure that no one "*without a Certificate, from the
Bishop of London,* of his being conforming to the Doctrine and Discipline of
the Church of England," would ever hold the office of clergyman.[40]

The attempt was not to give the governors control over the church. The
church was to be independent, but not separate. The objective was for the
governors to help the church help itself, and thus help the society. The role
granted the church was never to be compromised. Men without training or
ordination were seen as among the biggest threats. The vestry that administered each parish's affairs should not become an obstacle either. In fact, to
avoid this, each vestry was to have a clergyman among its members. This was
also to become a permanent post. No meeting of the vestry could occur in
the clergyman's absence. Meetings without him went ahead only because he
had knowledge of and had consented to these meetings. The entire executive
of government was to give the clergymen "good and Sufficient Stipends, &
allowances," allocations agreed upon by governor and nominated Council.[41]
The Assembly, at this point, should not have a say in the compensation for
the clergy. This was a matter beyond parliamentary debates.

No distinction was made between Jamaica's free and enslaved inhabitants in the instructions sent to the governors of the island. Both were to be
brought to a level of Christian observation acceptable by church standards.
Slaveholders were to be targeted along with their enslaved. Christianity and
slavery were not seen as incompatible.

Hickeringill had argued for church indoctrination along the same lines
that both slaveholders and enslaved should become loyal congregants of the
church. However, he accepted the racial hierarchy on which enslaved people
were inferior and their enslavers were superior. In Hickeringill's view, the
inferiority of enslaved people was the main reason for their enslavement in
the first place, and the main reason he thought of them as controllable using
hegemony. Enslavement was not an end; rather, it should serve a purpose,
which should be the exposure of the enslaved to the superior culture of slaveholders, in order for enslaved people to rise on the hierarchy of cultures. In
return, argued Hickeringill, the enslaved would work for slaveholders without the expectation of compensation, and without resistance.

David Eltis refers to this viewpoint as the rejection of the human condition of enslaved people. They were repositioned as "non-citizens," which
was perfectly acceptable to the English, despite their rejection of slavery in
England. They "re-accepted slavery" in the New World because they saw the

enslaved as "non-citizens," people who were neither English nor British.[42] This disqualified them from British freedom, a disqualification that was also justifiable because to be enslaved made one not exactly a person.

Hickeringill was very certain that the Anglican Church was the best church to become the hegemonic ally of slaveholding. He was known for his criticisms of other churches, once he became an Anglican cleric. However, Hickeringill was also critical of the Anglican Church. If he believed that its practices undermined its potential or its hegemonic role, he was critical of these practices. He reserved some of this criticism for the Catholic Church also because it was a state church in other countries in Europe, and because the Anglican Church, in his view, had adopted some of the practices of the Catholics. As McNulty states, Hickeringill indeed "launched theological and dogmatic attacks on established church practice," but this was not for the purpose of "exposing and undermining the cultural foundations of sacerdotal authority."[43] Hickeringill's criticisms were to make the authority of the state churches stronger. He exposed how these churches had been undermining themselves, how they were making themselves unpopular and insufficient in the eyes of the masses. Hickeringill's view was that state churches should become the most widely accepted and respected churches. They should be the churches to which the masses clung, and this should be done without discussion or reservation. Hickeringill's view was that the "popish" practices of these churches had been causing the reverse to happen.[44]

How was the Anglican mandate to be carried out in Jamaica? Hickeringill's discussion about this was really an early discussion about cultural imperialism. This relied on seeing nonwhite people as simpleminded, and this was the way that Hickeringill depicted Amerindians, the group that he had chosen for this discussion. According to Hickeringill, their simpleminded state made Amerindians ripe for enslavement. The matter of them not wanting enslavement was a nonissue. If they saw themselves as free, this was resistance that should be suppressed. Hickeringill also saw this as not true freedom, or as not the kind that the British had. Exposure to British freedom would make the enslaved aspire to get this. Their simpleminded state was the assurance that the aspiration was present, and that exposure to British freedom, through Anglican indoctrination, would also result in their pacification as enslaved people. Hickeringill had thus stated that "No other Caterer" would slaveholders need.[45]

Male Amerindians, according to Hickeringill, were already showing their readiness for enslavement in the fact that they were never without their "Bill and Bow." These were signs that they were prepared to hunt and gather for the benefit of slaveholders. Culturally, according to Hickeringill, Amerindians were showing their suitability for exploitation as slaves. Reserving his most caustic remarks of female Amerindians, Hickeringill left no doubt that he thought of the Amerindians as inferior, and this made their hegemonic exploitation also a relatively straightforward venture. This was Hickeringill's aim in his description of female Amerindians as "heedless," and as attiring themselves in a way that "all is bare." These indicators of their simplicity further made the point about their suitability for enslavement and hegemony. Hickeringill went on to state that though female Amerindians might be "Lovely" in appearance, settlers must bear in mind that they are also "Brown." Their skin color was thus the most visible sign of their inferior state. Adding to this was their intemperance. Hickeringill made this other point when he advised his readers to observe that, "If of your Wine and Brandy, you'll be free…They'll not leave till they Drunk as Beggars be." This was supposed to also apply to all Amerindians, females as well as males.[46]

The language of hegemony is deflection. Hickeringill made use of this when describing the Amerindian people as "true philosophers." However, he also used this to exemplify their simplicity, but without actually stating this. In the Guianas, this was very clear, where, according to Hickeringill, Amerindians lived in harmony with nature, and therefore had an attachment to the environment that was useful to slaveholders. This was another indication that they could be manipulated, and in this case, the purpose was manual labor. Slaveholders could use their attachment to the soil to their advantage. Furthermore, because of their limited aspirations, Amerindians, stated Hickeringill, could be put to work for the benefit of others with relative ease. According to Hickeringill, "not much they have…Nor do they want much, nor much do they crave." Their religious practices made their enslavement a necessity. Amerindians had the world upside down, as far as Hickeringill could see. They had a God for evil, known as "*Yerkin*," which, in Hickeringill's view, was a sign of their delusion. God and evil together was an oxymoron. The Christian view that Hickeringill had identified God as good and nothing else; there was no such thing as an evil God. Evil in the Christian worldview was signified by the Devil. Yet, as Hickeringill states, "They call the Devil *Yerkin*," and to make the matter worse, "him alone They Worship."[47]

Conclusion

Hickeringill gave no indication that he thought of enslaved people, Amerindian or otherwise, as "socially dead." Instead, Hickeringill insisted on using the culture of enslaved people to the advantage of slaveholders. They could be manipulated fairly easily because of this culture, which Hickeringill considered as inferior. Hegemonic controls provided the means to make this manipulation happen. Once the enslaved were exposed to Christendom, which Hickeringill thought of as superior, their resistance would diminish, and it might even disappear. The enslaved would never resist controls that gave them access to a culture that was vastly more advanced than theirs, that was basically for their own good.

Hickeringill based all of this on the racial hierarchy, which was the lens through which the English viewed the world. Hickeringill's confidence in his plan was also a sign that he had confidence in the lines that were drawn to divide the world into races. Jamaica's slave system, as Hickeringill stated, would profit from this racial division and its hierarchical structure. This hierarchy provided the way in which the enslaved was best perceived, and the means to bring about their effective pacification and domination. However, the assumption that was also implied by the hierarchy was that the enslaved would not willingly accept enslavement. A hierarchy was needed to engineer this willingness. The enslaved knew that they were free, and anticipated nothing that could permanently or effectively change this. In Hickeringill's view, this was the fact that made the racial hierarchy useful and hegemonic control always a necessity.

Centralizing the enslaved was the main point that Hickeringill made. His vision of the age of slavery was not about slave masters, but about the people that they tried to enslave. For this reason, Hickeringill wrote for the slaveholders, but about the enslaved. The making of a slave society anywhere was about how enslaved people should be controlled, about exploring the ways that control might be possible, about anticipating enslaved agency, resistance, and freedom. There would be no such thing as an age of slavery without these considerations. The Atlantic world and the productivity of enslaved people on which this world was based would remain as aspirations. The reality would be the same freedom that the enslaved maintained, and which frustrated the adventurism inherent in slaveholding. The slaveholders' desire was to control and dominate enslaved people, but this was desire, not the reality. As Hickeringill's book indicates, freedom was the condition that slavery had to counteract. Slavery did not invent freedom; rather, freedom made slavery the problem of an entire age.

The means through which abolitionism would happen was slave freedom. This was the only indication that freedom was under attack, the only sign that there was a need to start a campaign in freedom's defense. Abolitionism was the product of freedom, the freedom that the enslaved made visible for everyone to see, the freedom that was a constant annoyance for slaveholding.

Hickeringill would be very surprised that enslaved people have not been put into a more central position in the scholarship purporting to understand the age of slavery and its demolition. From 1661, Hickeringill had seen that to understand the colonized world meant understanding how enslaved people reacted to the measures put in place to destabilize their freedom.

Notes

1. Arthur Charles Dayfoot, *The Shaping of the West Indian Church* (Kingston and Gainesville: The Press University of the West Indies and University Press of Florida, 1999), 111; and Dale Bisnauth, *History of Religions in the Caribbean* (Kingston: LMH Publishing, 2006), 48, 49.

2. See especially Hart, *Slaves Who Abolished Slavery, Vol. 2*.

3. Gilien Matthews, *Caribbean Slave Revolts and the British Abolition Movement* (Baton Rouge: Louisiana State University Press, 2006); Claudius Fergus, "Dread of Insurrection: Abolitionism, Security, and Labor in Britain's West Indian Colonies, 1760–1823," *William and Mary Quarterly* 66:4 (2009): 757–80; David Ryden, *West Indian Slavery and British Abolition, 1783–1807* (Cambridge University Press, 2009); and Andrew Jackson O'Shaughnessy, *An Empire Divided: The American Revolution and the British Caribbean* (Pennsylvania: University of Pennsylvania Press, 2000).

4. See Michel-Rolph Trouillot, *Silencing the Past: Power and the Production of History* (Boston: Beacon Press, 1997); and Susan Buck-Morss, *Hegel, Haiti, and Universal History* (Pittsburgh: University of Pittsburgh Press, 2009), a book which expands on an earlier essay by the same author, "Hegel and Haiti," *Critical Inquiry* 26:4 (2000): 821–65.

5. See Trevor Burnard, "Powerless Masters: The Curious Decline of Jamaican Sugar Planters in the Foundational Period of British Abolitionism," The Elsa Goveia Memorial Lecture 2010, Department of History and Archeology, University of the West Indies, Mona, Jamaica.

6. See Christer Petley, "Gluttony, Excess, and the Fall of the Planter Class in the British Caribbean," *Atlantic Studies* 9:1 (2012): 85–106. See also Petley's earlier work, which he gives an appropriate title for what this study was really about: *Slaveholders in Jamaica: Colonial Society and Culture during the Era of Abolition* (London: Pickering & Chatto Ltd., 2009).

7. Edmund Hickeringill, *Jamaica Viewed: With All the Ports, Harbours, and Their Several Soundings, Towns, and Settlements Thereunto Belonging. Together with the Nature of Its Climate, Fruitfulness of the Soil, and Its Fruitfulness to English Complexions*, 3rd. ed. (London: Benjamin Bragge, at the Blew Ball, in Ave-Mary Lane, 1705 [1661]).

8. The idea that religion, specifically Christianity, is a form of liberation appears in these studies of Jamaica's history during and after slavery: Devon Dick, *The Cross and the Machete: Native Baptists of Jamaica, Identity, Ministry and Legacy* (Kingston: Ian Randle Publisher, 2009); Shirley C. Gordon, *Our Cause for His Glory: Chris-*

tianisation and Emancipation in Jamaica (Kingston: The Press University of the West Indies, 1998); Veront M. Satchell, "Colonial Injustice: *The Crown v. the Bedwardites, 27 April 1921,*" in *The African-Caribbean Worldview and the Making of Caribbean Society*, Horace Levy, ed. (Kingston: University of the West Indies Press, 2009), 46–48; and Horace Russell, "The Emergence of the Christian Black: The Making of a Stereotype," *Jamaica Journal* 16:1 (1983): 51–58.

9. ECCO 1738, Acts of Assembly, Passed in the Island of Jamaica; from 1681, to 1737, Inclusive. *Laws, etc.* London, printed by John Baskett, 1739, 73.

10. Ibid., 75.

11. Ibid.

12. Hickeringill, *Jamaica Viewed*, 30–32.

13. Burnard, *Mastery, Tyranny, and Desire*, 138.

14. Bridges, *The Annals of Jamaica*, Vol. 2, 100.

15. These are quoted from Dylan Thomas' famous poem, "Do Not Go Gentle Into That Good Night." The quotes are used here as metaphors for enslavement. See Ralph Louis Woods, *Famous Poems and the Little-known Stories Behind Them* (Portland, OR: Hawthorn Books, 1961), 235.

16. See Michel Foucault, *Discipline and Punish: The Birth of the Prison* (New York: Vintage, 1995).

17. J. Thorsten Sellin, *Slavery and the Penal System* (New York: Elsevier Scientific Publishing, 1976), 137.

18. Beckles, *A History of Barbados*, 13.

19. Richard S. Dunn, *Sugar and Slaves: The Rise of the Planter Class in the English West Indies, 1624–1713* (Chapel Hill: The University of North Carolina Press, 2000), 225, 227.

20. Williams, *Capitalism and Slavery*, 7.

21. ECCO 1709, An Account of the Number of Negroes Delivered in to the Islands of Barbadoes, Jamaica, and Antego, from the Year 1698 to 1708. Since the Trade Was Opened, Taken from the Accounts Sent from the Respective Governours of Those Islands to the Lords Commissioners of Trade, *Social Sciences*, London.

22. See Richard Jobson, *The Discovery of River Gambia* (London: Hakluyt Society, 1999 [1623]). Also see this later work by John Watts, *A True Relation of the Inhumane and Unparallel'd Actions and Barbarous Murders of Negroes or Moors, Committed on Three English-Men in Old Calabar in Guinny...* (London, 1672 [1668]).

23. Carl Bridenbaugh and Roberta Bridenbaugh, *No Peace Beyond the Line: The English in the Caribbean, 1624–1690* (New York: Oxford University Press, 1972), 233. See also pages 234–36 and 238–40.

24. Boggs, *Gramsci's Marxism*, 39.

25. Philip G. Cerny, "Dilemmas of Operationalizing Hegemony," in *Hegemony and Power: Consensus and Coercion in Contemporary Politics*, Mark Haugaard and Howard H. Lentner, eds. (Lanham, MD: Lexington Books, 2006), 68.

26. Mark Haugaard, "Conceptual Confrontations," in *Hegemony and Power: Consensus and Coercion in Contemporary Politics*, 4.

27. Antonio Gramsci, *Selections from the Prison Notebooks*, Quintin Hoare and Geoffrey Nowell Smith, eds. and trans. (London: Lawrence and Wishart, 1971), 9.

28. Hickeringill, *Jamaica Viewed*, 32.

29. Thomas Henry Lister, *The Life and Administration of Edward, First Earl of Clarendon; with Original Correspondence and Authentic Papers Never Before Published. In Three Volumes, Vol. 1* (London: Longman, Orme, Brown, Green, and Longmans, 1838), 501.

30. Ibid., 502.

31. Steve Hindle, "Exhortation and Entitlement: Negotiating Inequality in English Rural Communities, 1550–1650," in *Power in Early Modern Society: Order, Hierarchy, and Subordination in Britain and Ireland*, Michael J. Braddick and John Walter, eds. (Cambridge, UK: Cambridge University Press, 2001), 104.

32. J.L.C. McNulty, Hickeringill, Edmund (*Bap.* 1631, *D.* 1708), *Oxford Dictionary of National Biography*, [www.oxforddnb.com/view/article/13200, Accessed January 21, 2009].

33. Ibid. Also see Justin Champion and J.L.C. McNulty, "Making Orthodoxy in Late Restoration England: The Trials of Edmund Hickeringill, 1662–1710," in *Power in Early Modern Society*, 227–48; and John Morrill, Cromwell, Oliver (1599–1658), *Oxford Dictionary of National Biography*, [www.oxforddnb.com/view/article/13200, Accessed January 21, 2009].

34. Hickeringill, *Jamaica Viewed*, v.

35. Champion and McNulty, "Making Orthodoxy in Late Restoration England," 227; McNulty, Hickeringill, Edmund (*Bap.* 1631, *D.* 1708).

36. Vincent Carretta, "Writings of the British Black Atlantic," *Eighteenth-Century Studies* 34:1 (2000), 122.

37. Hickeringill, *Jamaica Viewed*, vi, ii.

38. Ibid., i-ii.

39. FP XVII, Jamaica (i) 1661–1739 (93–292), Instructions for Thomas Windsor, Lord Windsor, Governor of our Island of Jamaica, in the West Indies, 21 March 1661, 93.

40. FP XVII, Jamaica (i) 1661–1739 (93–292), Instructions for our Trusty & well beloved Sir Thomas Lynch, Knight, Our Captain General, & Governor in Chief, in and over our Island of Jamaica—and other the Territories depending thereon, in America.—1681, 95.

41. Ibid.

42. David Eltis, "Slavery and Freedom in the Early Modern World," in *Terms of Labor: Slavery, Serfdom, and Free Labor*, Stanley L. Engerman, ed. (Stanford, CA: Stanford University Press, 1999), 26.

43. McNulty, Hickeringill, Edmund (*Bap.* 1631, *D.* 1708).

44. Edmund Hickeringill, *The Ceremony-Monger, His Character in Five Chapters* (London: Reprinted the Year 1703, Humbly proposed to the consideration of the Parliament, 1703), see the title page, which goes on to state Hickeringill's many grouses with established church practices: *Chap. I. Concerning Bowing to the East.*

II. Of Implicite Faith. III. Concerning Reading Dons of Pul... IV. Concerning Bowing at the Name of Jesu, and the Power of the Keyes, The Church Keyes. V. Concerning Un-lighted Candles on the Altar; Organs, Church-Mufick, and other Popish-like and Foppish Ceremonies.

45. Hickeringill, *Jamaica Viewed*, 32.

46. Ibid., 32, 30.

47. Ibid., 30, 32, 33.

CHAPTER SEVEN

~

Colonization of the Church

Slaveholders in Jamaica did not widely accept the conversion of enslaved people in the church of state until the late eighteenth century. The change came about because of pressure from the British abolitionist movement after 1780, which added to the internal pressure from the clergymen of the state church. Anglican clerics, such as John Venn and John Lindsay, had advocated Christianizing the enslaved to improve the conditions of slavery.[1] This idea of improving slavery was known as amelioration, and when it began in Jamaica it was an important departure from the notion of slavery as effective only through the use of brutality and extreme punishments. Amelioration was essentially a plan to prolong slavery. The conversion of enslaved people was seen most clearly in the mass baptisms performed by the Anglican clerics after 1797, but when this occurred it became another means used by the enslaved people to express their freedom. This chapter is mainly about the ways in which that expression of slave freedom could be seen.

The idea that enslaved people took advantage of access to the church of state seems not to have been explored by the scholarship on the church's history in the Caribbean. Arthur Charles Dayfoot and Dale Bisnauth in their studies, for example, have rehearsed the view that the state church was also the "planters' church." They use this to argue that "the Church of England was the church of the Englishmen who resided in the colonies." It was "a Church in which the values and lifestyle of a vested interest, that of the planters, held control."[2] However, this argument does not consider the enslaved people who joined the church as a result of the campaign to baptize them. These enslaved people literally colonized the church, and this colonization was a sign that the church was undergoing transformation, moving away from the planters and toward becoming the church of the enslaved. The clergymen who baptized the enslaved people left ample accounts of this process. Some of the clerics saw it as a positive sign of the power of the church or its indoctrinating prowess. However, all of the clergymen observed how passionately enslaved people expressed their wish to become church members, and these accounts provide evidence of how the enslaved took advantage of a policy originally designed to make them into Christians who were passive or less inclined to embark upon acts of resistance.

The broader implication of enslaved people's colonization of the church is the exposure this gives to the limitations inherent in viewing enslaved resistance as the pursuit of freedom or the undermining of slavery. Resistance of course had these effects, as the studies by Gad Heuman, Michael Craton, Vincent Brown, and Claudius Fergus have all shown.[3] However, slavery is not the only lens through which to view resistance by enslaved people, and seeing resistance as the pursuit of freedom undermines the enslaved people's belief that they were free people, who could also use this freedom to challenge and overcome their enslavement. They showed this in their reaction to membership in the church of state. Access to this church was no match for slave freedom, and acceptance of church membership was both an act of defiance and an act of self-defense. Both exposed enslaved people's confidence in the resilience of their freedom. They knew that church membership would not make them passive; it would not give either the church or slaveholders the result that they wanted.

The acceptance of church membership by enslaved people signaled another aspect of the rise of freedom in the Atlantic setting in the late eighteenth century. This appears not to have yet received attention in the scholarship on freedom in the making of the Atlantic world. David Eltis and Kenneth Morgan, for instance, have adopted the view first proposed by H. Orlando Patterson that it was slavery that created freedom, rather than freedom's resilience and its use to challenge enslavement.[4] However, enslaved people knew about the power of the state church and its alliance with the slaveholding planters, yet they joined this church knowing that this was a risk. The acceptance of church access was not a sign of "social death" or the disappearance of freedom; rather, it answers Spivak's famous question in the affirmative: "Can the Subaltern Speak?"[5] The speaking took the form of action rather than words. Slavery and its supporting systems and institutions of domination, such as the church, were surmountable obstacles as far as enslaved people were concerned.

This chapter is organized into two sections. The first provides a brief outline of the campaign of mass baptism, through which enslaved people were able to join the church of state. This section is important to show the significance of Christian conversion for the church, the colonial and British governments, and the slaveholding planters. The significance of the resistance that enslaved people showed in their interaction with the clergymen can be seen in the formidable effort put into converting them into Christians. The second section discusses the reaction of enslaved people to mass baptism. It shows how the objective of the planters differed from the response of enslaved people, who used their notion of freedom, or simply put, slave freedom, to counteract the church while embracing it.

Mass Baptism: The Campaign

The Jamaica House of Assembly, which was dominated by wealthy, white sugar planters, decided in 1797 to embark on a policy to baptize the entire population of enslaved people in the island. This policy signaled the start of the island's amelioration policy, a start that came many years before the British government decided to propose its own amelioration plans in 1823.[6] The 1797 plan was revived in 1801 by another act of the Assembly promoting the work of the clergymen among the enslaved. This was another sign of the commitment to conversion in the state church, and the decision to use conversion as arguably the most important aspect of the island's amelioration policy.[7] Support from London came as a result of the view that Jamaica had undertaken its own Enlightenment in the form of amelioration. The slaveholders' intention, however, was not to use Christianization to emancipate the enslaved; rather, Christianity was seen as a way to strengthen the bonds between enslaved people and slavery. The church of state's indoctrinating power was believed by slaveholders to be the only way forward into a future where slavery would still exist. Abolitionism in Britain had been challenging the slave owners by highlighting their brutality toward enslaved people. Conversion was therefore seen as a way to silence British abolitionists, and hopefully delay their campaign to abolish first the British slave trade.

Jamaica's planters had begun to show signs of their willingness to accept the church as an ally from the early 1770s, departing from the longstanding antagonism between clergymen and planters, who viewed converting enslaved people as a threat to their power as slaveholders. Edward Long in his 1774 *History of Jamaica* made note of an aspect of the planters' change of attitude toward the church. This could be seen in the support given to the construction of church buildings in the parish capitals. In Hanover, for example, most of the £7,000 spent on building the church in Lucea its capital was donated by planters. Together the annual salary and surplus fees of the cleric in Vere was already at £200, or about £60 above the average of the island as a whole, mainly due to the support from the well-to-do white parishioners, most of whom were slaveholders.[8] J.B. Moreton, a plantation bookkeeper, writing during the late 1780s, observed the construction of a "tolerable elegant building" as the Kingston parish church, showing that acceptance of the clergymen was widening among the slave owners and others from the upper echelons of the parish, who had the financial resources to give the church some assurance that it had the means it needed to widen its presence among the entire population of Kingston.[9]

The argument of Mary Turner that the church neglected the enslaved in Jamaica in the same way it neglected the "home-heathen" in England is not supported by the decision taken in 1797 to perform mass baptisms among the enslaved.[10] This view also does not consider the struggle between clergymen and slaveholders over access to the enslaved for the purpose of conversion, which had been going on since the church's arrival in Jamaica shortly after the 1655 capture of the island from the Spanish. The argument Turner has is supportable only if by citing neglect her intention is to suggest that the church was not interested in converting enslaved people to promote the eradication of slavery. Nevertheless, the slave-owning people became fearful of converting enslaved persons because they saw this as a sign that at least some of the clerics harbored the desire to end enslavement altogether. This fear appeared in the decision to pass laws that appeared as early as 1681–1737, advising that "no slave shall be free by becoming a Christian."[11] These laws were passed when the Anglican Church was still the exclusive provider of Christianity in Jamaica, certainly before the arrival of the first notable group of nonconformists, the Moravians, in 1754—notable because they were allowed by planters to preach to enslaved people on their estates for the purpose of converting them.[12]

Anglican clergymen in Jamaica did not neglect the enslaved. Even John Lindsay, who was a supporter of the planters, wrote in his 1788 manuscript that Christianization was the "Great Desideratum—the vital Flame," which the planters must embrace, if they hoped for slavery's survival. Lindsay was clearly not interested in Christianity as immediate liberation for enslaved people. Nonetheless, this did not prevent him from viewing Christianization as a worthwhile project; it could, in Lindsay's view, "actuate the whole design" to fashion a less hostile system of slavery—one that would survive longer, but also aid in preparing the enslaved for freedom. Lindsay also advised that a special, watered-down version of the Anglican doctrine should be used on enslaved people. He did not see Africans in general as capable of comprehending the same doctrines taught to free and namely white members of the church. Lindsay's racist view of Africans appears in this statement advising that "it must not be forgot that a Negroes capacity must not be overloaded, for fear of perplexity and confusion: which would ruin all."[13]

Other clerics expressed the same disappointment that slaveholders did not see value in Christianizing the enslaved. Writing in 1724, Rev. John Kelly in St. Elizabeth reported to Bishop Gibson, bishop of London and therefore head of the Caribbean diocese, that it was "impossible to bring them [enslaved people] to any knowledge of the Christian Religion" due to the opposition from slaveholders. Rev. James White in Vere, writing in the same year, also informed Gibson that "None of the white Xians will admit them [the enslaved] to reciprocation of benefits, & freedom of conversion after baptism."[14] And Rev. William Reading, in a letter written in 1723, had stated that in spite of opposition, he had managed to baptize a few enslaved persons, adding that "I have first instructed them in the principles of Christianity."[15] There were also books imported by the Anglican cleric in Kingston in 1724 for use in the catechism of blacks as well as whites, books earmarked for the "catechetical Instruction of the Youth & particularly of the negro Children & others in the parish." A library was also established in Kingston with reading material for the "lately Converted," suggesting that some progress had been made in the effort to convert enslaved people.[16]

Nevertheless, conversion of the enslaved remained contested terrain until the 1797 decision of the Assembly. Writing in 1751, John Venn had informed the bishop of London about the struggle that the clergymen had been facing because of planter opposition to conversion for enslaved people. Venn's remarks do not concur with the view that the state church was the "planters' church." According to Venn, even if planters held this view and had supporters among the clergy, this was not the view of the entire clergy. Those who opposed the planters did so, Venn observed, on the basis of the interest that the enslaved had in baptism and conversion. According to Venn, "tho' it was most earnestly desir'd, yet it seems to be attended with insuperable Difficulties, which it is not in the Power of any Clergyman, however well dispos'd, to remove." Unlike Lindsay, who proposed a circumspect introduction of the enslaved to Anglican doctrine, Venn's position was that making the enslaved "Christians only in Name" was unacceptable. What was needed was sufficient instruction to ensure that genuine conversion occurred. Venn did not go on to state that he saw genuine conversion as a preparation for immediate emancipation from slavery. Like most clerics who advocated converting the enslaved, Venn's goal was to improve their morality, rather than to right away abolish their enslavement.[17]

Very surprisingly, Lindsay subscribed to the view that adequate indoctrination could safely transition these enslaved people into freedom through manumission. Lindsay advised that "the Manumised is still to Labour in Good Examples, for the Public by hiring himself as a Tradesman, or Labourer to some Honest, Faithful and Trusty Obedient Service—or till by his Industry he shall have made a purchase of some little convenient spot of Ground, whereupon he can himself, perhaps in time assisted by a Wife & Children—and to the full observation of an overlooking neighbourhood, he will very fairly & commendably support his Freedom."[18] Lindsay did not oppose using conversion to prepare enslaved people for freedom. He had enough confidence in the powers of the Christian religion to thoroughly indoctrinate the enslaved, so that they would not become threats to the social order if they were subsequently manumitted. This view was also due to Lindsay's racist stance that African people had limited intellectual capacities and were not driven by the kind of superior cultural traditions that would prohibit successful indoctrination. They could not undermine the social order if they became free people because of Christianity.

The planters in Jamaica finally embraced the notion that Christianization was a safe way to promote the social order and therefore protect slavery. They did not, however, express the wish to adopt Lindsay's radical proposition that promoting conversion was also a safe way to envisage freedom for the enslaved. The planters remained committed to slavery, but this began to manifest in the support that they gave to the church of state, so that its clergymen could baptize and convert the enslaved. Between 1813 and 1815, the Assembly again revised the decision taken just before the end of the eighteenth century to support the clergy. The salary of the clerics was almost doubled to £420 annually, and the "surplus fees" were acknowledged as lawful incomes in addition to the salary of each clergyman. The sources of these "fees" were services that included christenings, marriages, funerals, and baptisms, including those performed on enslaved people.[19] In 1813, the Jamaica Assembly had also enacted a curacy bill proposed by Parliament. This created the island's first curates, whose duty was to provide enslaved people with instruction in Christian knowledge, as part of preparing them for baptism in the state church. The Assembly reiterated its commitment to the curates in a new act passed in 1816 without British intervention. The salary of the curates was increased from £100 to £136 annually. This can be seen as part of the stimulus package to increase the number of baptisms that the clergymen performed after instruction was given to the enslaved people.[20]

In 1813, acting governor of Jamaica, Lt. Gen. Edward Morrison, had expressed that he was eager to report to the Colonial Office in London the liberty that the clerics had by then received to access the enslaved people for the purpose of baptism. Morrison's information suggested that baptizing enslaved people had become a virtual industry in Jamaica. And when the colonial secretary, Lord Bathurst, responded in 1817 to the information about conversion, he observed that only "inactivity and indifference" on the part of the clergymen could stand in the way of more baptisms in the future. Bathurst shared the view of the clerics and planters that the superior doctrine and principles of the state church also made it impossible for enslaved people to become threats to the social order after becoming Christians. Writing about this, Bathurst stated that "the purity of its doctrines is better calculated than that of any other persuasion," the church would "impress upon its communicants a strong sense of moral obligations, a cheerful submission to the laws, and that cheerful resignation to the will of Providence," and all of this was possible because of the church's doctrine, which "lightens the burthens of life, by rescuing affliction from the bitterness of discontent."[21]

This was the campaign of mass baptism that enslaved people were up against. The expectation that Christianity should result in manumission for the converted was discussed by at least one cleric, but this was not shared by other clergymen, or by the slaveholders, the Assembly, or the colonial secretary in London. Their view was to use conversion to increase the moral condition of enslaved people, with the expectation that this would also improve their condition as slaves. Slaveholders were expected to treat enslaved people better because they were also Christians. The most popular view of conversion was that it could support the slave system by ameliorating conditions for the enslaved. The improvements were expected to lessen the likelihood of resistance by the enslaved, and make it more difficult for antislavery campaigners to use the brutality of slave masters to petition against slavery. No one gave any adequate thought to how enslaved people themselves perceived conversion, but the clerics had quickly realized that enslaved people saw conversion as access to agency, and they demonstrated this agency in the ways that they took advantage of the conversion process.

Slave Freedom and Mass Baptism

One of the realities of mass baptism was that it gave the clerics, quite ironically, a sense of powerlessness. Writing in 1817, Rev. Dr. Edmund Pope, for example, reported that he had problems even with preparing a proper report about the baptisms he had performed. Pope himself was skeptical about the 1,678 baptisms he had done since his arrival as the clergyman for the parish of Westmoreland. He had been in that parish not more than three years. The figure he calculated when called upon by the governor to submit a report gave him ample reason to be cautious. He went to check this figure against the calculation of his predecessor. He was pleased by the confirmation, but this did not relieve Pope of the belief that he was merely the vessel that enslaved people had used to materialize their interest in church access.[22] It was also very hard for the clerics to falsify their records and they knew this. The start of the Returns of the Slave Registration in 1817 gave the Jamaican government and the Colonial Office a way to check the submissions of the clerics against the enslaved people registered in each parish. Registration was conducted at three-year intervals until the abolition of slavery in 1834.[23] It was a continuous reminder to clergymen that they were under the constant threat of exposure, if they attempted to submit reports about baptisms that they did not perform.

Rev. Stewart in neighboring St. Elizabeth found himself in only a slightly different situation to Pope's. He too found the number of baptisms he did almost unbelievable, but he also discovered that the enslaved born in Africa and those born in Jamaica responded to baptism with the same level of enthusiasm. Stewart initially thought that he had discovered a way to show how as a cleric he was instrumental in getting the enslaved people to join the church. He thought that if he separated the enslaved into the two groups, he could show that his sterling endeavors had paid off with the large number of Africans who also opted to join the church. The assumption here was that people with fresher memories of Africa were less likely to submit to Christian conversion. However, Stewart realized that his intervention would be impossible to prove because the presence of Africans with their more recent memories about African religious traditions also indicated a level of choice-making. In the end, Stewart presented only the data showing that both groups joined the church without any apparent hesitation.[24]

One of the considerations that Stewart made was probably the revelation concerning the practice among enslaved people that was known as "The Convince." The Moravian missionaries, who were also in St. Elizabeth and had been there since 1754, and who saw this practice, described it as one of the religious notions present among the enslaved without also highlighting that any group in particular had adopted it. The missionaries interpreted "The Convince" as evidence of African traditional practices, which had survived among the enslaved despite the rupture that slavery presumably caused. The missionaries were nonetheless unable to report on the practice without the usual bias of white preachers who encountered non-European practices. The missionaries had thus described "The Convince" as "much superstition intermingled with their religious exercises."[25] The report from the missionaries suggested that enslaved people made use of "The Convince" to show their closeness to God. The intention was to suggest that they could communicate with God and that the spirit of God had inhabited their bodies at critical moments when they needed to show the missionaries the presence of God in their lives. The practice became a way for the enslaved to show the European preachers that they too could communicate directly with God, and that the communication was a personal experience over which only God and they had control. The practice was thus empowering, as well as a sign to the missionaries of the survival of an African tradition and the powerlessness of slavery to destroy this.

The point here is that missionaries as well as Anglican clerics saw evidence of slave freedom and reported on these in their own ways. Both, however, revealed a good amount of cultural bias when making these recordings. Cultural bias was not limited to Anglican clergymen or to Protestant missionaries. However, while they were biased, this could not mask the empowerment that they were also seeing. James T. Light, a Moravian missionary, referred to the "gumbiah" as merely "a kind of drum" and expressed no joy for the fact that enslaved people played this "with the feet."[26] On the other hand, Light would also express how delighted he was whenever even "one soul" among the enslaved joined the church, and referred to each as an "infinitely precious" one. All Moravians in Jamaica had to contend with the fact that not many enslaved persons joined the church until over seventy years of their arrival in the island, and part of the reason for this was that the enslaved people clung to their own cultural practices. So whenever a Moravian, such as Light, expressed any bias toward African practices, he was also highlighting the strong influence of these practices, hence his great joy whenever even one enslaved person became a church member. Another missionary, Brother Koch, was more direct when making his assessment of Light's lack of progress, noting that Light "sees but little fruit of his labor."[27] Up to 1788, the Moravians in Jamaica had only 315 enslaved people in the church. The number would not begin to rise in any significant way until the 1820s. Noting the change, the missionaries said at that juncture that their situation was "certainly brightening," but again this was because more enslaved persons had at that point opted to join the church. The number climbed dramatically to 2,282 in 1823 because of the choice the enslaved people made.[28]

Through either acts of their own, or the suppression that they faced from the planters, the Protestant missionaries became unattractive to a large number of enslaved people until the 1820s. The change came when the British amelioration policy outlawed the attempts to prevent enslaved people from joining any ecclesiastical body. However, enslaved people had before this opted not to become members of churches that they knew were suppressed, or which had shown through their own actions that they were unwilling to support the idea of freedom. This was one of the problems that the Moravians faced. It was part of the reason that the Baptists, who arrived in Jamaica later than the Moravians arrived, but also in the eighteenth century, attracted a larger congregation of enslaved people nonetheless, though mainly from the 1820s onward.[29] As historian of the Moravian Church and missionary himself, Joseph E. Hutton, has recorded, the Moravians "never came forward as champions of liberty" at any time during slavery, "never pleaded for emancipation," and "never encouraged their converts to expect it." Hutton also stated that one of the main patrons of the church, Count Ludwig von Zinzendorf, was a "firm believer in slavery."[30] But along with this was the suppression that all Protestant missionaries in Jamaica faced until the 1823 British amelioration, suppression which made these churches unattractive to a large number of enslaved people. An example of the suppression was the ordinance that the Kingston Common Council passed in 1807, which imposed a £100 fine on Protestant missionaries who preached in the city and parish without a license. The Council had of course reserved the right not to issue this license.[31]

The Anglican Church faced opposition from planters, but this church was the church of state and therefore it never had to go through the level of suppression that was reserved for Protestant missionaries. The Anglican Church remained a more attractive option, even while facing opposition from planters. The planters did not oppose the presence of the church, as they opposed the presence of Protestant missionaries; rather, planters saw the Anglican advocacy of conversion as a threat to their power as slaveholders, and reacted in their consummate conservative fashion. However, once these objections began to subside, the response of the enslaved seemed to be a positive one. Planters of course viewed this as a sign that the clergymen were right about the church's power, but the clergymen were the first ones to highlight that the reality was totally different, and often without even realizing that there was a difference.

In the parish of St. Mary, for example, where Rev. Colin Donaldson baptized "one hundred" per annum between 1801 and 1815, this convinced Donaldson that the enslaved people had *"freely thrown away their African superstition and prejudice"* (his italics).[32] This was unlikely in light of practices such as "The Convince," but also important was the transformation that Donaldson himself underwent, seen in his admission that he no longer saw African cultural forms as obstacles preventing enslaved people from making genuine transitions into Anglican Christians. Donaldson did not realize his own transformation, or the fact that he made this on the basis of only one fact, which itself did not signal that enslaved people had abandoned their own cultural forms. The response that Donaldson had seen was slave freedom in action, its use to add a foreign culture that provided access into free society in Jamaica on some level, without any necessity to put aside one's belief system, which was a personal decision that only enslaved people themselves could make.

After seeing the choice-making power of enslaved people in the parish of St. Ann, Rev. Lewis Bowerbank said that he was certain that his report about the baptisms that he had performed were "defective," and he had to delay the submission of his report to King's House, the governor's chambers, for this reason.[33] He had unverified names in his records, people he may have baptized twice, once for themselves and another time for others not present for baptism, and who might have had no real interest in joining the church. Bowerbank said that he had the names of parents, but not their children. He had the number of children, but not their names, and because of this, he had no way to verify that these children were real. It was possible they were in his records to give him, the planters, and the government the false impression that he had baptized even the children of enslaved people. These people also knew how important baptism was to the clergymen, planters, and colonial government. Making the choice not to baptize either themselves or their children was an act of defiance, a way for the enslaved to circumvent the plans of the church, planters, and the state. Bowerbank himself, similar to his colleague Donaldson, was also transformed by enslaved people's choice-making capacity into a cleric who was much more cautious.

Rev. Henry Jenkins in St. James was one of the clergymen who reported on the matter of the baptism fees. According to Jenkins, it was the enslaved people who always paid these fees in that parish. It was clear to Jenkins that the enslaved in the parish wanted church membership, and this encouraged the cleric to change the way that the church conducted its business in at least St. James. This was the seventh largest parish of Jamaica's twenty-one parishes in 1817. Enslaved people had to travel long distances to reach the church on a Sunday morning in time for service. Many of them arrived late, and Jenkins himself found this disturbing, and despite making several attempts to stop the latecomers from coming to service unless they could arrive on time, the problem persisted. Jenkins realized that there was no way around this problem except to submit to the interest of enslaved people in church membership, which they had also been showing by their payment of the baptism fees. The decision Jenkins took was to have two services on a Sunday, one in the morning and another in the afternoon, a change made by the rector, but on the basis of the conduct of enslaved people.[34]

In St. Thomas-in-the-Vale, Rev. W.G. Burton became skeptical about his baptisms after realizing that these, as he said, "appear very great." Similar to Bowerbank, Burton was certain that he had performed many baptisms, but the number that he saw when his report was finished was unbelievable. The other point this cleric made was that he had much more work to do because of the enslaved people's eagerness to receive baptism. And adding to Burton's frustration, the enslaved people also insisted on first being baptized before they could think of themselves as actual church members. Giving these people instruction in the church prior to baptism was thus problematical for Burton, as well as his curate. The people simply refused to enter the church unless they were baptized in accordance with their interpretation of the qualifications for entry into the place where they would be worshipping, or "a notion prevalent amongst the slaves, that they may not come to church unless baptized, (that day excepted on which they present themselves for baptism)." Instruction was supposed to be an important part of the catechism campaign; part of the indoctrination that the clerics were supposed to provide so that planters, especially, would remain assured that conversion had benefits for enslavement. Burton's experience showed that instruction could take place only on terms acceptable to the enslaved people themselves, and this also made instruction less certain as a means of indoctrination. Its intended victims had already shown how much they could influence the process, and even showed that their unwillingness to allow themselves to be instructed, unless their conditions were met, could determine if instruction actually went ahead.[35]

Moravian missionaries at Bogue sugar estate in St. Elizabeth made almost the same discovery in 1813, when an enslaved man named Abraham insisted that he had to leave the church on the morning of his baptism, in order to dress himself in the way that he thought appropriate for the occasion. Abraham returned "out of breath," having "run so fast," according to the missionaries, so that he did not miss his baptism, and was dressed in full white, the shade of clothing that he wanted to wear.[36] It is possible that Abraham's choice of white clothing was symbolic of the association that he made between freedom and the shade of white. This might not have been what Abraham actually believed—that whiteness and freedom went hand in hand. However, most of free society in slaveholding Jamaica was white, signaling whiteness as a symbolic representation of one's freedom. Wearing white clothing on the same day that one gained full acceptance into the Christian church of white society was also a means through which to send the message that this acceptance was to also signal that one had access to white society and its freedom.

Addressing the baptism fees paid in the same parish as the missionaries, the Anglican clergyman, Rev. Thomas Stewart, added "that whenever I know, or have reason to believe, that the fee comes out of the pocket of the slaves, the acceptance has been, and always will be by me, invariably declined." Stewart felt that it was wiser to ensure that the planters and other slaveholders paid the baptism fees. This would signal to enslaved people the kind of benevolence that was beneficial to slaveholding people. It would encourage, Stewart hoped, the kind of response from the enslaved that was expected from the entire project to convert them into Christians. They would see masters as the ones who had invested in their progress into Christianity. Once again, this wish and the reality were quite different. Simply put, Stewart was enabling the enslaved to enter the church of state at the expense of slaveholders, while also having no assurance that enslaved people saw Christianization as a means of pacification. There was also Stewart's concern about making enslaved people feel even more empowered than they probably felt, in his interpretation, by handing them complete control over the basis on which they entered the church by allowing them, rather than masters, to pay the baptism fees.[37]

Stewart's main message was the inappropriateness of underestimating the significance of the baptism fees. However, writing about the same topic, Rev. John West in St. Thomas-in-the-East gave a more straightforward indication of its significance. West said that based on his observation, enslaved people "always value that *most* for which they pay their own money" (his italics).[38] In other words, one of the ways to ensure enslaved people took baptism seriously was to ensure that they paid the fees. Otherwise, they might never become the Christians that the clergymen, planters, and the state wanted them to become. In other words, Christianization's indoctrination might never have any real effect on them, except of course those effects that enslaved people themselves wanted this to have. This is the paradox of domination in whichever form it might take. There is always the people's views and choice-making to consider, or as James C. Scott would put it, there is always the important hidden "*Everyday forms of Peasant Resistance*," the "*Weapons*" of the people assumed to be "*Weak*," and the mere fact that this assumption is there also aids the people in their resistance, by keeping these hidden from their dominators, or the people who themselves can only assume that their domination is effective, or actually real.[39]

Baptism fees became part of the industry of mass baptism. Even the Assembly was forced to address the issue in the new slave law passed in December 1816. Enslaved people had extended their influence to the law-making body of the slave society in Jamaica by insisting that the baptism fees were seen as an important part of their conversion in the church of state. The Assembly's stipulation was that the fees should be 2s 8d for each enslaved person baptized.[40] When the cleric's reports were received, these reported the payment of fees which were both higher and lesser sums. The Assembly's attempt to regulate this part of the conversion process essentially failed. Enslaved people, who paid in most cases, paid whatever fees that they could or wanted to pay. In Vere, for example, Rev. G.C.R. Fearon said that he received various sums. He "never" had occasion or reason to believe that he could ask for greater sums; all of the fees that he received were "voluntarily tendered," rendering his interference unnecessary and unwise.[41]

Another dynamic that Fearon discovered in Vere was that both masters and enslaved people "voluntarily tendered" the fees paid for baptism. Resistance from planters was certainly at a minimum in this parish, signaling that they, too, were widely convinced that the enslaved people had taken the matter of baptism as seriously as they wished for them to take it. This made nonpayment an option hardly any planter in Vere explored. Instead, based again on enslaved people's conduct, planters were investing in a process with an outcome over which they could only hope that they had control. Worthwhile to also consider alongside the uncertainty of the planters' position was Fearon's other revelation that he had performed an additional 285 baptisms on people who paid nothing. Even the clergyman expressed a sense of powerlessness when writing about these 285 additional baptisms. The fact that he had done them without payment was only a part of the problem that these created. The other and more important issue was the disingenuousness that nonpayment signified. Fearon was one of the clerics who had seen enough evidence that enslaved people placed more value on the things for which they paid some kind of price. Even if this money was not theirs, but the planters', it symbolized an investment, which Fearon and other clerics knew was necessary to give them at least the feeling that the enslaved people took baptism as seriously as the church intended for them to take it.

Volunteering for baptism was widespread. Enslaved people did not resist entering the church of state. It was so widespread that it was tantamount to a colonization of the church. Between 1815 and 1817 alone, a total of 50,454 enslaved people were reported as having obtained baptism in the Anglican Church in Jamaica (Table 7.1). This was 16,818 per year during that period, and the total at the period's end was 16 percent of the slave population in that same year. The figures made the clergymen, slaveholders, and the state more enthusiastic and optimistic about converting the enslaved people. Plans were in place to conquer the entire enslaved population with baptism in the state church. However, these plans would make baptism appear even more

Table 7.1. Slave Baptisms in the Anglican Church in Jamaica, 1815–1817

Parishes	Three-Year Totals	Yearly Averages	Slave Population*
Port Royal	99	33	7,217
St. John	363	121	6,133
St. Elizabeth	511	170	20,143
St. Ann	1,051	350	24,814
Vere	1,259	420	8,056
Clarendon	1,285	428	19,397
St. Thomas (Vale)	1,441	480	12,241
Westmoreland	1,609	536	22,659
St. Catherine	1,772	591	9,679
St. David	1,928	643	7,758
St. George	2,359	786	13,640
St. Andrew	2,933	978	15,830
St. James	3,263	1,088	25,641
St. Thomas (East)	3,407	1,136	26,422
Kingston	4,641	1,547	17,954
Hanover	6,862	2,287	23,779
Trelawny	6,898	2,299	28,497
St. Mary	8,773	2,924	26,826
Total	**50,454**	**16,818**	**316,686**

*Shows slave population in 1817.
Source: HCPP 1818 (433), Return of the Number of Slaves Baptized in the under-Mentioned Parishes, for Three Years Preceding the 1st Day of November in the Present Year; Distinguishing the Number Baptized in Each of Those Years, 272.

like an industry, and this fact had consequences for the non-enslaved sections of Jamaica. More money from the government's budget was paid to both the clergymen and curates as time went on and as baptism became more taxing. This money came from the taxes paid by the legally free. They were literally paying the price for enslaved people to be received into God's church, and doing so with only the hope of accomplishing their own objective.

Even enslaved people who appeared to have had no urgent reason for baptism in the state church still wanted it. They had to have seen this as a transition that they themselves needed to make. They had to have a reason or reasons of their own, and the obvious question this raises is what possible reason or reasons could these have been? Take, for instance, the enslaved at Dean's Valley Water Works, a sugar estate in Westmoreland that was still owned by the Tharp family. John Tharp had made this estate profitable before his death in Jamaica in 1804, but he never lost sight of how much his profit margin depended on the people that he called his slaves. Tharp made a number of concessions to keep this estate and others that he owned profitable after the American independence of 1776, which increased production costs for West Indian planters all over the British Caribbean. This was due to the loss of cheap supplies from the mainland colonies, which since 1776 became a foreign country that was prohibited from legally trading with British colonies because of the Navigation Acts.[42] One of Tharp's concessions was the plans he drafted, around June 1798, for the construction of a hospital at his Good Hope estate in Trelawny. This was for the enslaved there, as well as for those from some of his other properties nearby, namely, Wales and Keith Hall estates in the same parish. This hospital was one of the first such facilities on a sugar plantation anywhere in the northwest of the island. In 1803, Tharp had also reported on how the enslaved people had been massaging his ego by calling him "Daddy Tharp," which he liked, but which made him vulnerable, and he knew it. Even as Tharp reported that the enslaved on his estates had "increased, and are very happy," he was also admitting how much this was due to the choices that the enslaved people made, and for which Tharp had to make a number of allocations.[43]

Yet, when Rev. Pope visited Dean's Valley, he reported no difficulty baptizing the enslaved at the estate. Clearly, they saw some kind of benefit or benefits in the baptism that Pope came to offer. No force was applied to make them accept baptism, and as Pope indicated, none was necessary. He performed 211 baptisms in 1817, and expected the others to follow in due course.[44] Regrettably, Pope gave no information about the motivations of the enslaved people he baptized. He was understandably more impressed with the turnout for baptism, which he seemed not to have anticipated, probably because he knew about John Tharp's experiences.

However, other clerics suggested what they thought the enslaved saw that made them interested in baptism. Rev. Daniel Rose in Hanover, for example, also writing in 1817, observed what he thought was an apparent connection between the fact that the planters paid for the baptisms and the interest of enslaved people. Rose said that the fees were "paid by the master and not by the slaves," and what was paid was always whatever "they think proper."[45] In other words, the enslaved people felt that it was right and just for the planters to pay. The interest was not really in the church or baptism; rather, baptism and the church were means to an end. The enslaved used these to extract payments from the planters. Rose did not indicate any specific reasons to explain why enslaved people wanted the planters to make the payments, whether for slavery in general, or for specific acts of brutality. Nevertheless, the planters were paying and enslaved people were taking these payments by becoming baptized church members. Baptism was a form of reparations.

The point Rose made is important to understanding the power relations between enslaved people and enslavers. This power was not a one-way relationship in which masters had all of the power and enslaved people were powerless or socially inept. Power shifted from master to the enslaved at many intervals, and one must always bear in mind that masters relied on enslaved people for most things, including money, status, and sex, three human wants that are treated as needs. However, Rose also appears to have had little faith in the willingness of enslaved people to use the church to connect with the blessings that God could bestow, which is surprising, given the fact that Rose was a cleric. Writing in the 1820s, Peter Duncan, the Methodist missionary, advised that part of the problem William Hammett, the first Methodist preacher in Port Royal, faced, was that he could not inspire people, including the enslaved, to have enough faith in the church as one of the houses of God. Hardly anyone joined the church, and Duncan suspected that if Hammett had been given the resources, especially a proper house of worship, his experience would have improved.[46] Duncan's point was that appearance could mean the difference between failure and success. Churches which appeared Godly, such as the adequately supported Anglican churches, attracted more attention in the form of followers, and a lot of this was because of the impression of religiosity. People simply expected God to be present in any church, and for the church to show in its appearance that God would want to make an appearance there.

Also important was custom. The Anglican clergyman in Port Royal performed only ninety-nine baptisms between 1815 and 1817 (Table 7.1). Port Royal was known for its debauchery and worldly customs, negating to some extent the importance of church membership in the lives of the inhabitants, and though this was the legacy of the parish's history of piracy, which was long past, it was still a factor that is worth considering in any explanation for the low turnout of enslaved people for baptism, even in the church of state. St. John's parish, which had fewer enslaved people, nevertheless had 363 baptisms during the same period. St. John did not have Port Royal's history. Enslaved people in St. John saw some value in church access, or more value than the enslaved in Port Royal could see. The enslaved in Clarendon showed some of this value to Rev. Thomas Williams, the Anglican rector of that parish, who reported in 1817 that, "with very few exceptions," the enslaved, rather than planters, paid the baptism fees. Furthermore, they were sending their children to become baptized, and paying fees for these baptisms as well. According to Williams, up to "one-third" of his baptisms were performed on young people under the age of sixteen. Williams' assessment was that this showed that the "desire for religious instruction is great," and so great that he was taxed "to discharge even the common functions of office."[47]

The issue of being taxed came up often. Clergymen complained about having too much work to do because of enslaved people. Mass baptism was taking a toll on the clerics even as they discharged this duty under a mandate. They were to inculcate enslaved people with enough Christian dogma to ensure that they became passive and dutiful enslaved people, but it was as if the clergymen were involved in a scheme that was turning on itself. The dominators were feeling the stress of domination. Keeping the enslaved submissive was not easy work, and there were signs that the suppression was not working. In Portland, Rev. Phillip Humphries said that "every Sunday" he had to contend with a "crowd" at the church. There were enslaved people gathered "round the doors and windows on the outside" of the church.[48] Not only were they coming for baptism, they were also coming to church. The crowd was intimidating. Humphries was pleased by the turnout, but the interest was clearly more than baptism, and enslaved people were eager to hear every word that the clergyman said. He had a captive audience, but one that was also demanding from him words that they could use. Humphries' concern was that at some point, he had to decide which master to serve: the slave, his master on earth, or the master in heaven. The crowd at the church was making the decision both easy and difficult. The presence of the crowd made the decision easy, but the crowd also made Humphries feel taxed. The church itself was changing because of the sheer pressure from the presence of enslaved people, but so were the clergymen as well.

Rev. A. William Pownall, rector of St. David's parish, said in 1817 that the "true nature of christianity [sic]" was difficult to teach to enslaved people.[49] Pownall was rehashing an old prejudice, but one that also explains how the clergymen vocalized some of the pressure that they felt from the enslaved people in the church. Teaching Christianity to enslaved people was more challenging as far as Rev. Pownall was concerned, and because they had competing activities, customs, and notions about religion, as well as commitments linked to enslavement. Some slave masters made the enslaved work on a Sunday, much to the dismay of the clergymen, and some masters were so immoral that they infected enslaved people with these immoral practices. One of the most common was the sexual relations masters forced upon enslaved women. The enslaved themselves had their Sunday marketing, another annoyance for the clerics. But whether the cause was the master or enslaved people themselves, Christianization of the latter was made more challenging for the clerics, and Pownall expressed this in his own prejudicial fashion. However, he expressed as well the necessity to transform the way that the church approached the matter of teaching its doctrine and principles, or it had to accommodate itself to the condition and experiences of enslaved people in order to have any effect on them.

Matthew Lewis, absentee owner of two estates in Jamaica, suspected that the failure to connect with enslaved people specifically on their terms explained the position of the Moravian missionary at Mesopotamia sugar estate, Westmoreland. Lewis visited this estate while on his first visit to Jamaica in 1816, and when he arrived there, he was told by the missionary that "seldom more than ten or a dozen" enslaved people would "attend his lectures at a time." The estate had a population of 200 enslaved people, and Moravians had been there since the mid-eighteenth century. Nonetheless, the missionary who was there in 1816 reported performing baptisms on "not more than forty persons." Lewis became skeptical about even the prospects of the Anglican clergyman on his own properties. Knowing that he himself had to institute a "new code of laws" on his two estates, he also knew that any kind of procedure attempted with the enslaved depended on how they viewed those procedures.[50]

The "Church lights," another revelation from the Protestant missionaries, were also signs to these teachers of religion that enslaved people had their own views about the churches, and had developed their own ways to take advantage of the ecclesiastical landscape. This landscape presented enslaved people with choices, meaning they could choose to become Baptists, Methodists, Moravians, or join the Church of England, for example, but the "Church lights" chose not one, but two or more of these churches. Peter Duncan, the Methodist missionary, reported that the "Church lights" attended morning service on a Sunday and the afternoon service on the same day, but in different churches. They went to the Sunday market when they were not at service. This way, they also took care of their temporal needs, and did so without forgoing their spiritual wants. In Duncan's report, a Church light was depicted as a manipulator of the churches' eagerness to win the allegiance of enslaved people, a Church light was the representation of choice-making, and a person who accepted that homage to God was important, but also accepted the idea that God would help the people who helped themselves.[51]

The Church light represented the realization of enslaved people that competition for their allegiance was big business for the churches in Jamaica. This competition shaped the churches during the age of slavery. They were providers of Bible knowledge, access to God, and through Christian instruction offered the advantage of literacy to enslaved people who could not read and write.[52] However, providing these made them competitors, and enslaved people indeed made them compete. Each church had to show how it was better than its competitors, how enslaved people might better off joining that church rather than the others. The Moravians, for example, tried to distinguish themselves by offering enslaved people the chance to become preachers as well. However, the Anglican Church and Baptist Church also offered the post of deacon to enslaved people that they said would have to join the church and show that they qualified for this position. The Anglican Church went a step further by appointing enslaved people to the role of curate or cat-echist to teach other enslaved people Bible knowledge in classrooms set up as part of the system of education during slavery. The creation of these positions for enslaved candidates was a sign of the changes that the churches made while adjusting to the realities of dealing with people demeaned but not disempowered, and because these posts suggested alternative ways to bring about the indoctrination plans of the churches, enslaved people benefitted from the belief within the churches that they were implementing additional measures from which their own plans could profit.

The churches had no control over how enslaved people interpreted their roles as deacons, native assistants, helpers, or whichever name was used to describe these posts offered to the enslaved. The Moravians realized this when one of their best native assistants, an enslaved man named George Lewis, began to integrate what the missionaries discussed as African "super-stition" into his preaching. Lewis was their itinerant helper and had become "the means of leading many" to "enquire after the right way." He was also manumitted when the missionaries collected £100 and used this to pay for Lewis' freedom. Lewis profited from the church in a very real way, and prior to this he would "express what the gospel imports," the missionaries re-corded, leaving no doubt in their minds that Lewis understood and believed in the "truths of the gospel." It is not that the missionaries thought Lewis abandoned his faith. They were annoyed at the fact that he had begun to interpret the gospel in a different way, and added African belief and customs to the Moravian doctrine.[53] Brathwaite would describe this as an empowered response to Christian certitude; an exemplification of "creolisation" and its role in the process of empowerment.[54]

Moravian missionaries often complained how enslaved people were serv-ing "two masters" and most times, this had nothing to do with slaveholders. Brother Koch referred to this by quoting from Matthew 6:24 in a sermon that he delivered at Spice Grove sugar estate, Manchester, in 1822. According to Koch, this was the passage which stated that, "No man can serve two masters" (his italics). Brother James T. Light, mentioned before, added in his own sermon on the same issue, the story of an enslaved man at Irwin sugar estate, who had acquired "two or three hundred pounds in gold and silver coins," and owned "considerable property," yet was "very unhappy in his mind," and called on the missionaries to pray for his soul when he was dying.[55] It took a law passed by the Assembly to ban Sunday marketing by enslaved people, but they simply shifted the practice to Saturday.[56] The "Church lights" also continued to serve more than one master. They asserted their right to remain as churchgoers, and to choose from the churches the ones that they should attend, choices also made while taking care of life's demands, heeding the warning in Jeremiah 17:5 to always cleave to God, but to do so without neglecting life's worldly demands. Part of the difficulty that the Moravian missionaries faced was the rigidity of their doctrine, Zinzendorf's principle of *Erfahrung*, for example, which placed a heavy demand on enslaved people, by insisting that the "experience" of faith was the most vital "qualification for baptism." Most enslaved people simply lacked the time to demonstrate as fully as the Moravians wanted that they knew the "truth" of the gospel, which they could show by attending church regularly, for instance.[57] Church attendance was one way to demonstrate slave freedom, but it was not the only way, and competing with the churches were the many secular means through which slave freedom could also be shown, such as the independent economic activities that enslaved people had also been doing on Sundays, and the ability to choose from among the churches, a performance of slave freedom shown most clearly by the presence of the "Church lights."

Anglican Bishop Edmund Gibson had castigated Moravians and Methodists in England for ironically inviting the "*Sheep out of all nations, out of all Professions, out of all Parties, out of all National Churches*" to join their congregations.[58] Aside from showing that he was upset by their competitiveness, Gibson's statement was also a sign of Anglican elitism. In Jamaica, this elitism worked in the church's favor. Enslaved people gravitated toward it because of the impression that joining was upward social mobility. The clergymen placed less emphasis on the demonstration of faith. For instance, they were more concerned about baptism than regular attendance on a Sunday. The enslaved found this flexibility quite useful. Church membership did not have to interfere with their secular pursuits and even if they had these to do on a Sunday. The clerics rallied against Sunday marketing specifically and as a principle argued that Sunday should be the day of worshipping. However, church attendance was not essential, especially for the enslaved, whose numbers the churches were having difficulty accommodating in any case. Observing Sunday as the Sabbath could be done at home.

Aside from its flexibility, the elitism of the Anglican clergymen also served as an attraction to the church, and Moravian missionaries confirmed some of this elitism when expressing joy that the Anglican rectors had visited their chapels, and while there had announced their wish "to see" the missionaries return the visit, to see them "at the parsonage."[59] The term "sectarian" was used in Jamaica to draw a clear distinction between the Anglicans and Protestant missionary churches.[60] This term was a representation of Anglican elitism, and a reminder to enslaved people and other churchgoers that the Anglican

Church was the state church, the first to arrive in the colony, and the only church that had the social power to influence colonial attitudes. Enslaved people knew that when they joined the Anglican Church, they were submitting to the power that the clergymen promoted on the church's behalf, but also establishing an alliance that was potentially of greater advantage to them. Henry Williams, an enslaved man, was reminded of this power by the vicious Anglican cleric, Rev. George Wilson Bridges, in the 1820s, when Williams was sent to the workhouse, where he was flogged, all of which was engineered by Bridges, who had even admitted that he had "used his influence" to that effect. According to Bridges, he had tried "to induce Henry Williams to leave the sectarians because he was an intelligent person."[61] In his own unfortunate way, Bridges reminded Williams that he had no protection if he remained outside of the Anglican Church. However, the fact that Williams remained outside of the church was an expression of free will, showing his determination to decide how he worshipped God, in spite of the risks, which he knew.

Conclusion

Alfred Caldecott's study, *The Church in the West Indies*, published in 1898, examined the church's relationship with slavery, but did not explore how enslaved people who joined the church used this access to demonstrate agency, resistance, and especially slave freedom.[62] Slave freedom is a completely new concept in the history-writing on the church of state in Jamaica and other colonies in the Caribbean. It does not appear in the later scholarship of Dayfoot and Bisnauth, for example. These scholars have also done fine work on the history of the church, but have placed emphasis on examining how the church remained the church of planters throughout the age of slavery, a view that gives no consideration to enslaved people's interactions with the church outside of stating that attempts were made by the clergymen to indoctrinate the enslaved.

In this chapter, I have shown some of the ways in which enslaved people showed their agency through church access, focusing on how these illustrated the view of the enslaved themselves that they were free people who had slavery to overcome. The enslaved used church access to assert freedom, rather than to pursue it. This is one of the fundamental features of slave freedom, the assumption of enslaved people that enslavement did not mean the loss of freedom; rather, it was an obstacle that was destructible. Historians of resistance among the enslaved have also raised awareness of the importance of resistance and agency, but have argued these signaled the pursuit of freedom and the counteraction of slavery. Slavery is presented as the institution that shaped the experiences of enslaved people; slavery is the start and the end, so to speak. And while this is fine to express the importance of enslavement, it is less than acceptable as an optic through which to understand the enslaved themselves. We cannot assume that enslaved people thought of slavery as effective or permanent, especially since slavery was designed to extract labor without compensation, and was therefore inherently unjust. Enslaved people knew that slavery was injustice, and their acceptance of church membership was one of the ways through which they demonstrated this awareness.

The mass baptism campaign of the Anglican Church in Jamaica was part of the domination during slavery. Not all clergymen supported using the church to prolong slavery, but all of them viewed Christianization as a way to establish the essentialism of the social order. In other words, even if slavery had ended, the social order would survive because the former enslaved people would not abandon the work that they did on the estates. The productivity of the plantation economy would continue, whites would remain the upper echelons of society, colonialism under British rule would continue. These had been the original mandate of the church from the time of the English capture of Jamaica in 1655. Initially, slavery was the means through which the survival of the social order was envisaged. However, during the British Enlightenment and the abolitionist challenges it brought, slavery became less attractive, and some of the clergymen had from even before that increased their advocacy of converting enslaved people in the church to prepare for the day when slavery was no longer necessary as a means through which labor could be extracted. They argued that conversion would ensure that enslaved people remained loyal to the social order, but this argument would also make sure that enslaved people remained at the center of the most important change in the history of the Atlantic setting, the demolition of slavery, and its replacement with freedom. However, slave freedom preceded this change and helped to shape the way enslaved people responded to church access and its attempt, for whatever reason, to provide assurances that the enslaved were in fact dominated. However, slave freedom showed that domination was wishful thinking.

Notes

1. FP XVIII, (ii) 1740–undated (1–242), John Venn to the Bishop of London, Jamaica, 15 June 1751, 47–48; John Lindsay, "A Few Conjectural Considerations upon the Creation of the Human Race. Occasioned by the Present British Quixotical Rage of Setting the Slaves from Africa at Liberty. By an Inhabitant of Jamaica. The Reverend Doctor Lindsay Rector of St. Katherine's in that Island. St. Jago de la

Vega," 23 July 1788, 173, 227–30. For recent scholarship on Lindsay and his advocacy of slave conversion, also see B.W. Higman, *Proslavery Priest: The Atlantic World of John Lindsay, 1729–1788* (Kingston: University of the West Indies Press, 2011).

2. Dayfoot, *The Shaping of the West Indian Church*, 111, 90; Bisnauth, *History of Religions in the Caribbean*, 48.

3. See the following studies: Heuman, ed., *Out of the House of Bondage*; Craton, *Empire, Enslavement, and Freedom*; Craton, *Testing the Chains*; Brown, *The Reaper's Garden*; and Fergus, "Dread of Insurrection." Also see Alpers, Campbell, and Salman, eds., *Slavery and Resistance in Africa and Asia*.

4. Patterson, *Freedom in the Making of Western Culture*, 3; David Eltis, *The Rise of African Slavery in the Americas* (Cambridge, UK: Cambridge University Press, 2000), in which African freedom is discussed as a factor in the decision of western Europeans to enslave Africans, but this slavery is then treated as the sole re/creator of the abolition of slavery, see pages 281–84. Morgan, *Slavery and the British Empire*, see especially pages 199–204, where the ongoing infleunce of the legacy of slavery is discussed as the means through which freedom evolved as the important trope of post-slavery societies in British Caribbean colonies.

5. Gayatri Chakravorty Spivak, "Can the Subaltern Speak?" in *Marxism and the Interpretation of Culture*, C. Nelson and L. Grossberg, eds. (Basingstoke, UK: Macmillan Education, 1988), 271–313. For the concept of "social death," see Patterson, *Slavery and Social Death*, 8.

6. HLRO HL/PO/JO/10/8/115, Copy of Letter from Simon Taylor, Henry Shirley, George Murray, and Lewis Cuthbert, Esquires, to the Earl of Balcarres; Dated 12th December 1797; and Transmitted in His Lordship's Letter to the Duke of Portland, of December 1797, *Circular Letters to the Governors of the West India Islands*, London, 1800.

7. FP XVIII, (ii) 1740–undated (1–242), An Act to Regulate the Ecclesiastical Regimen of the Clergy, 19 November 1801, 112–20.

8. Edward Long, *The History of Jamaica. Or, General Survey of the Antient and Modern State of That Island: With Reflections on Its Situation, Settlements, Inhabitants, Climate, Products, Commerce, Laws, and Government*, Vol. 2 (London: Printed for T. Lowndes, 1774), 69, 211.

9. J.B. Moreton, *Manners and Customs in the West India Islands. Containing Various Particulars Respecting the Soil, Cultivation, Produce, Trade, Officers, Inhabitants, &C., &C. With the Method of Establishing and Conducting a Sugar-Plantation; in Which the Ill-Practices of Superintendents Are Pointed Out. Also the Treatment of Slaves; and the Slave-Trade* (London: J. Parsons, W. Richardson and J. Walter, 1793 [1790]), 38.

10. Mary Turner, *Slaves and Missionaries: The Disintegration of Jamaican Slave Society, 1787–1834* (Urbana: University of Illinois Press, 1982), 10.

11. ECCO 1739, Acts of Assembly, Passed in the Island of Jamaica; from 1681, to 1737, Inclusive, 1738, 80.

12. Buchner, *The Moravians in Jamaica*, 21, 24; Joseph E. Hutton, *A History of the Moravian Church* (Grand Rapids, MI: Christian Classics Ethereal Library, 2000 [1872]), 128.

13. Lindsay, "A Few Conjectural Considerations upon the Creation of the Human Race," 227, 229, 231.

14. FP XVII, Bermuda, 1695–undated (1–92), Jamaica (i) 1661–1739 (93–292), Queries to be Answered by every Minister, 220, 234.

15. FP XVII, Bermuda, 1695–undated (1–92), Jamaica (i) 1661–1739 (93–292), William Reading to Henry Maule, Palmores Hutt, Jamaica, 15 February 1723, 159.

16. FP XVII, Bermuda, 1695–undated (1–92), Jamaica (i) 1661–1739 (93–292), Catalogue of Books and Instructions Sent with Mr. Barrett, Jamaica, 1724, 175–80.

17. FP XVIII, (ii) 1740–undated (1–242), John Venn to the Bishop of London, Jamaica, 47, 48.

18. Lindsay, "A Few Conjectural Considerations upon the Creation of the Human Race," 220–21.

19. HCPP 1814–15 (478), No. 14 – Jamaica. Copy of a Letter from Lt. General Morrison to Earl Bathurst; Dated Jamaica, 28 January 1813; with Twenty Enclosures, *Jamaica, Papers Relating to the West Indies*, 12 July 1815, 103.

20. HLRO HL/PO/JO/10/8/302, Stipendiary Curates Bill, Print with MS Amendments, 284.

21. HCPP 1818 (433), Copy of Circular Letter from Earl Bathurst to the Governors of West India Colonies. Downing-Street, 7 April 1817, Great Britain, 142.

22. HCPP 1818 (433), Enclosure No. 12, Rectory, Westmoreland, 8 July 1817, Rev. Edmund Pope, 184–96.

23. Higman, *Slave Population and Economy in Jamaica*, 47, 181.

24. HCPP 1818 (433), Enclosure No. 22, Rectory, St. Elizabeth, 9 June 1817, Rev. Thomas Stewart, 202–203.

25. Buchner, *The Moravians in Jamaica*, 50.

26. *Periodical Accounts Relating to the Missions of the Church of the United Brethren, Established among the Heathens*, Vol. IX (London: W.M. McDowell, for the Brethren's Society for the Furtherance of the Gospel Among the Heathen, 1823), 138.

27. *Periodical Accounts Relating to the Missions of the Church of the United Brethren, Established among the Heathens*, Vol. VIII (London: W.M. McDowell, for the Brethren's Society for the Furtherance of the Gospel Among the Heathen, 1821), 123.

28. *Periodical Accounts Relating to the Missions of the Church of the United Brethren, Established among the Heathens*, Vol. II (London: W.M. McDowell, for the Brethren's Society for the Furtherance of the Gospel Among the Heathen, 1796), 16, 83; *Periodical Accounts Relating to the Missions of the Church of the United Brethren, Established among the Heathens*, Vol. IX, 137.

29. Phillippo, *Jamaica, Its Past and Present State*, 290.

30. Hutton, *A History of the Moravian Church*, 128.

31. HCPP 1814–15 (478), City and Parish of Kingston—an Ordinance for Preventing the Profanation of Religious Rights and False Worshipping of God, under the Pretence of Preaching and Teaching, by Illiterate, Ignorant, and Ill-Disposed Persons, and of the Mischiefs Consequent Thereupon, 105.

32. HCPP 1818 (433), Enclosure No. 15, Rectory, St. Mary, 4 July 1817, Rev. Colin Donaldson, 198.

33. HCPP 1818 (433), Enclosure No. 5, Piddingham, St. Anne's, 30 July 1817, Rev. Lewis Bowerbank, 178.

34. HCPP 1818 (433), Enclosure No. 1, Montego Bay, St. James's, 4 June 1817, Rev. Henry Jenkins, 171, 172.

35. HCPP 1818 (433), Enclosure No. 19, St. Thomas's Vale, 5 June 1817, Rev. W.G. Burton, 200.

36. *Periodical Accounts Relating to the Mission of the Church of the United Brethren, Established among the Heathen*, Vol. VI (London: The Brethren's Society for the Furtherance of the Gospel Among the Heathen, 1814), 64.

37. HCPP 1818 (433), Enclosure No. 22, Rectory, St. Elizabeth, 9 June 1817, Rev. Thomas Stewart, 202.

38. HCPP 1818 (433), Enclosure No. 6, Rectory, St. Thomas in the East, 4 June 1817, Rev. John West, 177.

39. See Scott, *Weapons of the Weak*, see title.

40. HCPP 1818 (433), Enclosure No. 2, Rectory, Vere, 12 June 1817, G.C.R. Fearon, 172.

41. Ibid.

42. Ward, *British West Indian Slavery*, 46.

43. NLJ MS2115/R55.7.124.2, Crop Book for the Tharp Estates, *Tharp Papers*, 1791, 182. Also see Ray Fremmer, "Slave Trade in Old Falmouth," *Daily Gleaner*, March 1965, 23; and Alan E. Furness, *The Tharp Estates in Jamaica*, Kingston, National Library of Jamaica, Unpublished Manuscript, Ch. 12, 3.

44. HCPP 1818 (433), Enclosure No. 12, Rectory, Westmoreland, 8 July 1817, Rev. Edmund Pope, 193, 94.

45. HCPP 1818 (433), Enclosure No. 3, Rectory, Hanover, 10 June 1817, Rev. Daniel Rose, 173.

46. Duncan, *A Narrative of the Wesleyan Mission to Jamaica*, 10, 14.

47. HCPP 1818 (433), Enclosure No. 4, Rectory, Clarendon, 9 June 1817, Rev. Thomas Williams, 176.

48. HCPP 1818 (433), Enclosure No. 8, Portland, 10 June 1817, Rev. Phillip Humphries, 180.

49. HCPP 1818 (433), Enclosure No. 21, Rectory, St. David's, 13 September 1817, A. William Pownall, 202.

50. Lewis, *Journal of a West India Proprietor*, 113, 114, 145.

51. Duncan, *A Narrative of the Wesleyan Mission to Jamaica*, 20, 127.

52. Some of these advantages are examined in the studies examining the role of Protestant missionaries in British colonies: Turner, *Slaves and Missionaries*; Shirley C. Gordon, *God Almighty, Make Me Free: Christianity in Preemancipation Jamaica* (Bloomington: Indiana University Press, 1996); Keith Hunte, "Protestantism and Slavery in the British Caribbean," in *Christianity in the Caribbean: Essays on Church History*, Armando Lampe, ed. (Kingston: University of the West Indies Press, 2001),

106–15; Maureen Warner-Lewis, *Archibald Monteath: Igbo, Jamaica, Moravian* (Kingston: University of the West Indies Press, 2007); Larry Gragg, *The Quaker Community on Barbados: Challenging the Culture of the Planter Class* (Columbia: University of Missouri Press, 2009); Andrew Porter, *Religion versus Empire? British Protestant Missionaries and Overseas Expansion, 1700–1914* (Manchester, UK: Manchester University Press, 2004), see especially pages 317–19. For similar work on the role of Protestant missionaries among enslaved people in Brazil, see José Carlos Barbosa, *Slavery and Protestant Missions in Imperial Brazil*, Trans. Fraser G. MacHaffie and Richard K. Danford (Lanham, MD: University Press of America, 2008), and my review of this book in *Church History and Religious Culture* 90:4 (2010): 723–25.

53. Gordon, *God Almighty, Make Me Free*, 18; United Brethren in Christ, *Instructions for Members of the Unitas Fratrum, Who Minister in the Gospel among the Heathens* (London: Printed for the Brethren's Society, for the furtherance of the Gospel among the Heathens, 1784), 16; Buchner, *The Moravians in Jamaica*, 31, 48, 49.

54. I am referring here to this famous study, Brathwaite, *The Development of Creole Society in Jamaica*, see pages vii, 306, 307. For more detailed research specifically on "creolisation" in the churches, see Jon Sensbach, *A Separate Canaan, the Making of an Afro-Moravian World in North Carolina, 1763–1840* (Chapel Hill: University of North Carolina Press, 1998), see pages 113 and 114 to start.

55. *Periodical Accounts Relating to the Missions of the Church of the United Brethren*, Vol. IX, 28, 243.

56. See these studies for discussions about the economic activities of the slaves, including the importance of Sunday marketing: Sidney Mintz, "Slave Life on Caribbean Plantations," in *Slave Cultures and the Culture of Slavery*, Stephan Palmié, ed. (Knoxville: The University of Tennessee Press, 1995), start with page 15; McDonald, *The Economy and Material Culture of Slaves*, see page 31 to start.

57. Arthur J. Freeman, *An Ecumenical Theology of the Heart, the Theology of Count Nicholas Ludwig Von Zinzendorf* (Bethlehem, PA: The Moravian Church in America, 1998), 44, 98, 285; Craig D. Attwood, *Community of the Cross, Moravian Piety in Colonial Bethlehem* (University Park: The Pennsylvania State University Press, 2004), 44; and Buchner, *The Moravians in Jamaica*, 31.

58. Edmund Gibson, *Observations Upon the Conduct and Behaviour of a Certain Sect, Usually Distinguished by the Name of Methodists* (London: Publisher Unknown, 1740), 7, 20.

59. *Periodical Accounts Relating to the Missions of the Church of the United Brethren, Established among the Heathens*, Vol. X, 36.

60. Ibid.

61. Ibid., 256, 257.

62. See Alfred Caldecott, *The Church in the West Indies* (London: Frank Cass & Co. Ltd., 1970 [1898]). Also see these other studies of the Anglican Church, which examine the enslaved in the church, but not using agency, or resistance, or slave freedom: William Moister, *The West Indies, Enslaved and Free* (London: T. Woolmer, 1883); Henry Paget Thompson, *On the Other Side: The Story of the Church in the*

West Indies (London: Junior Work Department, the Society for the Propagation of the Gospel in Foreign Parts, 1929); John E. Levo, *The Romantic Isles: A Sketch of the Church in the West Indies* (London: SPG and SPCK, 1937); Frances Rosemary Perrin, *For Christ and His Church: Twelve Lessons on the Church in the West Indies for Boys and Girls of 8–11* (London: The Society for the Propagation of the Gospel in Foreign Parts, 1952).

CHAPTER EIGHT

~

Slave Laws and Amelioration

In the late seventeenth century, through to almost the mid-eighteenth century, whenever a person was sentenced to execution for murder in Jamaica, that person was entitled to "the Benefit of the Clergy," unless the victim was an enslaved person. The phrase, "the Benefit of the Clergy," meant the entitlement to a visit by the clergyman, who would pray for the soul of the person who was facing execution after being convicted for murder.[1] However, the enslaved were not seen as human beings, so no one who had killed an enslaved person was convicted of having committed a real murder and was not robbed of "the Benefit of the Clergy." The enslaved was property, and killing the enslaved, without just cause, was seen as a property-loss issue. The killer merely owed the slave owner compensation for the loss.

However, the other significance of this, and which was not intentional, was the fear of the enslaved that the disregard showed. The intention was to send a clear message to enslaved people that they were property, and not human beings, who might have rights and/or entitlements, such as the right to freedom. Their bodies, minds, and even souls belonged to their masters. Thoughts of freedom were inimical and damaging to this kind of arrangement. The fear of the enslaved extended even to his or her death. As Vincent Brown has recently shown, death indeed played symbolic roles during the age of slavery.[2] For instance, it was viewed by the enslaved and masters alike as an important act from which resistance could spring. Enslaved people could use British fears of death as forms of symbolic terror from the afterlife, which the laws passed by the Assembly of Jamaica tried to prevent by making sure that the death of an enslaved person was not seen as the death of an actual person. These laws stood as signs of the perilousness of slavery, due mainly to the enslaved people and their power that the slaveholders unwillingly acknowledged, and tried to shield themselves against.

This chapter is about the powerlessness that these slave laws, as they were called, represented, and the ultimate admission of this powerless that came in the attempt to ameliorate the conditions of slavery after many years, the last important modification of slavery before its abolition in 1834. The chapter examines the uses that the enslaved people in Jamaica made of the slaveholders' amelioration policy, and assesses the importance of these uses as further signs of slave freedom and its powerful role in the campaign of the enslaved to erode and eradicate the system of slavery. The next chapter will focus on two additional demonstrations of slave freedom during the amelioration period: manumission and slave marriage. These have not been mentioned in any of the previous chapters, but they also showed the ongoing struggle of the enslaved to assert their freedom in a very real way with respect to manumission, and by their entry into a social institution that was reserved only for the legally free, the institution of marriage.

An important point that the present chapter addresses is the central role that slave freedom played in the reshaping of the colony, which in this case was seen in the modification of slavery using the amelioration policy. Though amelioration was indeed the slave owners' choice, it was adopted on the basis of the decision that the enslaved had made to resist the domination of slavery. Due to this resistance, slavery was problematical from its very beginning, and predicting and then seeing these problems caused by the enslaved, advocates of slavery among the Anglican clergy in the island had promoted the use of Christianization as a means of hegemonic control over enslaved people. However, the slaveholders had resisted conversion and placed countless obstacles in the way of the clerics who supported it. The slaveholders, especially the sugar planters, who owned the majority of the enslaved people, counteracted the entire body of clerics regardless of the reason they wanted to convert the enslaved.

It was indeed true that the clergymen were divided on the purpose of converting enslaved people, who by the end of the seventeenth century were completely of African origin. Some clerics, such as Hickeringill and John Lindsay, saw Christianity as a way to aid the enslavers, but also to save the African from the alleged "backwardness" of their traditional cultures. Christian conversion was seen as a means through which slavery could be protected from the resistance of the enslaved, a way to prolong the life of the institution. However, other clergymen, such as John Venn, viewed conversion as a way to prepare enslaved people for a safe transition into freedom. Christianization would bond them to the social order; it would ensure that they remained tied to the plantations, for example; so that, if and when slavery was abolished, the economic, social, and political domination of whites in the colony would continue, but without the immoralities that had become common practices of the slaveholding people.

None of the clerics who supported conversion did so without some notion of domination in mind; either direct domination in the form of a prolonged, though milder version of slavery, or indirect in the form of capitalist domination over a newly formed working class comprised of former slaves, who would work because of loyalty and because of the sheer need for their subsistence. These were the two poles of thought circulated by the Anglican clergy when amelioration was finally adopted by the slaveholders in Jamaica in the late eighteenth century, both showing the centrality of the concern about the agency of the enslaved, both showing the expectation that if the slaveholders did not act first, the enslaved would. They would change the system and possibly end it because of their rejection of enslavement, but which was aggravated, or so it was believed, by the brutal practices of the slaveholders.

The Slave Laws

The slave laws signaled that slavery was in peril from its earliest stages. The necessity for these laws was the realization of the power of the agency and resistance of enslaved people. The laws tried to counteract slave freedom in this way. In these laws, the slaveholders made sure to point out that slavery was lawful, and enslaved people resisting enslavement were the ones who were guilty of unlawful conduct. The legalization of slavery was in fact the legalization of the attempts to undermine the natural right to freedom that enslaved people knew that they had, and had been showing that they had this knowledge through their resistance. Resistance, and the mere expectation of it, drove fear into the slaveholders, who produced the slave laws as a way to protect slavery, as well as themselves, from the enslaved.

In his 1740 *A New and Exact Account of Jamaica*, Charles Leslie's advice had implied that the slaveholders must acknowledge that they were not as in charge of the colony as they might have thought that they were. The laws passed by the Assembly represented the presence of this virtual powerlessness. This same powerlessness, Leslie implied, had forced the slave masters to adopt their increasingly repressive tactics, and to seek the legitimization of these practices using the artifice of the slave laws. One such law, which was quoted by Leslie, stated that "No Master of any Ship or Vessel shall presume to carry off this Island, any Slave or Slaves, without a ticket under the Governor's Hand."[3] This clause had added another layer of protection for the owners of enslaved people, by banning the removal of the enslaved from the island without authorization, which had to be issued by the top executive branch of the colonial government. However, the clause was also directed at the enslaved people, by the fact that it mandated the top executive's involvement in any kind of plan to place the enslaved on vessels that were bound for sea travel. Preparations had to be made for this to happen, and these preparations were necessary because of the likelihood of insurrection aboard these vessels. Worse, the insurrections might also spread onshore because of the additional empowerment that a successful revolt anywhere gave to its enslaved participants, as well as others who were not at the time involved. Even when the laws did not directly mention insurrection, they were always in some way connected with the persistent fear of that equally tenacious realization.

The early English geographer, John Fransham, who did not even reside in the colonial world, wrote about the fear of the enslaved and their agency, though in a totally different framework. Fransham's 1741 *The World in Miniature*, was a clear celebration of the idea of the British Empire, an eighteenth-century discourse on the British success at globalizing the planet, starting with the western hemisphere, from the seventeenth century onward. The necessity for this kind of discourse was the interesting part of it. It was due to the urgent need to remind British readers of their accomplishments on the world stage, in order to shore up the machinations through which the empire became, or was to become, a new reality. However, at the same time that he was celebrating the empire as a great achievement, Fransham also warned about the dissatisfactory demographic arrangement in the colonies within the empire. He mentioned that in Jamaica in 1740, for example, the white population stood at a mere 50,000 people.[4] This was clearly not a sufficient number to ensure that the empire was maintained and continued to grow, and it was certainly not the kind of number that made the business of empire a safe and secured adventure in comparison to the number of enslaved and other nonwhite people in the colonies.

Other writers, such as Nathaniel Crouch, also paid close attention to the issue of the demographic imbalance in the western colonies. In his *The English Empire in America*, Crouch mentioned that the nonwhite population in Jamaica, for instance, had already reached the frightening number of 150,000 before the year 1741.[5] The fear of nonwhites was due to the overwhelming number of enslaved Africans and their descendants in this group, and this fear extended even as far as the thoughts about the prospects of the British

Empire as a whole. This fear was based on the knowledge that enslavement had assumed that the enslaved viewed themselves as slaves, and that they had accepted that enslavement was simply their lot in life. Counteracting this assumption, however, was the prospect and the reality of resistance, its clearly visible power to change the social arrangement that was established on the basis of slavery, and its power to demolish even the empire, or at the very least, to render the empire a promise that could never be fulfilled. The perilousness of slavery had put the entire business of empire under duress. These advisories about the demographic disparity were among the first warning signs of the fragility of enslavement in the face of the determination of enslaved people to show that freedom was their natural state, and that slavery was an imposed and temporary setback.

It is unsurprising, therefore, that among the laws passed in Jamaica as early as 1703, were laws encouraging white males to migrate to the colony; laws discouraging the emigration of white males; and laws also stipulating in stringent terms that able-bodied white males were to be hired at the same time that specified numbers of enslaved people were purchased. It was known that white rule in the colony was heavily dependent on the suppression of nonwhites, and especially on the suppression of the enslaved. It was from the enslaved especially that whites forcibly extracted labor so that they could turn a profit. Their entire existence—economically, socially, and politically—was tied to the labor that enslaved people, in particular, provided. The status of slaveholders, namely the sugar planters, was attained because of their exploitation of the enslaved. Their political influence was due to their economic prowess and social status. The basis of white prosperity was indeed black suppression, and larger numbers of white males were therefore needed, especially on the sugar plantations where the numbers of the enslaved were also largest, in order to provide at least some assurance that white rule could be and would be maintained. In broader terms, the concentration of large numbers of enslaved people on the plantations was viewed as one of the most dangerous events in the British colonial enterprise; and one of Jamaica's contributions to the endeavor to eradicate this danger were the laws stating that, for instance, one white male was to be hired for every twenty slaves that were purchased.[6]

And even this was not seen as enough. White taxpayers in Jamaica were asked to come up with an additional sum of £500 initially to be put toward the creation of the island's first police force in the early eighteenth century. This constabulary was to help in the suppression of black dissent, especially if there was a small insurrection involving the enslaved on one of the estates. In addition, a law was enacted for any vessel plying Jamaica's coastal waters with enslaved people as the crew. This law stated that the captains were required "to keep one white Man, qualified to bear Arms," onboard these vessels and the penalty for breaking this law was set at 40s per month, until compliance was confirmed.[7] Emma Christopher's study of slave ships has shown that the fear of insurrection aboard sea vessels was a constant phenomenon, and was more whenever African people served as crew members. In Christopher's study, these vessels, known as slavers, were the ones that made the journey across the Atlantic, a trip that historians now refer to as the Middle Passage. This voyage was notorious for the loss of life among the enslaved onboard as the cargoes. Some committed suicide by throwing themselves overboard, others died because of diseases caused by mainly the insanitary conditions in the holds of the ships, and some were cast overboard deliberately for the insurance, if they became sick or feeble-looking, and the captains felt that they would not sell for much when the ships arrived at their destinations in the Americas. Christopher's study has shown that the Africans among the crew on these slavers are not to be seen solely as sellouts because of their participation in slave trafficking. Participation is obviously undeniable, but these same black crew members also inspired resistance, and through this, added to the constant danger of insurrection aboard these vessels. Black crew members were persistent reminders of black freedom; it seemed to the enslaved cargoes that they could do as they pleased; and because of this impression, based on their mere presence, black crew members could incite insurrection among the enslaved cargoes.[8]

Even the livestock pens, with far fewer enslaved people than the plantations had, were not left out. Verene Shepherd, in her study of these pens, has shown that they were vital components of the slaveholding regime.[9] However, pens also served as signposts of the central role of resistance among enslaved people during the age of slavery. Clauses within the slave laws passed during the late 1600s and early 1700s specified that "One white Servant man" was to be hired for the first sixty head of livestock, and another white male was to be hired "for every Hundred after the first Sixty." These white employees were also "to be resident where such Stock are or shall be kept." This revealed mostly the fear of the enslaved and their numbers—numbers that grew with the addition of more heads of livestock on the pens—and another 40s per person was the fine for not hiring the stipulated number of whites to work on these pens.[10]

In addition, these stipulations were an indication of the deep involvement of the government in the suppression of the agency of enslaved people. Even the pens had to be included, showing in yet another way the far-reaching effects of even the mere assumption that the enslaved would not accept slavery, and would continue to undermine slaveholding with acts of sabotage and insurrection. The colonial legislators in Jamaica became very guarded about their right to govern the colony independently of Britain, but they also thought that they could best materialize this capacity for self-rule if they could control the enslaved people. Colonial governance was thus tied to the suppression of slave freedom, and white settlers saw their freedom in terms of their capacity to perfect the domination of the enslaved.

However, Paul Knaplund and David W. Galenson have both suggested that the ideology of white self-rule in New World colonies was acquired almost in isolation. Enslaved people were absent for the most part from the considerations made about self-government in the colonial settings; they certainly did not play a central role. Their exploitation was not the means used to determine white freedom. Instead, the settlers, according to Knaplund, were "Adventurous, aggressive men and women," who "rejected Whitehall dominance over their government and economic life."[11] Galenson also suggests that colonial Virginia's acquisition of "a General Assembly" in 1619, based on an "extraordinary liberal suffrage," came about largely because of the self-directed commitment of the free white population to self-rule.[12] However, the laws directing that whites were to take every precaution against the enslaved told a different story. These laws showed the awareness that white self-government was inextricably linked to the suppression of slave freedom. Not surprisingly, the suffrage in the colonies, extraordinarily liberal as they might have seemed, excluded everyone except for white males, associating even gender bias to the matter of suppression, adding the view that only white males had the mental and physical wherewithal to control the rebellious enslaved. Until the 1730s, mixed race or colored people in Jamaica could not vote, and within a few years after this, the vote was taken away from them once again. No one, except for white males could serve in the executive, legislative, or judicial branches of the colonial government until the 1820s. If the settlers were adventurous and aggressive, they became this way after their arrival in the unfamiliar terrain of the New World, where their difficulties with dominating and exploiting the landscape were aggravated by their inability to tame untamable people.

The Maroons had arguably dealt the most effective blow to colonial self-governance and slaveholding in Jamaica before the mid-1700s. They forced the British in Jamaica into signing a peace treaty in 1739. This ended one of the longest wars that the British had ever fought anywhere in the Americas before, during, and after the eighteenth century. And if we should adopt the viewpoint of the Maroons themselves, this war had been going on since the British captured Jamaica from the Spanish in 1655, at which point the

Maroons had taken to the mountainous interior in larger numbers and built their formidable communities in the Windward and Leeward sections of the island. The Maroons today argue that the British began to fight them as soon as they arrived, and because they could never defeat them, they signed the peace treaty in the early eighteenth century.[13]

Barbara Klamon Kopytoff has argued that the Maroons became allies of the British because of the treaty's obligations, and this has today remained a scar on the Maroons in the view of many citizens from the rest of Jamaica.[14] However, the treaty still stands as a symbolic representation of the African determination to assert their freedom. There was no other display of black unity to fashion civil defiance in early eighteenth-century Jamaica that was more spectacular, more efficient, and more effective than the First Maroon War, which in the records from the colonial archives lasted about a decade, but in Maroon oral history, had lasted eighty-four years. Coinciding with the beginning of this war, an attempt was made by the Jamaica Assembly to strengthen its campaign against what they referred to as African rebellious-ness. This law, passed in 1730, highlighted further the African commitment to showing that they were free people. The law was passed specifically "for the better suppressing and reducing the rebellious and runaway Negroes."[15] Other laws passed during the same decade tried to also "Better" regulate the enslaved, and to use even free blacks and coloreds, along with the Maroons at the end of the decade, in the suppression of enslaved African people and their descendants. The use of other nonwhites in the campaign of suppres-sion was appropriately described as making these groups "More Useful" to the society.[16]

This and the treaty with the Maroons in 1739 were signs of the adoption of craftier hegemonic means of suppression, designed specifically to stem the hemorrhaging of the slave system. Together, these signaled social change, or the fact that slavery was changing and the modifications were caused by the enslaved. Awareness of slave freedom and its power brought about the change that was seen. This awareness was also viewable in the suppression of even the hegemonic allies because of the fear that they might use their posi-tion to aid the enslaved, rather than the slaveholding regime. For instance, as Gad Heuman has stated, the ordinance that was passed in 1730, and then quickly amended in 1733, was an attempt to suppress all "free blacks and coloreds" even while they were seen as potential allies of the slaveholders. They were not allowed to "participate in politics," and "they were not eli-gible to sit in the legislature." Furthermore, "they lost the right to vote" as soon as the ordinance was amended, which was a mere three years after its enactment.[17] In 1793, free blacks and coloreds were still seen and treated as noncitizens in Jamaica, even while they were expected to aid slaveholding. For example, they could not testify in court cases in which whites were the ones on trial for any offence, but whites could testify if the cases were about free blacks and coloreds.[18]

The prospect and the reality of black rebelliousness were the main reasons for the slave laws, as well as those laws which were passed in order to mandate the employment of more white males along with the growth of the enslaved population. When the prospect of a war with the Maroons turned into reality, these laws were revised and reinstituted with harsher penalties for any infractions.[19] The laws, including those which later tried to generate alliances with the Maroons and other nonwhites, stood as further vivid examples of the trepidation that slaveholders felt because of the enslaved. They either perceived or had seen the power of slave freedom, and because of this, they had only one objective in mind, which was to suppress it.

However, when Tacky's revolt broke out in 1760, the slaveholders in Jamaica were again forced into reexamining and taking stock of their position in the colony. Tacky's revolt was a war against both slaveholding and white rule in Jamaica, a reminder of the weakness of the laws which were designed with suppression in mind. Tacky's war exposed the perilous state of slavery and showed the power of the enslaved people's conviction that they were free, and thus they should be freed from slavery. James Knight had warned in his 1726 *The State of the Island of Jamaica* that slaveholding was indeed in danger even during that early period, and the only way to save the system from dissolution was if the slave masters should cease the brutal measures and terror tactics that they had been using to protect slavery. Knight connected the rebelliousness of the enslaved to the ill-treatment meted out by the slaveholders. He was also one of the early deniers of slave freedom in this sense, one of the writers who undervalued slave freedom with the idea that better treatment could generate conformity among the enslaved. Knight did not think that enslaved people could have thoughts about freedom unless these came as a consequence of enslavement. A similar view reappears in the thesis of Patterson that freedom was culturally manufactured because of the extremeness of slavery in the Americas.[20]

Knight chose not to put his name anywhere on the book, probably because of his perspective which did not correspond with the current dispensation of most slaveholders in Jamaica. Furthermore, Knight viewed colonial independence or self-government as having weakened the position of slaveholders, and therefore British intervention was urgently needed. This intervention, he argued, could aid the slaveholders in their remaking of the slave system, in their instituting of the change away from brutality and toward indoctrination, or toward measures tantamount to a cautious amelioration policy. Writing that the book was addressed "to a Member of PARLIAMENT" was Knight's way of suggesting the need for assistance from London. He also pointed out the disappearance of some 15,165 enslaved people from the island, people who were lost to "the *Spaniards* in the *West-Indies*." This loss had occurred "*during the peace with France and Spain*" (his italics), and was a consequence of the obvious disgruntled state of the enslaved population of Jamaica.[21]

Addressing the need for a different approach, Leslie had also advised in 1740 that "No country excels" the island-colony of Jamaica "in a barbarous Treatment of [the] Slaves." Leslie saw no value in preventing the enslaved from practicing in their traditional cultural practices, for example, in their "Sacrifices, Libations etc.," which he argued were "at this Day in Use among the Negroes." Like Knight, who wrote before him, Leslie had warned "that Slavery is the ruin of Society." However, Leslie's interest was not in abolishing the institution of slavery. Instead, Leslie thought that it was possible for the slaveholders to improve the conditions of slavery. They could, for example, eradicate the harsh methods that they used to punish the enslaved, and the latter would automatically respond to the change with loyalty and less inclination toward rebellion.[22] Both Knight and Leslie were, ironically, following the trend of underestimating the enslaved while at the same time observing the evidence of the capacity of enslaved people to think and act independently. Of course, slaveholders themselves also adhered to this hazardous trend. Their only difference from Knight and Leslie was their neurotic obsession with brutality. On the other hand, Knight and Leslie were proponents of amelioration, but similar to the Anglican clergymen, who also criticized the extremities of the slave masters, Knight and Leslie made an irrational assessment of the enslaved by thinking that amelioration could work in the way that they had planned it, that it could become a successful form of domination that would pacify the enslaved people and prolong the life of slavery.

Tacky's war stood as a reminder of the fact that the enslaved people had never stopped thinking about the ways that they could assert their right to freedom. The revolt was planned while slave masters concocted more aggressive measures to suppress the enslaved. None of these measures produced the outcome that slave masters wanted, none could make enslaved people lose sight of their freedom. The revolt was success because of the fact that it happened, and because of what it did to the slaveholding people. It revived the fear of slave freedom in a sudden, unexpected, and catastrophic way. It sent the colonial government scrambling to assemble troops of the colonial militia to dispatch to the affected areas in western Jamaica, and after the fighting the

Assembly passed a new slave law. This contained some of the most extreme suppressions up to that point. Bans were placed on gaming, drinking, and the playing of drums by the enslaved. They were prohibited from blowing shells and horns, which were interpreted as ways for them to communicate across the plantations, ways to send messages about their plans to rise up in rebellion at any given moment. Other clauses in the new law stated that only the enslaved who sold fresh milk and fish could be issued tickets by masters to travel on Sundays away from the plantations. The Anglican cleric, Rev. George Wilson Bridges, in his *Annals of Jamaica* written in the 1820s, described the new law as nonetheless "imperfect and precarious." In other words, it was a clear waste of resources. While the slaveholders made themselves merry with the view that they were victorious over Tacky and his fighters, the new slave law told a completely different tale. The law was an admission of defeat, as far as Bridges was concerned. Its aggression showed this clearly, alongside the fact that it was necessary for the colonial government to also execute and transport off the island scores of Tacky's forces who were not killed during the fighting. But the new law itself, Bridges argued, could "seldom inspire virtue" and could "never be expected to restrain vice."[23]

Elsa Goveia has suggested that Bridges was neurotic, that he lived in a world of nightmares in which enslaved people were villains who harangued himself and other whites who were trying to create the perfect colony. Most of this is true. However, Bridges was not in any way neurotic. In fact, he was among the sanest of the colonial whites of Jamaica. He saw the power of slave freedom very clearly, hence his trepidation, hence the "nightmare" world in which he felt that he lived.[24] Tacky's war was a reminder that this world existed and could change the practices of slaveholding at any time. Historian Richard B. Sheridan has also noted that there were many other acts of rebellion besides Tacky's war. In fact, as Sheridan states, revolts were "nearly endemic" in the second half of the eighteenth century. A revolt erupted "on an average of every five years" and usually "involved about 400 slave participants." In addition, hidden or silent acts of resistance were frequent, such as "malingering, petty theft, sabotage, arson, poisoning, running away, suicide."[25] Each demonstrated the disapproval of slavery, the effort to undermine the institution, but also the determination of the enslaved to have their freedom recognized by the people who had assumed that they could enslave them. Freedom was the ultimate cause of resistance in any shape or form, slavery was the institution that the enslaved counteracted, slavery made showing the existence of this freedom urgent and necessary, but it did not create or generate the freedom of the enslaved, nor the desire that they had for this freedom.

Tacky led the most spectacular exhibition of African freedom in Jamaica during the eighteenth century after the cessation of the war with the Maroons. He chose to attack slavery in a violent and direct way; the only strategy that he felt could immediately and effectively end the institution. His inspiration was his belief in his freedom, and because his followers had the same conviction, they continued to fight after Tacky was shot and killed. Bridges had also recorded this because he viewed it as an important event in the recounting of the revolt. Tacky might have captained the revolt, but he was not the reason for it. His followers were inspired by the same feeling that they were free people unfairly forced to defend their freedom because of slavery. After Tacky's death, his followers had "soon rallied, and rose again, in various directions," from where they continued to fight with "desperate fury" because of their determination to die rather than to continue living in slavery.[26] The fact that Tacky was killed by the Maroons, not the colonial militia, was also important. This event was, without a doubt, a poor reflection on the Maroons. However, it also exposed the fact that the slaveholders had started to accept the view that counteracting the resistance of the enslaved would require assistance from anywhere that they could get this. Overall, they had come to the realization that different strategies were needed from the ones that they had been using, and eventually, they adopted the idea of using a tactic that was suppressive but which, in their view, was not brutal. Neither the slave laws nor the daily brutalities of slaveholding seemed to them to have been working in the way that they wanted these to work.

The resolution to implement amelioration, which came almost at the end of the eighteenth century, showed that the slaveholders had waited a long time before they had finally decided to fully acknowledge that they needed help. The long period that came before the amelioration policy was a clear sign of the intransigence of the slaveholders, but it was also a sign of their fear of slave freedom. This fear manifested in their need to carefully consider all of the possible outcomes of any major change, and the fact that they were permanently mindful that changing course could produce effects that none of their plans might be able to prevent. The one constant feature of slaveholding was the resistance of the enslaved, and the slave masters had learned to expect this resistance in any form that it could take, and regardless of any decision that they themselves took as slaveholders. On the other hand, amelioration, when it was finally enacted, stood as another admission by the slaveholders that they were losing their power over the enslaved, and were quite possibly losing the power that they felt that they had over the society as a whole.

The Adoption of Amelioration

The contribution of J.B. Moreton, a plantation bookkeeper in Jamaica, to the discussion about amelioration in the island in the 1790s, came at a time when the slaveholders had already decided that ameliorating slavery was the only way that they could save the institution from destruction by the enslaved people. Moreton's contribution was to show the wisdom of this decision. He suggested applying to the enslaved the same kind of thinking that had resulted in the treaty with Captain Cudjoe, the leader of the Leeward Maroons, in 1739. Moreton wrote that he had met with Cudjoe, and that he was impressed that this former enemy had become a friend and ally of the English king and the slaveholders in Jamaica. According to Moreton, Cudjoe described his relationship with the king of England as a friendship that was "good," and had added that they would even exchange gifts on occasion, an expression of their high regard for each other.[27] Whether Moreton was lying or was truthful is beside the point. He might have misread Cudjoe's remarks, or Cudjoe might have deliberately made those comments knowing that these were the kind of remarks that Moreton, a white employee of a slave plantation, had wanted to hear. However, the most important point is that Moreton took Cudjoe's pronouncements seriously, and Moreton believed that the Maroon leader was truly an ally of the English in Jamaica and England.

Moreton's point of view regarding the adoption of amelioration, when dealing with the enslaved, coincided with Adam Smith's well known advocacy of ending slavery to some extent. Smith was one of the thinkers of the British Enlightenment, and arguably he was its foremost economist. Smith's proposition, in his 1776 *An Inquiry into the Nature and Causes of the Wealth of Nations*, was that slavery should be abolished and a waged labor arrangement should be implemented as its replacement. The objective was to protect bourgeois investments in production, such as the huge investments in sugar cultivation in the Caribbean colonies. Smith was convinced that because the laborers would need to work to maintain themselves, slavery was unnecessary.[28] Though Moreton most certainly did not go as far as to propose abolition, while addressing *the Treatment of Slaves*, he nonetheless proposed reducing the longstanding reliance on brutality, and replacing this with concessions, which he expected would stimulate the enslaved to work without resistance, or in the same manner that wages were expected to stimulate laborers to work without complaint.[29]

The amelioration that was adopted by Jamaica's slaveholders in 1797 was directly connected with the pressure that they were facing from the resistance of the enslaved people. Slave freedom was the main motivation for the bill that the four wealthy planters had proposed in December of that year, which was passed by the Assembly in that same month. The bill had proposed Christian indoctrination of the enslaved and the importation of enslaved people who were no older than twenty-five years, based on the assumption that these enslaved people could better withstand slavery because of their youth, and they would be less likely to rebel as a result. Both propositions were adopted and appeared in the act when it was passed.[30] External factors, such as the impact of British abolitionism, which began in the 1780s, and the slave rebellion in St. Domingue that erupted in 1791, were considered when the bill was first proposed. However, these were seen as secondary to the concern about slave freedom. The outside factors were seen as annoyances, but which the planters felt that they could overcome in the course of time.

Following the initial fear that the rebellion in neighboring St. Domingue might spread to Jamaica, the prices of sugar and coffee on the world market increased. The freedom of enslaved people in St. Domingue had, ironically, created a favorable set of economic conditions that helped to stimulate the revival of the sugar and coffee industries in Jamaica. Higman has recorded, for instance, that the per capita product of Jamaica did in fact revive in the years after the outbreak of rebellion in St. Domingue. He notes that the "Jamaican per capita product doubled to £29.2" nine years later, or at the start of the nineteenth century.[31] Also important was the fact that British abolitionism was not about amelioration before the 1820s. The decision of the slaveholders in Jamaica to adopt amelioration was connected with abolition only because it was a way to avoid abolition altogether. Smith had proposed abolishing slavery, not the modification of the institution, and Condorcet, another one of the important voices of the Enlightenment, was also a proponent of abolition, who "criticized the institution of slavery" as an absurd "obstruction to progress," the kind of institution that could not possibly be improved.[32] Abolitionism had turned to ending the slave trade in the 1790s, while the slaveholders in Jamaica were contemplating amelioration. The abolitionists felt that ending the trafficking of slaves would starve slavery into nonexistence, and when this did not happen, the abolitionists turned their attention to ending slavery itself.

When the slaveholders in Jamaica and other colonies acted in response to abolitionism, they did so with the formation of the West India Interest in 1786, not with the amelioration of slavery. This lobby group came into existence to counteract the information about slavery that came from the abolitionists, information that the slaveholders and the British merchants who did business with the slave plantation system considered as propaganda.

The enactment of a "New Consolidated" slave "Act" by the Assembly of Jamaica in 1784 was one of the earliest and visible signs that the slaveholders had begun to take amelioration seriously, but this new slave law was passed two years before the slaveholders showed that they were affected by British abolitionism.[33] Furthermore, before this slave law came into existence, a select number of slaveholders in Jamaica had already begun to implement amelioration policies on their estates. These included the brothers William Foster and Joseph Foster-Barham, owners of Bogue and Mesopotamia sugar estates in St. Elizabeth and Westmoreland, respectively. As Moravians themselves, they had invited Moravian missionaries to convert their enslaved people into Christians, with the hope that this would pacify the enslaved because they would interpret conversion as part of improving the conditions of slavery, improvements for their benefit. These missionaries had begun to arrive in Jamaica from 1754.[34]

In addition, some of the Anglican clerics had reported from before that that they too had converted a small number of the enslaved people, and they were able to do this because of the slaveholders, who had expressed interest in using the Christian doctrine to facilitate improving the conditions of slavery, which they hoped would pacify the enslaved or make them less rebellious. This was amelioration at its very rudimentary stage, long before British abolitionism started. In 1739, for example, Rev. Lewis de Boneval had reported that he was even approached by the governor, Edward Trelawney, about his attempts to Christianize the enslaved. According to Boneval, Trelawney had "told me with some sharpness that he was Surprised I should preach a doctrine that tended to Sedition," but to which Boneval said that he responded by informing the governor that he was merely trying to aid the governments of Britain and Jamaica, as well as the slaveholding people. According to Boneval, he was attempting "to inculcate in them the doctrine of turning from all their evil ways & of rendering to God the things that are God's & to Caesar the things that are Caesar's; [and] that by Caesar," added Boneval, "I always told them was to be understood the King[,] his representative, & their masters."[35]

Writing to one of his sons in 1803, the slaveholder John Tharp made the link between his adoption of amelioration from many years before that and the conduct of the enslaved people on his own estates. Tharp stated that the enslaved people had named him "Daddy Tharp" mainly because of his allocations. As a result, he was able to report with some amount of confidence that his people had "increased" through natural means and "are very happy." Nevertheless, he had not lost sight of the fact that his people's happiness was a spectacle. The moment that they turned him into "Daddy Tharp" was when this had started, and they reserved the right to withdraw the name as often as they pleased.[36] Matthew Lewis' experiences were very similar. However, he had responded initially with the warning that the enslaved were "perverse" because productivity had declined on his estates instead of increased as he expected, and this was after Lewis' introduction of a "new code of laws" on both of his estates.[37] As mentioned in earlier chapters, James B. Wildman, an absentee planter similar to Lewis, owned three estates in Jamaica—Salt Savannah, Papine, and Low Ground—which he visited in the 1820s. Wildman was called upon by the enslaved people to make a range of changes on his properties. Turner has noted that because of the enslaved people, Wildman had to choose "to abolish flogging as a punishment for women," introduce measures to "control" the use "of the whip to extract slave labor," and had even decided to control the use of the whip for "the extraction of animal labor." Wildman eventually consented "to abolish night work" as well, and did so on the basis of petitions from enslaved persons. He supported "Religious education," which the enslaved people on his estates embraced.[38]

Brown argues, in *Moral Capital: Foundations of British Abolitionism*, that the work of the abolitionists changed slavery and then ultimately ended it.[39] However, this view does not give enough consideration to the changes brought about by amelioration, and therefore to the central role of slave freedom, or slave resistance, in the decision to move in the direction of these changes. While William Wilberforce, for example, was petitioning for the abolition of the slave trade, starting from 1796, the enslaved people in Jamaica had been using their agency to undermine, erode, and abolish the practices of slaveholders from long before that, and the effect of this resistance was seen in the decision taken by the slaveholders to adopt fully amelioration in 1797.[40] However, the amelioration that was introduced was designed mainly to indoctrinate enslaved people using Anglican instruction and baptism, and this was in order to protect the institution of slavery. In other words, when amelioration materialized, the objective was to prolong the life of slavery by eradicating the acts of brutality committed by slave masters, a goal that was seen as achievable only if the enslaved people were also Christianized. Despite everything, amelioration did have a moral feature attached to it, and one that was supposed to change slaveholders' attitudes toward the enslaved, while also, of course, changing the enslaved themselves. Fundamentally, amelioration was viewed by slaveholders as another form of domination. However, nowhere in the policy was there any consideration of how the enslaved people would respond to amelioration in light of their proven determination to show the slaveholders that they were free.

The London agent for the slaveholders in Jamaica, Robert Sewell, wrote to the Colonial Office in 1797 to inform them that the Christianization of enslaved people in the island was indeed seen as the most important part of the amelioration policy adopted by the Assembly. Sewell wrote that the policy had proposed to place "the Clergy in Jamaica on the most respectable footing," and added that the goal was to "instruct in the doctrines of the Christian Religion such Negroes as may be willing to be baptized on every Sunday, and at a time to be appointed by the Rectors." Through this latest consideration by the assemblymen, as Sewell also added, the governor was to now have more power "to censure, suspend, or remove, any Clergyman who may become a just object of complaint."[41] The purpose of this was to provide at least some assurance that clerics who might fail to carry out the Christianization project would be removed from their posts. Converting the enslaved was now seen as one of the most important policy decisions for the future of the colony.

This future was supposed to be one in which the slaveholders were still in charge of the island, or one in which slaveholding would remain the most important activity. It was slaveholding that would protect the social order, so slavery had to be maintained. The assumption made was that the amelioration would succeed and the only way that it could possibly fail was if the clerics, who were assigned to carry out its most important feature, had themselves botched the performance of their duty. Sewell's message was confirmation of the absence of any serious contemplation about how the enslaved people would react, even though it was the agency of the enslaved that had brought the slaveholders to the point of implementing measures that would modify the slave system in a permanent way. However, this was one of the perennial features of slaveholding in Jamaica and other British colonies: the refusal to acknowledge in any overt way the presence of slave freedom and its influence on the present and future state of the society.

This refusal was rehearsed by Sewell as well, who stated in his letter that the Christianization of the enslaved would require no use of force. Enslaved people were expected to "be willing to be baptized on every Sunday," and the most important role of the clergymen was to simply become available to facilitate the desire of the enslaved for their conversion to Christianity. This assumption of compliance without resistance would however help the enslaved to hide the fact that they were resisting the Christian indoctrination even while they appeared to be conforming by accepting the invitation to join the church. Whenever dominators assume success, the dominated are given more room in which they can maneuver and manipulate the process that is designed to dominate them. While the slaveholders were confident about the power of the church to indoctrinate the enslaved people, the latter were able to use the church to their advantage. Another consistent feature of enslavement was the view that Carmichael would write about in her *Domestic Manners and Social Condition of the White, Coloured and Negro Population of the West Indies*, published in 1833. As already mentioned, according to Carmichael, the enslaved were seen as "stupid beings," but she warned about the inadequacy of such a view and explained that even when the enslaved conformed, they were resisting. Carmichael wrote that their capacity to make intelligent choices appeared in the compassion that they showed to the "kind benevolent owners of negroes" and this was one of their activities that most certainly should not be underestimated.[42] These acts of compassion, which included taking food crops to masters who were facing economic hardship, were to be seen as investments that the enslaved people were making in their future. Simply put, they expected returns from these investments, and legal freedom was one of them. Carmichael was writing about the enslaved people in St. Vincent and Trinidad, where she stayed, but her intention was to provide observations that could be applied to the entire British-colonized Caribbean.

Sewell's message was important, nonetheless. It contained an inadvertent acknowledgement that the decision to change slavery in Jamaica had been brought about by the enslaved people. The amelioration policy came into being because of the need to modify how the slaveholders treated the enslaved, and the response of the latter to Christianization was viewed as the most important adjustment that could be made for the foreseeable future of the colony. At the same time, the slave owners in the island made no attempt to experiment with measures to force the enslaved to embrace the Anglican version of the Christian religion. They assumed that force was unwise, in addition to being unnecessary. Because the use of force was not present, the slaveholders had shown that they were aware of the power of the resistance of the enslaved. As a whole, amelioration was heavily dependent on this awareness. Amelioration was an admission of powerlessness by the slaveholders, and an admission that necessitated the adoption of a new type of domination strategy.

Conclusion

The slave laws of Jamaica contained early evidence of the perilous nature of slaveholding in the British colonies of the Caribbean. These laws were proof of the commitment that slave owners had to make to extreme measures of suppression because of slave freedom. Some of this commitment was based on prophesizing, or on actions which were taken because of the expectation of resistance, rather than because of its reality. Either way, the fear of the en-slaved shaped the system of slavery and the lives of the slave owners in more ways than they had ever admitted. Slave ownership produced the conceited-ness among the slaveholders that made them unwilling to disclose that they were always on their guard because of the choices that the enslaved people made, and mainly the decision not to remain in slavery.

The amelioration policy in Jamaica continued to expose the fears of slave-holders, even though this policy was implemented by slave-owning people and for the purpose of making their domination of the enslaved produce the kind of effects that they wanted to see. Once amelioration was embraced, it became the main means through which slavery was to proceed for the future, and the main defining feature of the institution until it was abolished in 1834. However, in spite of the presence of amelioration, the enslaved con-tinued to resist enslavement. They did not act in the ways that slaveholders expected them to act. The most important part of amelioration was the use of Christianity as offered by the Anglican Church as a form of indoctrina-tion. However, as the previous chapter has shown, enslaved people used the invitation to join the state church to initiate their own colonization of the church, and throughout the process of their entry into the church they influ-enced how the clerics performed their duties with respect to the amelioration policy. The next chapter continues the examination of the enslaved people's responses to amelioration, using manumission and marriage. These were two other demonstrations of slave freedom during what we can indeed describe as the declining period of slavery in British colonial Jamaica, and the slave world of the British Atlantic as a whole.

Notes

1. ECCO, 1738 [1739], Acts of Assembly, Passed in the Island of Jamaica; from 1681, to 1737, Inclusive, 1738, 80.

2. Brown, The Reaper's Garden, 41, 167.

3. Charles Leslie, A New and Exact Account of Jamaica, 3rd Ed. (Edinburgh: R. Fleming, 1740), Letter VII, 228.

4. John Fransham, The World in Miniature: Or, the Entertaining Traveller. Giving an Account of Every Thing Necessary and Curious; . . . With Several Curious and Use-ful Tables . . . The Second Edition Much Enlarg'd: Also the Addition of a New Sett of Cutts, 2 Vols., Vol. 1 (London: Printed, and sold by John Torbuck; Mess. Astley and Austen; T. Osborne; A. Millar; and J. Hodges and T. Harris, 1741), 140.

5. Nathaniel Crouch, The English Empire in America: Or, a View of the Dominions of the Crown of England . . . Illustrated with Maps and Pictures. By R. Burton, 5th. Ed. (London: Printed for Nath. Crouch, 1711), 190.

6. ECCO, 1738 (1739), An Act to Encourage the Importation of White Men. No. 113. Acts of Assembly, Passed in the Island of Jamaica; from 1681, to 1737, Inclusive, 99.

7. Ibid., 5, 99.

8. Christopher, *Slave Ship Sailors and their Captive Cargoes*, 52.

9. Verene A. Shepherd, *Livestock, Sugar, and Slavery: Contested Terrain in Colonial Jamaica* (Kingston: Ian Randle Publishers, 2009), see especially chapters two and five.

10. ECCO, 1738 (1739), An Act to Encourage the Importation of White Men. No. 113, 99.

11. Paul Knaplund, "Great Britain and the British Empire," in *Material Progress and World-Wide Problems 1870–1898*, F.H. Hinsely, ed. (Cambridge, UK: Cambridge University Press, 1962), 407.

12. David W. Galenson, "The Settlement and Growth of the Colonies: Population, Labor, and Economic Development," in *The Colonial Era*, Stanley L. Engerman and Robert E. Gallman, eds. (Cambridge, UK: Cambridge University Press, 1996), 136.

13. This assessment is based on the oral history of the Maroons, which was recounted at a panel discussion following a public lecture, to which I was invited to participate as one of the panellists. See Devon Dick, "Role of the Maroons in the Morant Bay Uprising: You Shall Know the Truth and the Truth Shall Set You Free," St. Thomas Co-operative Credit Union Commemorative Paul Bogle Lecture, Anglican Church Hall, Morant Bay, St. Thomas, Jamaica, Wednesday, October 26, 2011. The Maroon leaders in Jamaica, who were also invited to participate on the panel, were Colonels Sterling, Lumsden, Prehay, and Williams.

14. Barbara Klamon Kopytoff, "Colonial Treaty as Sacred Charter of the Jamaican Maroons," *Ethnohistory* 26:1 (1979), 46, 48. For example, the treaty of 1739 stipulated that the Maroons were "to convey [enslaved] runaways taken up by them, within five days, to the next magistrate in the parish where they are found, and be paid 40 s. for each runaway (or less, at discretion of the magistrate); and mile-money, at the rate of 7½ d. per mile." See ECCO, 1793, An Abridgment of the Laws of Jamaica; Being an Alphabetical Digest of All the Public Acts of Assembly Now in Force, from the Thirty-Second Year of King Charles II. To the Thirty-Second Year Of . . . George III. Inclusive, as Published in Two Volumes, . . . Jamaica. *Laws, etc.*, St. Jago de la Vega, Jamaica: printed by Alexander Aikman, 127.

15. ECCO, 1738 (1739), An Act for the Better Suppressing and Reducing the Rebellious and Runaway Negroes, *Passed in the Month of March, in the Year of our Lord One Thousand Seven Hundred and Thirty, and Which Was Continued by One Other Act Intituled*, an Act to Continue Part of Act. No. 320. Acts of Assembly, Passed in the Island of Jamaica; from 1681, to 1737, Inclusive. *Laws, etc.*, London, printed for John Baskett, 255.

16. ECCO, 1738 (1739), An Act for the Better Regulating Slaves, and Rendering Free Negroes and Mulattoes More Useful; and Preventing Hawking and Peddling; and Enlarging the Time for the Commissioners Collecting the out-Standing Debts. No. 292. Acts of Assembly, Passed in the Island of Jamaica; from 1681, to 1737, Inclusive. *Laws, etc.*, London, printed by John Baskett, 236.

17. Gad J. Heuman, *Between Black and White: Race, Politics, and the Free Coloured in Jamaica, 1792–1865* (Westport, CT: Greenwood Press, 1981), 5.

18. ECCO, 1793, An Abridgment of the Laws of Jamaica; Being an Alphabetical Digest of All the Public Acts of Assembly Now in Force, from the Thirty-Second Year of King Charles II. To the Thirty-Second Year Of . . . George III, 32.

19. ECCO, 1738 (1739), An Act to Oblige the Several Inhabitants of This Island to Provide Themselves with a Sufficient Number of White People, or Pay Certain Sums of Money in Case They Shall Be Deficient; and for Laying a Duty Upon Shipping, and Applying the Same to Several Uses. No. 317. Acts of Assembly, Passed in the Island of Jamaica; from 1681, to 1737, Inclusive. *Laws, etc.*, London, printed for John Baskett, 254.

20. Patterson, *Freedom in the Making of Western Culture*, Vol. 1, 3.

21. Anonymous (James Knight), *The State of the Island of Jamaica, Chiefly in Relation to Its Commerce, and the Conduct of the Spaniards in the West Indies* (London: H. Whitridge, 1726), 49–52 and the title page.

22. Leslie, *A New and Exact Account of Jamaica*, 1, 11, 41; and Elsa V. Goveia, *A Study on the Historiography of the British West Indies to the End of the Nineteenth Century* (Washington, DC: Howard University Press, 1980), 52.

23. Bridges, *The Annals of Jamaica*, Vol. 2, 91, 92–93, 100.

24. Goveia, *A Study on the Historiography of the British West Indies*, 106.

25. Richard B. Sheridan, "The Jamaican Slave Insurrection Scare of 1776 and the American Revolution," *The Journal of Negro History* 61:3 (1976), 290, 291.

26. Bridges, *The Annals of Jamaica*, Vol. 2, 95, 98.

27. Moreton, *Manners and Customs in the West India Islands*, 133, 134.

28. Smith, *An Inquiry into the Nature and Causes of the Wealth of Nations*, Vol. 2, 60.

29. Moreton, *Manners and Customs in the West India Islands*, see title.

30. HLRO HL/PO/JO/10/8/115, Copy of Letter from Simon Taylor, Henry Shirley, George Murray, and Lewis Cuthbert, Esquires, to the Earl of Balcarres, 5, 53.

31. Higman, *Plantation Jamaica, 1750–1850*, 2.

32. Luster, *The Amelioration of the Slaves in the British Empire*, 1.

33. Ibid., 4.

34. Buchner, *The Moravians in Jamaica*, 21, 24.

35. FP XVII, Jamaica (i) 1661–1739 (93–292), Lewis de Boneval (Bomeval?) to Bishop Gibson, 14 November 1739, 287–88.

36. NLJ MS2115/R55.7.124.2, Crop Book for the Tharp Estates, 182.

37. Lewis, *Journal of a West India Proprietor*, 141.

38. Turner, "Planters Profits and Slave Rewards," 244, 245.

39. See Brown, *Moral Capital*.

40. Luster, *The Amelioration of the Slaves in the British Empire*, 4. Luster provides the date 1796 for Wilberforce's first submission to Parliament of the bill to abolish the British slave trade.

41. FP XVIII, (ii) 1740–undated (1–242), Robert Sewell, Agent for Jamaica, to the Duke of Portland, 12 April 1798, 100, 101.

42. Carmichael, *Domestic Manners and Social Condition*, Vol. 2, 66.

CHAPTER NINE

~

Amelioration, War, and Individual Freedom

In this chapter, I will examine the relationship between amelioration and attempts by enslaved people to end slavery, and more importantly, to end it on their own terms. The chapter thus contributes to the discussion about slave freedom, and focuses on the assertions of this freedom through both illegal and legal measures. For the illegal means, the chapter uses the 1831–1832 rebellion, which was the final violent uprising of enslaved people in Jamaica. The legal assertion of their freedom is examined using manumission and self-purchase, which occurred during slavery and the apprenticeship period, respectively. Apprenticeship will be explained later, but briefly, it was designed as a transitional phase from slavery to full freedom, and was similar to amelioration in the sense that it was imposed on the enslaved, now known as apprentices, without any regard for their expectations with respect to the abolition of slavery. The resistance to apprenticeship was therefore a resistance against freedom on terms set by the former masters or the governments of colonial Jamaica and Britain. Additionally, the chapter explores slave marriage, which was a silent though not hidden form of protest and overcoming, or the strategic alliance of acculturation with resistance and part of the search by the enslaved for a variety of ways to assert their right to freedom.

Amelioration and War

Amelioration was one of the last signs from the slaveholders telling of the perilousness of slavery prior to its abolition in 1834. However, enslaved people continued to send reminders about their determination to be allowed to live as free people and the powerlessness of slave masters to prevent them from becoming agents of social change, who were pursuing the destruction of slavery individually as well as collectively. The last rebellion of enslaved people in Jamaica showed this determination to be free quite vividly. Traditionally known as Sam Sharpe's rebellion, after the enslaved man who led the uprising, this final act of violent mass resistance erupted in December 1831 and continued until January 1832. According to one recent account by Devon Dick, the rebellion involved "about 60,000" enslaved participants, which signified that this was not a small undertaking, and furthermore, the participants came "from approximately 200 estates."[1]

Dick is one of the historians who have been advocating the renaming of the rebellion into the "Baptist War." This, as he argues, is necessary to indicate the rebellion's legitimacy as a fight for the natural right of freedom, and a fight against unnatural enslavement.[2] The renaming would certainly indicate more clearly other important aspects and effects of the rebellion, such as the leadership by Sharpe, who was not only enslaved, but more importantly, a deacon in the Baptist Church. Using his understanding of Protestant Christianity, or his hermeneutical appraisal of the gospel, Sharpe had developed the view that slavery was contrary to the teachings of the Bible, and a contradiction of the Christian status of enslaved people who had joined the churches. The rebellion was a crucial demonstration of enslaved people's use of conversion to subvert the slave system, a complete rejection of the purpose of amelioration in this respect. You will recall that Jamaica's amelioration was planned as a way to prolong slavery using primarily Christian indoctrination in the Anglican Church.

As for the effects of the Baptist War, these were almost carbon copies of the effects of Tacky's revolt in 1760. Sharpe and his followers embarked upon a war by the enslaved that was the costliest one that the colonial government of Jamaica had experienced up to that point. The cost of suppressing the war reached a total of £161,570. But this was no match for the death toll; the cost in terms of lives lost was 207 enslaved people, who were killed during the fighting, and another 500, who were executed afterwards for having participated in the war.[3] As in 1760, the suppression symbolized the trepidation of the regime. This latest rebellion could not have happened at a more inappropriate time for slaveholding in Jamaica. This was during the amelioration, but also when both the Jamaican social order and the British government had introduced ameliorative measures—measures that they felt could make slavery better. The war by the enslaved was a rejection of this idea that slavery could be made better. Anything short of unfettered freedom was seen by the enslaved as unacceptable. This was slave freedom at one of its highest points in terms of illustrating in a forceful way the wish of enslaved people to have their freedom acknowledged by the law.

If the cost of the war and the death toll are not convincing evidence of the far reaching effects of this violent demonstration of slave freedom, the destruction to property provides more evidence of the same result. Richard Hart has estimated that over £1 million worth of property damage was recorded as a direct and indirect consequence of the war by the enslaved.[4] Real estate was one of the clearest signs of slavery: the sugar and coffee plantations, and the livestock pens. Destroying these, mainly by arson, was a direct attack on the power structure that was supported by slavery, a toppling of enslavement by the burning of the architectures through which slavery was maintained, and which stood as constant reminders of the gains made from enslavement. Enslaved people knew, for example, that the profit margin was one of the most important support mechanisms for slavery. They knew that once slavery became unprofitable, it would have to end, and the war was used to create this chain effect.

However, there was also the destruction that resulted from the reprisals. These added to the destructiveness of the war by extending it beyond the actual fighting. This destruction took place after the war had ended. It was also arguably worse than the destruction during the war because it was conducted by the slaveholders and their supporters. They attacked the Baptist and Methodist meeting houses and places of worship, justifying the reprisal with the accusation that the missionaries of these two ecclesiastical bodies had encouraged the enslaved people to rise up in rebellion. The churches themselves submitted an initial estimate of £20,000 as the cost of the damage and destruction to their property by the combined force of slaveholders and their supporters. Parliament, however, agreed to compensate the churches with £12,740 for the damaged and destroyed buildings.[5] This did not satisfy the churches, since it was only barely over 50 percent of what they had asked for, and furthermore this money, whatever the figure might have been, was in no way compensation for the victimization that missionaries themselves had suffered individually and as a group. There were reports of stones being hurled at the missionaries and their houses, and at least one report about a missionary being threatened with tarring and feathering.[6]

Some of these vicious attacks were done by the members of an organization formed in January 1832 for exactly that purpose. Known as the CCU, it stood as a reflection of the viciousness and intransigence of slaveholding, but also as a strong rehearsal of the fears of slaveholders with respect to slave freedom. Even though the CCU did not attack enslaved people, its assaults on the missionaries were, nonetheless, indicative of its view that enslaved people had supporters, who were aiding them in their effort to undermine and abolish slavery. These supporters thus needed to be suppressed, which along with the recent suppression of Sharpe's war, would hopefully end the entire project to abolish the slave system on terms set by the enslaved.[7] Some slaveholders had begun to accept that slavery's days were numbered; this view had appeared in the cogitations of proslavery advocate James Macqueen published in 1824.[8] However, they all shared the desire to bring about abolition only when they felt that this was necessary; only, as they argued, when the enslaved were really ready. The view expressed here was simply an admission of the wish by slaveholders to preserve the status quo, and even if slavery had to come to an end.

The CCU was banned in January 1833 by the government through a proclamation which was issued by the British crown.[9] The CCU became such an embarrassment that news of its activities reached London and the monarchy. However, it was not banned because of its reactionary stance on slavery; rather, the ban was due to the decision taken at the beginning of the nineteenth century to promote religious tolerance in the colonies. The CCU was a complete rejection of the freedom of the people in slavery, but was banned because of its negation of Enlightenment ideas about freedom, and more precisely, freedom of worship. In this way, the CCU's presence and banning showed that enslaved people were the ones most prepared for the abolition of slavery.

In the end, the promotion of freedom for the enslaved depended mostly on the activities of the enslaved themselves. They were the ones who had reminded both the colonial and British governments that slavery was immoral. Adding to the embarrassment caused by the CCU was the fact that at least one Anglican clergyman was known to have been involved in the organization. This was Rev. Bridges, who was described as the CCU's "Rev. 'Trooper'."[10] And the view was expressed that his involvement was quite a poor reflection on the state church, the same church that was the state church of imperial England.

Dick's perspective, which is also shared by Thomas C. Holt, that overall the Baptist War "was the catalyst that led to the Act of Emancipation in 1833" is not an exaggeration; not in light of the effects of this war, when all of these effects are considered together.[11] Holt puts the same view in another, more cautious way: "The authors of the abolition law cited the Christmas revolt of 1831 as a major factor compelling their action."[12] Among the war's most important implications was the violent way in which the enslaved people affirmed their freedom. The message was that freedom had to extend to the people enslaved; otherwise, the Enlightenment would remain merely rhetoric. There was no justification for proposing liberalism as the most vital component of western culture going into the future, while at the same time maintaining the enslavement of Africans and their descendants in the west. This was a deliberate rejection of the dialectical struggle, the coming into being and the terminating, the struggle between the modern and old that Germany's Enlightenment philosopher, G.W.F. Hegel, was writing around the same period.[13] It was an attempt to force an unnatural outcome, preserving practices of the past and negating the liberalizing mission that Western Europe itself had been embracing. The enslaved were the ones who were most forcefully exposing the illogical and contradictory nature of western thinking with regards to slavery.

Manumission

Examining the functions of manumission in the Roman Empire, David Daube, writing in the 1940s, argued that manumission was mainly a legislative device, and one through which enslaved people were able to acquire their freedom.[14] The same kind of assessment, in which manumission is identified as primarily the "acquisition" of freedom, rather than the "assertion" of freedom, is found in the study by Sumner Eliot Matison published later in the same decade. For instance, Matison states that the "legal right to manumit" had arisen "out of the inherent right of the property holder to abandon title to his property."[15] Because of the view of slaveholders that the enslaved were essentially property, manumission has also been examined as mainly a legal process, and one through which freedom was established not by the enslaved, but by the people who claimed that they owned the enslaved as their property.

If we should fast-forward to the scholarship in the late 1970s, we will see a slight change in the perspective. At this juncture, manumission is treated as much more than a legal process. The scholarship was beginning to view manumission as a social undertaking. This meant that the scholarship had to seriously analyze the role of the enslaved. Lyman L. Johnson's work on manumission in colonial Buenos Aires, for example, recounted manumission as a change that was initiated by enslaved people and not the slave masters. Johnson noted that up to 60 percent of the 1,482 manumissions in Buenos Aires, between 1776 and 1810, had resulted from self-purchase. In other words, enslaved persons had taken control of their manumissions, had been using their own money to buy themselves out of slavery.[16] In an article published a decade later, Rosemary Brana-Shute, using examples from

Suriname, also highlighted the importance of viewing manumission from the perspective of the enslaved. Brana-Shute presented her approach as an individualized perspective, and the main point that she made was that the manumissions in Suriname had resulted from negotiations that the enslaved people had initiated with the slaveholders.[17] In this way, the enslaved took control of their manumission and it became their achievement, while masters functioned mainly as facilitators, a role that most if not all masters also played unwillingly.

This signified another turn in the scholarship on manumission. The study of manumission had now moved away from assessing manumission from the slaveholders' point of view, to the standpoint that the enslaved themselves were the central participants. This was done without negating the role of the enslavers. There is no way that we can or should ever completely erase the slave masters from the picture. However, following the trend of the historic turn of the early 1970s, the people at the bottom of the social ladder, so to speak, were investigated with more sensitivity, and the conclusion was that they had appropriated in strategic ways a process that their overlords had continued to think of as their process. It was subversion without the subversives recognized or acknowledged as subversive. This, of course, benefitted the subversives.

We are now, therefore, at the point where manumission can be assessed as almost exclusively the endeavor of the enslaved. The trend has been established in some of the recent scholarship, such as the studies by James H. Sweet and Herbert S. Klein in collaboration with Clotilde Andrade Paiva. Sweet argues that even Africans far away on the continent, or Africans who were not taken into slavery, participated in manumitting their enslaved relatives in the Americas. They initiated these transactions that extended across the Atlantic. They arranged with the captains of slave ships to buy their relatives out of slavery; and the enslaved themselves had to prove that they were indeed the kin of the relatives who were back in Africa. This was the role of the enslaved in the manumissions that materialized out of these transatlantic transactions.[18]

The reporting of the manumissions in Jamaica during amelioration shows the necessity for an approach that considers the role of the enslaved, or more broadly, an African perspective. Between 1808 and 1830, there were approximately 10,793 manumissions in Jamaica. Except for the period 1811–1813, these had remained fairly consistent, averaging above 1,000 manumissions every three years until 1828. The same average was reported for the final two-year period of 1829–30 (Table 9.1). Not surprisingly, these manumissions were listed by the colonial government of the island under two

Table 9.1. Manumissions in Jamaica, 1808–1830

Period	Manumissions
1808–1810	1,819
1811–1813	490
1814–1816	1,302
1817–1819	1,998
1820–1822	1,460
1823–1825	1,334
1826–1828	1,334
1829–1830	1,056
Total	**10,793**

Source: HCPP 1823 (347), (No. 3) – a Return of All Manumissions Effected by Purchase, Bequest or Otherwise, since 1st January 1808, 8-129; HLRO HL/PO/JO/10/8/988, Return of All Manumissions Granted in Jamaica between 1817 and 1830, 15 August 1832, Main Papers, Session 1831-32: Nos. 832-858. Lords Journals Vol. LXIV, 13 August 1832–16 August 1832, 463.

main categories: those which were described as "bequeathed" based on the wills of the slaveholders, and those that were described as "purchased." There were others that did not fit any of these two categories and were thus listed as "Otherwise." No attempt was made from within the circles of officialdom to link either the unclassifiable manumissions or the other two categories to the enslaved in any direct way. Even those described as "purchased" were presented with the slave masters as the focal points. Furthermore, the list of bequeathed manumissions, or those that were allegedly due to slaveholders in a more direct way, were listed as accounting for the majority, for more than half of the total manumissions recorded.

Higman is the historian who, through his work, has given us some of the most important information about manumission in Jamaica, but his study focuses on the issue of the complexion of the manumitted, and he has adopted fully the categories of the colonial government. Higman has noted that the enslaved most frequently manumitted were coloreds, or those with lighter skin complexions, and this was due mainly to their white fathers.[19] However, based on the terms under which even the so-called bequeathed or willed manumissions were acquired, none of these were attained without the enslaved people themselves fulfilling the stipulated criteria. In other words, without their input, or without them doing the actual work to accomplish their freedom, none of the manumissions that were reported by the government would have taken place.

These examples will illustrate some of the work that was done by the enslaved, and through which they were able to obtain their manumissions. The colonial government owned enslaved people as well, and one of them named Prince William had obtained his manumission in 1816. Based on the report from Governor Manchester, there can be no doubt that William's manumission was almost completely his doing. William worked for his manumission by displaying the kind of submissiveness that he was expected to display as an enslaved person. He was therefore described by Manchester as a deserving candidate for manumission. Manchester wrote, for example, that it was "expedient and proper that such meritorious conduct should be suitably rewarded."[20]

Enslaved people used submission as their resistance, which appealed to slaveholders who, after viewing the defiance of other enslaved people, were nothing short of impressed by those among the enslaved who showed them obedience and respect. We can assess William's conduct as among the ultimate sacrifices that enslaved people made in their effort to have their freedom acknowledged under the law. William's acquisition also included his winning of lifelong support for his subsistence from the government. In other words, taxpaying slaveholders, for instance, would have to pay for William for the remainder of his life. William was to receive £10 annually following his manumission.[21] This was by no means adequate compensation for slavery, but it was an accomplishment nonetheless. It was certainly better than if he had received nothing.

In other cases, the sacrifices that the enslaved made were seen in the periods that they had to wait before the manumissions, which had been willed to them, had materialized. One should also bear in mind that these waiting periods also came after many years of enslavement, which, when added to the additional time before the manumissions came into effect, increased the payments (made in kind, rather than with cash) that these enslaved people made for their manumissions to occur. Some of these were quite lengthy periods, such as the fifty years that Fidelia Graham had waited before she had finally acquired her manumission in 1809. In 1819, four other enslaved persons, Old Poly, Ann M'Carthy, Florence Taylor, and Caroline Mullings, were informed as well that they would have to await "the death of a devisee" before they could acquire their manumissions. This particular stipulation, "the death of a devisee," appeared quite frequently in the wills of the slaveholders. It meant more hardship or more payment for the enslaved; or that even after the slaveholder's passing, the enslaved had to work for an additional period—until the death of the slaveholder's heir(s)—before their manumissions materialized. Manumissions acquired in this way could not have been signs of freedom which was given. Rather, they stood as signs of the additional work that the enslaved had to perform in order to earn their manumissions or the acknowledgement that they were free.[22]

However, the reality that all manumissions were worked for and earned by the enslaved does not show as clearly as possible the subversion of amelioration that manumissions also represented. This is shown more clearly in the money that was spent on the manumissions that occurred in Jamaica. The total sum was £246,874, or an average of £6,458 annually between 1808 and 1822 (Table 9.2). Manumission thus became a virtual industry in the colony, and the money that was earned by this industry represented a significant sum that was taken directly out of the slaveholding complex, including the earnings from the plantations and livestock pens. In other words, this enterprise, known as manumission, was carried out with money extracted from slaveholders, and the beneficiaries were the enslaved persons who obtained their manumissions.

Nevertheless, the slaveholders, as well as the colonial government, earned significant sums from the industry that was created as a result of manumission. In other words, the enslaved had been contributing to the economy of the colony even while they were subverting this same economy and its social model in another way. Their assertion of their freedom had put an additional £15,261 into the coffers of the government between 1808 and 1822, an average annual sum of £1,017 for the period. Along with this were the phenomenal earnings of the slaveholders, which can be seen in the table below. Together, all of these figures also represented the exploitation that was occurring while the enslaved pursued the legal recognition of their freedom. These struggles exposed the purpose of manumission from the perspective of the slaveholders. It was another type of exploitation. The form which this took was the extension

Table 9.2. The Money Earned by the Government and the Slaveholders from Manumission, 1808–1822 (earnings in £s currency of Jamaica)

Period	1808–1810	1811–1813	1814–1816	1817–1819	1820–1822
Government Earnings	5,129	4,573	5,155	258	146
Slaveholders' Earnings	56,984	18,391	52,552	68,397	50,550
Total	**62,113**	**22,964**	**57,707**	**68,655**	**50,696**

Source: HCPP 1823 (347), (No. 3)—a Return of All Manumissions Effected by Purchase, Bequest or Otherwise, since 1st January 1808, 8-129.

of the domination of the enslaved, the criminal delay of their freedom on top of the grave injustice of their enslavement. Slaveholders instituted immoral but calculatedly long waiting periods, which had the potential to frustrate enslaved people out of their determination to live in legal freedom.

The colonial government, in its reporting of the money paid out and earned due to manumission, did not calculate or even estimate how much of this sum was paid directly by the enslaved. We do not know exactly how much money enslaved people invested from their own pockets in the manumissions that were reported. Giving even an estimate of this sum would have divulged too much of the centrality of enslaved people in the manumissions that took place. The government's main concern was to show how the slaveholders had been facilitating the changes in the society under their amelioration policy. This policy had to be advertised as the slaveholders' doing, rather than the accomplishment of the enslaved, and this was necessary to ward off criticisms about the wisdom of allowing slavery to continue for any period in the future.

Nevertheless, using the bits of information provided, I was able to estimate that enslaved people paid an average of £50 to £60 in the cases where they paid directly for their manumissions. These cash transactions indicated that there was a good deal of money within the enslaved community, most of which probably came from the provisions and small farm animals that they sold in the markets, and from work that they did as jobbing slaves if they were located in towns, such as Kingston. What was very clear was that some of the highest sums paid for manumission were paid by the enslaved themselves. Slaveholders seemed unwilling to make it easy for enslaved people to purchase their emancipation. Jane Williamson, for example, paid £400 for herself and children in 1809, and Beck paid a whopping £1,260 for herself and eight children in 1818. In Beck's case, since we know the number manumitted, if each paid the same, this sum was £140 per person, or £70 to £80 more than the average that I was able to estimate.[23] In other words, manumission was not an easy route to legal freedom; slave owners discouraged it even while advertising that they supported amelioration. When manumissions occurred, especially if these were paid for by the enslaved, slave owners knew that it was impossible to hide the fact that these indicated the abolition of slavery by enslaved people themselves.

Manumission was one of the biggest threats to the survival of slavery. As this became clearer to the slaveholders, they increased the obstacles or made these harsher and thus harder to overcome. Nevertheless, the manumissions continued. An enslaved man named Port was told that he would have "To work until he procures the money to discharge the full expense of his manumission papers," which meant that Port's request was to be delayed because the sum demanded by the slave owner went above the money that Port had offered for his manumission. The sum was set by the slave owner to keep Port working as a slave for as long as possible. In other cases, the stipulation was that the manumitted had to find other enslaved people to replace them. In 1817, an enslaved woman named Sibella was given that very same instruction, and in 1820, William Bain was also told in no uncertain terms that he would be manumitted, but only "if it" was "possible" to find "a negro slave" to replace him.[24]

Both Sibella and Bain were colored. Slaveholders also used manumission to divide the enslaved community on the basis of color, increasing the hardship that the enslaved people in general faced as they pursued their legal freedom through the manumission process. Slaveholders made sure that manumission affected not only them, but all enslaved people, both those pursuing manumission and those who did not use that process. This was part of the function of the fact that coloreds were more likely to be manumitted. The implication for the enslaved was that the legal freedom of some meant the perpetuation of the enslavement of others. Arguably, no other stipulation by the slave owners could have been more difficult for the enslaved than this one. Both the manumitted and their replacements paid a price in these cases. For the manumitted, it was the knowledge that they were legally acknowledged as free because others had sacrificed their own freedom for this to occur. For those still enslaved, the price was more obvious: they had to remain in slavery, at least for a period until they too could buy themselves out of slavery.

In the French colonies in the Caribbean, where manumissions also occurred, the slaveholders applied the term *rachat* to refer to manumission. This term meant "redemption," which signified the way that the enslavers wanted the manumitted to view the process through which they became legally free. The manumitted were never to be given the impression that they were freed in the eyes of the law by any means except as a gift, and that this gift was from their owners. The term *rachat* was symptomatic of the struggle between masters and the enslaved over freedom.[25] Masters knew that the enslaved had developed the view that manumission was their process, their acquisition of legal freedom, and that this was a source of empowerment and an encouragement for other enslaved people to pursue legal freedom through the same mechanism. In British-colonized Jamaica, slaveholders tried to take control of manumission using a range of stipulations, all of which showed the enslaved that they could only receive their legal freedom if the slaveholders, and the colonial state, had agreed to this. One of these precautions that the state also approved of was the stipulation, as an enslaved woman named Betty Gandon was told in 1818, that they would be "made free," a very careful choice of words. Furthermore, as Gandon was also told, to be "made free" also involved finding a free and preferably white "person or persons to enter into the usual security to the churchwardens."[26] With this additional provision, the message was clear that no manumitted person was to assume that their legal freedom materialized because of their own initiative and effort. They were free because their masters, and the state, wanted them to be free.

The politics of manumission was indeed one of its most important features. The fact is that when an enslaved person obtained manumission, this affected free white society as much as it affected the enslaved community. Manumission had a reach that transcended class and color boundaries, and everybody, enslaved and free, black, colored, and white, knew about manumission's reach. Male slaveholders, who had fathered colored children, used manumission to free even themselves from the moral burden that came from the fact that they had fathered children whom they had ignored and had allowed to remain as enslaved people. The white father of Mary and Peter Knight, for example, wrote in his will in 1817 that "I request my executors to free my reputed children, now on Mesopotamia estate, if it is any ways possible." The term "reputed" appeared in these requests quite frequently, indicating the reluctance to admit that they had fathered children with enslaved women, and had made the situation worse by ignoring these children, so that they remained in slavery.[27] Another implication was that, in theory, the practice of primogeniture might have given the males among the children rights to their white fathers' estates upon the death of the latter. This was not a situation most slaveholders wished to contemplate.

Overall, all manumissions were acquired rather than given. Essex, who was manumitted in 1817, had acquired his "at the end of three years" and only after the death of his master, "not before."[28] Ordinarily, we would classify this manumission as one of the bequeathed manumissions, but Essex, similar to every other manumitted enslaved person, obtained his legal freedom by fulfilling the criteria that was stipulated. They all did some kind of work, made some kind of payment, and fulfilled these because of the value that they placed on their freedom. One of the most important factors that the slaveholders did not put into their considerations about manumission was the value that the enslaved placed on freedom. They were prepared to undertake almost any activity to assert that they had the right to be free.

Marriage

Under the laws of England used in the British Empire, a marriage was defined as a "voluntary social union" between "a man and a woman." It was assumed that couples who got married entered the marriage by free will. If these were enslaved people, marriage symbolized a type of freedom or at the very least, a defiance of the slave masters who believed that they controlled every aspect of the lives of the enslaved. Furthermore, a marriage was to have no time limit, and could only be "annulled or dissolved by a competent tribunal or by legislation."[29] In other words, slaveholders who objected to the marriages of enslaved couples were powerless to dissolve these legally, unless they brought their objections to court. If this happened, it was an additional cost, both in time and money, which the slave owners did not need. Marriages of enslaved couples were even harder to dissolve if these were solemnized in the church of the state. The Anglican Church was the only church in the colony with this kind of authorization during slavery. Enslaved couples who got married in this church chose well. It was the only church that could shield their marital contracts from any effective disruption by masters, unless this was done with the assistance of the courts.

When Governor Manchester reported on the marriages of enslaved couples that had been occurring during amelioration, one of the facts that he highlighted was that these had taken place in the state church. Of course, Manchester was also interested in using these marriages as a sign of the success of the colony's decision to ameliorate the conditions of slavery, and as a sign that the church of state was now opened to the enslaved and free alike. However, marriage by the enslaved was not legalized until 1823, the slave laws were silent on the issue of marriage by the enslaved, and the general understanding was that enslaved people were not allowed to marry unless they received permission from their masters. However, Manchester's report showed that there were 3,596 marriages of the enslaved performed by the Anglican clergymen between 1808 and 1822.[30] This made the point that the enslaved had acted in defiance of normal practice. Also significant was the fact that none of these marriages were done in secret. The law stipulated that the clergymen had to publish the banns ahead of the marriages. This was to provide protesters the chance to raise their objections, either before or during the marriage ceremonies. The enslaved who got married in the state church therefore did not have the benefit of using these marriages as hidden forms of resistance. These were known acts of defiance. Nonetheless, they were strategic acts of resistance in light of the decision to marry in the state church rather than in one of the other Protestant churches, none of which had the power of the Anglican Church.

To be enslaved and married was a form of moral renewal. It was a commitment to a social condition that slavery had been trying to destabilize and destroy. It provided the enslaved with a way to escape from the well-known sexual liberties that especially white male slaveholders took with enslaved women. Marriage itself, as Trevor Burnard has observed, was not one of the common institutions in Jamaica during the early period of English settlement of the island. There was a general disavowal of marriage, and this was one of the reasons for the demographic failure of white society in early English Jamaica.[31] Accompanying this was the longstanding practice of white male slaveholders retaining a "chère amie," as Maria Nugent called the practice. Nugent disclosed that this was still common during the early nineteenth century when she was living in Jamaica with her husband, the governor. Nugent observed that "no man here is without one," an enslaved woman who was kept as a mistresses, a practice done in the open. Interestingly, Nugent seemed aware of the importance that the enslaved themselves placed on marriage and supported encouraging them "to marry."[32]

However, Nugent felt that marriage was a way to prevent enslaved people from rebelling, as they had done in neighboring St. Domingue in 1791. Therefore, for Nugent, granting enslaved people the right to marry was a way to ameliorate their condition and hopefully bring about their pacification. Acknowledging that marriage was a departure from the norms of slavery, Nugent was nevertheless convinced that the institution could act as a safety measure to maintain the social order established under slavery. This was the kind of interpretation that benefitted the enslaved and namely couples that wished to marry.

Manchester's report did not show the number of whites that got married during the same period, but it did show the number of free blacks and coloreds who chose to marry and opted to have these done in the state church (Table 9.3). The comparison that this gives us a chance to do is important, though one should bear in mind that the enslaved was significantly vaster in number than the other two groups combined. Regardless, the point can be made that while free blacks and coloreds faced fewer obstacles than the enslaved confronted, they were not marrying as frequently as enslaved people, and this raises the question, what did the enslaved see in marriage that was so important? Viewing the marriages recorded in St. Thomas-in-the-East and Kingston can provide some of the answers. These two parishes had the largest number of marriages on Manchester's list.

St. Thomas-in-the-East had 1,612 marriages of enslaved couples by the end of the period. This parish also had one of the largest slave populations in the island. Higman records that the population stood at 23,306 in 1832 and the parish of St. Ann, with largest number of enslaved people, had 24,708 in the same year.[33] The number of marriages in St. Thomas-in-the-East reflected the size of the enslaved population in this parish. Manchester's list provided no information for St. Ann that could give a better basis for the comparison, but it appears that the larger the enslaved population was the larger the number that got married. This indicates that they chose to

Table 9.3.   Marriages in the Anglican Church of Jamaica, 1808–1822: Enslaved People, Free Blacks, and Free Coloreds

Parish	Enslaved	Free Blacks	Free Coloreds
Kingston	1,348	190	247
St. Andrew	405	12	53
St. George	47	2	14
Port Royal	2	11	1
St. James	2	—	21
Trelawny	1	1	13
Manchester	8	1	2
St. Dorothy	3	—	—
St. John	1	—	—
St. Thomas (Vale)	—	—	6
Vere	1	—	2
Clarendon	2	1	9
St. Mary	35	—	8
St. Ann	—	—	17
St. Elizabeth	—	—	25
Portland	27	3	2
Hanover	—	—	25
St. David	102	—	2
St. Thomas (East)	1,612	26	21
Total	**3,596**	**247**	**468**

Source: HCPP 823 (347), No. 4 – Return of Number of Marriages Legally Solemnised between Slaves, and Also between Free Black and Coloured People, since the 1st of January 1808, 130-31.

marry when conditions were conducive, when their community, in terms of number, could support the wish to marry, objections by the slaveholders notwithstanding.

Kingston showed this better. This parish had 1,348 marriages during the period. Most of Kingston's enslaved were not attached to plantations. Mostly an urban parish, with the island's largest town and highest population density, Kingston had 2,089 enslaved people per square mile in 1832, in addition to one of the lowest male to female ratios for the enslaved, which was 78:100 in 1829–32.[34] The advantage that the enslaved took of these was seen in the larger number of marriages in the parish. Facing fewer restrictions due to the absence of the work regimen of the plantations, they had a better chance of living either with or close to their partners provided that these people resided in the parish. The population density and low sex ratio also made it easier to find partners than in the other towns and nonurban parts of the island.

Overall, the enslaved capitalized on the opportunity to marry when conditions made this possible. They opted to use marriage to live in a way that they felt that free people should be able to live, and since marriage brought them closer to freedom, establishing this freedom was one of their motivations to marry. The decision was an act of self-definition in addition to resistance, shown also by the presence of these marriages despite the hostility from slaveholders, who had the support of the law. Before 1823, the marriages of enslaved people were "not recognized by the laws of the land," as J.H. Buchner, the Moravian missionary, reported in his history of the missionaries in the island.[35] The wish to control how their lives went was more visible when the conditions in which most enslaved people lived were considered. Burnard states that high "death rates" and "family instability" were common features "aggravated by the hard conditions under which the slaves worked."[36] Michael Craton also paints a dismal picture in his study of Worthy Park estate in St. Catherine, where death rates were high, and birth rates low.[37] In other words, getting married took determination, conviction, and courage, all representing the view that marriages showed "a virtual emancipation," according to Cecilia A. Green in her research on the heated discussion about these marriages in British Bahamas around 1816, which also showed the importance of the issue.[38] It had significant implications for the future of slavery.

This form of agency by the enslaved was not expected. They were expected to revolt, for example, but the urgency to live in the same social institutions reserved for free people took the slave masters by surprise. The enslaved had disregarded slavery in a very visible way and were forcing the slaveholders to come to grips with this. They had put slaveholding into yet another state of frenzy. The masters had to begin discussions about the marriages of the enslaved, and the possibility that these signaled that the enslaved were preparing for the end of slavery. How many other forms of preparation were in existence, and how many had escaped from notice even though the enslaved were not hiding these? The campaign for emancipation was done openly with the marriages in the state church.

Marriage was connected with the desire to have a family life. Enslaved people lived together in households or family situations even if they were not married. Higman discovered 814 household units at Old and New Montpellier estates in St. James, and Shettlewood Pen in Hanover, and 204 of these resembled the western idealized nuclear family.[39] The bonds that held these units together were already strong; marriages were not necessary for these enslaved people to establish and maintain these families. The bonds which most commonly held these together were bonds of blood and common law. The latter was an agreement based on romantic affections between partners or commitments to partners and children, and even if these children were the products of previous relationships. The best way to see marriage in light of all of this is that the enslaved used marriage to confirm unions that were already in existence, but which did not need the marriage contract to be maintained.

Enslaved people who chose to marry in the state church aided this church in its bid to become the church of the entire society. In this way, the enslaved participated in revitalizing the church's role and its mission to improve the moral standing of the inhabitants of the colony. Slavery was responsible for the rampant immorality that the preachers of all of the churches complained about and used in their arguments for the colonial government to take the matter of public morality as a serious issue. One example was the Baptist missionary Phillippo, who complained about the "unblushing licentiousness" that was visible "from the Governor downwards through all the intermediate ranks of society," and which was carried on "in the broad light of day" to make these practices much more "notorious."[40] Enslaved people aligned themselves to social change under the guidance of the churches, and especially under the auspices of the Anglican Church in the case of the couples who opted to get married in this church.

As for the benefits of marriage, research on enslaved people in other places can be helpful in the attempt to understand the views of the enslaved in Jamaica. David Chandler's examination of the issue in colonial Columbia indicates that enslaved couples got married to raise their living standards. Enslaved people who chose to get married were highly regarded, a trend noticeable among the Jesuit missionaries, who also owned slaves. The missionaries went on a campaign to stamp out common law unions, viewing these as contrary to Christian principles. The enslaved people who entered marriages were thus seen as having crossed a significant social obstacle that was promoted by slavery, and in return, they were awarded with lighter work-related tasks and treated with some amount of respect.[41] In her study of the enslaved in Paraiba, Brazil, Alida C. Metcalfe states that marriages protected a number of enslaved women from sexual exploitation by masters and enslaved men. Marriages promoted stable family life, which provided constant emotional and material support. The family income was generally larger than the earnings of individuals living alone.[42]

An enslaved man in Jamaica named Archibald Monteith defied the odds by becoming financially prosperous on his own. He was able to purchase land on which he built a house and was known as a man of good character inside and outside of the church. Monteith had joined the Moravian Church and was appointed by the missionaries as one of their native assistants.

The missionaries saw him as a true Christian, someone who had made a genuine conversion to become a committed church member, and could therefore help the missionaries with preaching the gospel to other enslaved people. However much these stood as signs of agency that had produced self-improvement, Monteith wanted more from life. He decided to marry Rebecca Hart, who was enslaved herself, on January 8, 1826 at the Anglican parish church, Black River, St. Elizabeth.

This marriage was another act of resistance against the norms and values that slavery had been trying to impose upon enslaved people. Monteith and Hart used the marriage to assert their right to be acknowledged as free people. By getting married, the couple showed that they could live in the same way that any free person might be expected to live. Furthermore, they refused to become burdens on the state, parish, or slaveholders; the marriage was symbolic in this respect, an expression of the couple's self-reliance. They used even the decision about where to marry as another demonstration of their independence and desire for self-definition. It showed that they wanted to marry on terms that only they had decided. They chose to marry not in the Moravian Church, as was expected since they were also Moravians, but in the state church, or the church that Monteith described as the only one in the parish with an actual chapel, the church that had status both structurally and in terms of state recognition. It was the church that could best communicate the significance of their marriage, the church where the officiating pastor was an ordained Anglican clergyman, or someone that even other enslaved people feared to some extent, even if they did not respect him. This was shown on the day of the marriage, when the clergyman quelled the crowd of enslaved people outside of the church, after they began to criticize the couple for thinking that they were white, because they had married in the church still seen as "the planters' church" by the enslaved who were not its members.[43]

How the marriage worked was another accomplishment. Hart and Monteith were attached to different plantations. Though these were located in the same parish of St. Elizabeth, Hart was attached to Paynestown estate and Monteith to Dunbarken estate. Their marriage trumped the division due to this difference. In time, Monteith also chose to buy his freedom even while knowing that legal freedom was about to materialize. This decision was made in 1837, a year before full freedom or emancipation. And Monteith, while making the transaction, refused to pay the purchase price set by his former master. He paid the price which he thought was fair, £50 instead of the £90 that his former master had initially demanded, and became legally free on his own terms on June 1, 1837.[44]

Apprenticeship

The abolition of slavery in Jamaica in 1834 did not immediately result in full freedom. Parliament accomplished not unfettered freedom, but apprenticeship. The system of slavery was replaced with a transitional period, known as apprenticeship. All British colonies in the Caribbean adopted Parliament's suggested apprenticeship system, except for the island of Antigua. Viewing unfettered freedom for the enslaved as the safer alternative, Antigua's slaveholders decided to embrace this rather than risk denying the enslaved their freedom any longer. The Bermudans took the same decision. Under apprenticeship, the former slaveholders were granted forty hours and thirty minutes of free labor. The rest of the time belonged to the apprentices, and they could use this time to work outside of the plantations on their own or for other people, if this was their wish. All formerly enslaved people became apprentices, except for those below the age of six, who became fully free as of August 1, 1834. The apprenticeship system was scheduled to end for field laborers or praedials in 1840, and for other apprentices, known as non-praedials, in 1838. However, it ended for all in the latter year.[45]

The acts of resistance of the apprentices were the last actions taken to show their determination to live as free people before the complete collapse of slavery. This resistance was the main reason apprenticeship itself ended prematurely. The apprentices made it clear that nothing but complete or unfettered freedom was acceptable to them. Some chose to show this by resisting the attempts that former masters made to control them and to continue to make them work under poor conditions similar to slavery. Others opted out of the system before its scheduled end, and Archibald Monteith was one of these examples. More than any of the others, these apprentices were the ones who exhibited their view that freedom could never be granted. It was an inalienable right and one that they had never lost sight of, even though they were enslaved.

The year before the non-praedials were to gain full freedom, British antislavery advocates, Joseph Sturge and Thomas Harvey, who toured Jamaica, reported that "the term of apprenticeship is decreasing."[46] By this, they meant not only that the time was expiring, but also that the apprentices had been shortening the period by entering into transactions with former masters to immediately buy their freedom. One of the examples that the visitors gave was William Hamilton. He had purchased his freedom at the very beginning of apprenticeship.

Hamilton would have been a non-praedial apprentice, a "mechanic and copper-smith." This meant that Hamilton knew that his time in apprenticeship would be four years, and that this time was shorter than the period that the larger number of field laborers or praedials would have to spend before they too became fully free. Yet, Hamilton opted not to wait for the four-year expiration of apprenticeship. He wanted the law to recognize his freedom immediately; he wanted his freedom on his terms. This decision was not surprising. During slavery, Hamilton was one of the enslaved people who had openly defied the norms of the institution. Sturge and Harvey, when they heard about him, described William Hamilton as an exception to the rule. The truth is that he wasn't. He might have been "the only slave on the Bog Estate who dared to attend a place of worship; the only one upwards of 400 negros who dared to live with his partner in marriage."[47] However, other enslaved people had made the same choices, maybe not at Bog estate, but as Manchester's list had shown, the number of married enslaved people had increased to more than a thousand by 1822. Hamilton and these other enslaved people had used marriage, along with church membership (which in the case of the Anglican Church stood at 50,454 enslaved converts in 1817), as forms of resistance and essentially to assert their self-determination.

And none of these decisions were made without consequences. Yet, the enslaved people and later, the apprentices, continued to defy the imposed circumstances of slavery and apprenticeship, respectively. Masters and former masters were powerful in the sense that they could raise these obstacles to protect slavery and apprenticeship. However, they were also powerless to prevent the enslaved and apprentices from using their agency to improve their present and future condition. William Hamilton, for example, had organized an independent valuation of himself, which was £209, but the overseer at Bog estate increased this and asked for £500, thinking that the revised sum would deter Hamilton from his objective. Hamilton paid the price demanded by the overseer, and then paid another £22 10s for the freedom of his fourteen-year-old son. Again, this was an inflated amount. The valuation that Hamilton had arranged had put the price for his son at £8.[48]

Self-purchase was quite common during apprenticeship, and the valuations organized by the apprentices were always lower than the money requested by the former masters. The valuation itself was a source of resistance. However, the failure of this act of resistance did not lead to the abandonment of the objective. Apprentices either paid the sums that former masters asked for, or they negotiated until a mutually agreeable sum was reached. Sturge and Harvey estimated that 1,580 apprentices purchased their freedom between August 1, 1834 and November 1, 1836. The total sum that they paid was £52,216, which told the other part of the story. If all of them paid the same amount, on average each of these apprentices would have paid £33 for their freedom.[49] This was much lower than the prices asked for by the former masters in the cases that are known, such as the case of Hamilton and that of Monteith. This figure represented the success of the negotiations with the former masters.

Special magistrate, E.B. Lyon, one of the supervisors of the apprenticeship appointed by the colonial officials in London, advised that self-purchase by the apprentices had become infectious. He stated having "anxiously watched the conduct of those, who have released themselves by purchase from their apprenticeship, not alone from the influence their example would naturally have upon the remaining bondsmen."[50] The only problematical part of this assessment was the assumption Lyon made that the apprentices needed external encouragement to pursue self-purchase. If external influence was needed, what accounted for the many that sought self-purchase and became the external encouragement? Self-purchase resulted from the apprentices' desire for freedom. The success that other apprentices had with their self-purchase simply made the goal appear more achievable. Historian Douglas Hall has observed that none of the obstacles from former masters prevented the apprentices from using self-purchase to free themselves under the law, especially not "the system of illegal valuation" that Governor Sligo reported as "still very prevalent" in 1836.[51]

Where did the apprentices get the money to purchase their freedom? Some of them used savings from mainly the sales in the markets, while others took out "loans," and in both cases the implication was that they viewed legal freedom as an investment in their future.[52] They were confident that they could repay the loans, for example, if they were legally free, which to them meant that they would have a greater number of economic as well as social opportunities.

Though apparent, the assertiveness of the apprentices is hard to find in the discussions about apprenticeship while the system had existed. The two American representatives of the antislavery society in that country who also visited Jamaica in 1837, James A. Thome and Joseph H. Kimball, exposed the "harsh" experiences of the apprentices and even described some of these as worse than slavery. However, these injustices were presented as part of the stimulation for self-purchase. The apprentices in Manchioneal, Portland, for example, knew that they would receive "no justice" from the "special magistrates" and had the impression that "there was no law in Manchioneal."[53] True as these grim depictions were, these abuses by the former slaveholders and their allies among the special magistrates were not the stimulators of self-purchase. Apprentices were not miraculously changed into different people by apprenticeship. They were the same people who were enslaved and had resisted that attempt to destroy their freedom as well. The sense of fairness and justice which had prompted these acts of resistance against slavery continued during the apprenticeship period, part of the supposed "great experiment" with freedom.[54] The enslaved and apprentices certainly did not need an experiment to know the meaning of freedom.

The apprentices who felt that they were treated fairly by ex-masters gave these former masters the impression that they were pacified by the better treatment. One overseer stated that "he was getting along well" and the "people" on the estate were "industrious and obedient," and the "plantation was never better cultivated." However, resistance was evident in other areas of their lives. The apprentices who were parents refused to allow their children who had obtained legal freedom in 1834 (because they were below six years of age) to do work on the estates or to be hired by anyone else. This rebuttal of child labor was a rejection of the capitalist practice of using any kind of labor that could be acquired, and the apprentices interpreted this practice as similar to the greed for labor that was responsible for the persistence of slavery. Reporting on the rebuttal, the overseer stated that "the parents are jealous there is some plot laid for making them [their children] apprentices, and through that process reducing them to slavery." The overseer had no doubt that this "feeling" would "continue till the apprenticeship is entirely broken up, and the people begin to feel assured of complete freedom."[55]

Full freedom continued to be the primary goal of the apprentices. Those who found that they faced obstacles also came up with creative ways to overcome these. There was one couple, for instance, who wanted to marry in the Anglican parish church in Portland, and when the rector, Rev. S.H. Cooke, refused "to publish the banns," the couple went to the Baptist chapel in Yallahs, in the neighboring parish of St. David, and got married there. The disadvantage was that this was "a marriage which the law" did "not recognize as legal," since only the Anglican clergy could legally perform marriages, regardless of the race, class, or status of the couples. For the apprentices who were determined to marry, this was an obstacle that they knew they could overcome and did as they pleased, even though some of these same couples also resided "on different estates."[56] These were some of the acts of resistance that made the abandonment of apprenticeship a change that "the Jamaica Assembly" welcomed in 1838.[57]

Conclusion

Amelioration in Jamaica was conceived as a new form of domination. However, the response of the enslaved made amelioration the system of improving the conditions of slavery that it was actually supposed to be. This response was seen in the manumissions and marriages that took place during the time of amelioration. The changes made to slavery during this period were not due to the slaveholders, even though the amelioration was their policy. These changes were brought about by the enslaved people, who made the sacrifices to obtain their manumissions, and got married even in the state church and while there was no law granting enslaved people the right to marry. Both manumission and marriage were visible acts of resistance, but because the enslaved people made use of the principle of improvement under amelioration in these acts of resistance, the slaveholders, for the most part, saw the manumissions and marriages as activities that they either controlled or which were not essentially threats to slavery.

The last rebellion of the enslaved people stimulated a very different response from the slaveholders. They rehashed the intransigence of previous years and drew upon some of the most extreme forms of repression to suppress the rebellion. The idea that the rebellion was suppressed does not accurately depict its impact on slaveholding in Jamaica, or the wider British-colonized Caribbean for that matter. This rebellion was discussed in the parliamentary deliberations about the abolition of slavery, which was enacted in 1833 to take effect in 1834. In other words, the abolition act came into being the year after the rebellion had ended. And the influence of the rebellion was also seen in the apprenticeship system, which was implemented to basically train the enslaved how to behave as free people. This was based on the fear that slave freedom, seen in a most violent way in the recent rebellion, would destroy the social and economic order fashioned during the many years of slavery in Jamaica and other British colonies in the Caribbean.

A similar determination not to allow their freedom to be compromised by any newfound system of domination characterized the actions of the apprentices between 1834 and 1838. Just as a number of enslaved people ended their enslavement through manumission, a number of apprentices ended their status as apprentices using self-purchase. Other acts of defiance were recorded by the ex-slaveholders and their allies, such as the special magistrates. Among these were the persistent refusals of apprenticed parents to allow their children to enter the workforce, despite the attempts of especially the sugar planters to hire these children as laborers on the estates. Because of the apprentices, the system of apprenticeship became too problematical to continue, and the decision to end it completely in 1838 was an acknowledgement that only full freedom would ever satisfy the former enslaved people.

Notes

1. Dick, *The Cross and the Machete*, 5.
2. Ibid.
3. Patterson, *The Sociology of Slavery*, 273.

4. Hart, *Slaves Who Abolished Slavery*, Vol. 2, 323.

5. HCPP 1831–32 (582), No. 5.-Copy of a Memorial from the Baptist Missionary Society to Viscount Goderich, Dated 23 April 1832, *Jamaica: Slave Insurrection*, 30; HCPP 1833 (540), Return to an address of the Honorable the House of Commons, dated 25th July 1832;—for, memorial and statement of the Baptist missionaries in Jamaica; dated 19 April 1833, 5; HCPP 1834 (476), An Estimate of the Sum Required to Enable His Majesty to Make a Grant to the Baptist Missionary Society, and to the Wesleyan Missionary Society, on Account of Expenses Incurred in the Erection of Certain Chapels Destroyed in the Island of Jamaica, 10 July 1834, 457.

6. HCPP 1833 (540), Return to an address of the Honorable the House of Commons, dated 25th July 1832;—for, memorial and statement of the Baptist missionaries in Jamaica; dated 19 April 1833, 3, 4, 5.

7. *St. Jago de la Vega Gazette*, 11–18 February 1832, 4; *The Watchman and the Jamaica Free Press*, 28 March 1832, 8; HCPP 1833 (540), Return to an address of the Honorable the House of Commons, dated 25th July 1832;—for, memorial and statement of the Baptist missionaries in Jamaica; dated 19 April 1833, 3, 4, 5.

8. M'Queen, *The West India Colonies*, xi.

9. *The Kingston Chronicle and City Advertiser*, 21 January 1833, page unknown.

10. *The Watchman and the Jamaica Free Press*, 28 March 1832, 8.

11. Dick, *The Cross and the Machete*, 7.

12. Thomas C. Holt, *The Problem of Freedom: Race, Labor, and Politics in Jamaica and Britain, 1832–1938* (Baltimore. MD: The Johns Hopkins University Press, 1992), 14.

13. G.W.F. Hegel, *Hegel's Science of Logic* (London: Allen and Unwin, 1812), 185.

14. David Daube, "Two Early Patterns of Manumission," *The Journal of Roman Studies* 36 (1946), 64.

15. Sumner Eliot Matison, "Manumission by Purchase," *The Journal of Negro History* 33:2 (1948), 146.

16. Lyman L. Johnson, "Manumission in Colonial Buenos Aires, 1776–1810," *The Hispanic American Historical Review*, 59:2 (1979), 260, 261.

17. Rosemary Brana-Shute, "Approaching Freedom: The Manumission of Slaves in Suriname, 1760–1828," *Slavery & Abolition*, 10:3 (1989), 44–48.

18. Herbert S. Klein and Clotilde Andrade Paiva, "Freedmen in a Slave Economy: Minas Gerais in 1831," *Journal of Social History* 29:4 (1996), 933, 944; and James H. Sweet, "Manumission in Rio De Janeiro, 1749–54: An African Perspective," *Slavery & Abolition* 24:1 (2003), 54, 55. For other recent studies taking the enslaved-centered approach to manumission, see Bernard Moitt, "Freedom from Bondage at a Price: Women and Redemption from Slavery in the French Caribbean in the Nineteenth Century," *Slavery & Abolition* 26:2 (2005), 251; Emily Blanck, "The Legal Emancipations of Leander and Caesar: Manumission and the Law in Revolutionary South Carolina and Massachusetts," *Slavery & Abolition* 28:2 (2007), 237, 248; Robert Olwell, "Becoming Free: Manumission and the Genesis of a Free Black Community in South Carolina, 1740–90," in *Against the Odds: Free Blacks in the Slave Societies of the Americas*, Jane G. Landers, ed. (New York: Routledge, 1996), 1–19.

19. Higman, *Slave Population and Economy in Jamaica*, 176.

20. HCPP 1818 (433), An Act for Manumising a Slave Named Prince William, Belonging to the Public, 11 December 1816, 51.

21. Ibid.

22. HCPP 1823 (347), (No. 3) – a Return of All Manumissions Effected by Purchase, Bequest or Otherwise, since 1st January 1808, 78, 119.

23. Ibid., 21.

24. Ibid., 119, 122.

25. Moitt, "Freedom from Bondage at a Price," 251.

26. HCPP 1823 (347), (No. 3)—a Return of All Manumissions Effected by Purchase, Bequest or Otherwise, since 1st January 1808, 122.

27. Ibid., 117.

28. Ibid., 123.

29. William Pinder Eversley and William Feilden Craies, *The Marriage Laws of the British Empire* (London: Stevens and Haynes, 1910), 1–2.

30. HCPP 823 (347), No. 4 – Return of Number of Marriages Legally Solemnised between Slaves, and Also between Free Black and Coloured People, since the 1st of January 1808, 130–31.

31. Trevor Burnard, "A Failed Settler Society: Marriage and Demographic Failure in Early Jamaica," *Journal of Social History* 28:1 (1994), 63, 65.

32. Philip Wright, ed., *Lady Nugent's Journal of Her Residence in Jamaica from 1801 to 1805* (Kingston: The University of the West Indies Press, 2002), 29, 26, 86.

33. Higman, *Slave Population and Economy in Jamaica*, 53.

34. Ibid., 53, 58.

35. Buchner, *The Moravians in Jamaica*, 44.

36. Burnard, "A Failed Settler Society," 77.

37. Michael Craton, "Hobbesian or Panglossian? The Two Extremes of Slave Conditions in the British Caribbean, 1783 to 1834," *William and Mary Quarterly* 35:2 (1978), 343.

38. Green, "'A Civil Inconvenience?'," 5, 15, 16.

39. Higman, *Slave Population and Economy in Jamaica*, 159. Also see Higman, "The Slave Family and Household in the British West Indies, 1800–1834."

40. Phillippo, *Jamaica, Its Past and Present State*, 124–25.

41. David Chandler, "Family Bonds and Bondsmen: The Slave Family in Colonial Colombia," *Latin American Review* 16:2 (1981), 112.

42. Alida C. Metcalfe, *Family and Frontier in Colonial Brazil: Santana De Paraiba, 1580–1822* (Berkeley: University of California Press, 1992), 155.

43. Archibald John Monteith, "Archibald John Monteith: Native Helper and Assistant in the Jamaica Mission at New Carmel," *Callaloo* 13:1 (1990), 108–10. For a full discussion about Monteith, see Warner-Lewis, *Archibald Monteath*.

44. Monteith, "Archibald John Monteith," 111–13.

45. D.G. Hall, "The Apprenticeship Period in Jamaica, 1834–1838," *Caribbean Quarterly* 3:3 (1953), 142, 143.

46. Joseph Sturge and Thomas Harvey, *The West Indies in 1837; Being the Journal of a Visit to Antigua, Montserrat, Dominica, St. Lucia, Barbados, and Jamaica; Undertaken for the Purpose of Ascertaining the Actual Condition of the Negro Population of those Islands* (London: Hamilton, Adams, & Co. Paternoster Row, 1838), Section IX, lxxxiv.

47. Ibid.; Hall, "The Apprenticeship Period in Jamaica," 142, 143.

48. Sturge and Harvey, *The West Indies in 1837*, Section IX, lxxxiv.

49. Ibid., Section XI, lxxxvi.

50. Ibid.

51. Hall, "The Apprenticeship Period in Jamaica," 148.

52. Sturge and Harvey, *The West Indies in 1837*, Section XI, lxxxvi.

53. James A. Thome and Joseph H. Kimball, *Emancipation in the West Indies: A Six Months' Tour in Antigua, Barbadoes, and Jamaica, in the Year 1837* (New York: The American Anti-Slavery Society, 1838), 401.

54. See William A. Green, *British Slave Emancipation: The Sugar Colonies and the Great Experiment, 1830–1865* (London: Oxford University Press, 1976). Green views the abolition of British slavery in its Caribbean colonies as an experiment with freedom; but this assumes that freedom did not already exist within the enslaved and apprenticed communities; it downplays how much value the enslaved and apprentices placed on their freedom and their conviction that a compromise, such as apprenticeship, was unnecessary.

55. Thome and Kimball, *Emancipation in the West Indies*, 415.

56. Sturge and Harvey, *The West Indies in 1837*, Section XII, lxxxviii, lxxxix.

57. Hall, "The Apprenticeship Period in Jamaica," 166.

CHAPTER TEN

~

Conclusion

This study has examined the role played by the enslaved people in the un-making of slavery in British-colonized Jamaica. It has examined this role through the optic of slave freedom, the idea that the enslaved never accepted slavery, never saw themselves as slaves, and that the slaveholders expected that they would resist slavery from the beginning years of the institution. The study has proposed that violent revolts by the enslaved are a narrow way in which to view slave freedom. The agency of the enslaved was demonstrated in a variety of ways, some violent, others nonviolent, some overt, others hidden. The one consistent feature of the lived experiences of the enslaved was their desire to have their freedom acknowledged and their use of what-ever means that they could find to pursue this objective. This was slave freedom, which shaped and unmade the history of Anglo-Jamaica during the age of slavery in the Atlantic world. Slave freedom existed in thought and manifested in action, and slaveholders themselves were always aware of its existence and were perpetually reacting to this reality.

This awareness came from the rejection of monarchical absolutism and Anglican authoritarianism in England, from the idea that freedom was important, necessary, and inalienable, views which were still present in Eng-land when Jamaica was captured by the English in 1655. The English who became the colonial dominators of Jamaica knew that for slavery to succeed, they would have to find the means through which to suppress the enslaved effectively. Categorizing them as slaves would not be enough. Legislation would be needed in order to legalize and legitimize enslavement, pre-existing denunciations of nonwhite people on the basis of their race would have to be brought in to add another level of validation, and hegemonic controls would be necessary if the domination would have any hope of survival and success. But, regardless of the brutal and covert methods used to fashion an effective system of slavery, slave freedom survived. In fact, the brutality and later improvements to the conditions of slavery made by the slave masters, as this study has shown, were themselves a representation of the relative powerlessness of the slaveholders when they were confronted with the persistent reality of slave freedom.

The brutality was shown in the immediate aftermath of Tacky's war against slaveholding in 1760, when the Jamaica Assembly moved quickly to enact the most suppressive slave law since the inception of any kind of slavery in the colony. However, the slave laws before this were not significantly different in terms of their objective. This was to maintain white domination over the enslaved population, now exclusively African and their descendants. Other laws, such as the laws to increase the white male population, laws to also ensure that enough whites males were on sea vessels plying the coastal waters of Jamaica, were all passed to provide the same support for the white suppression of enslaved African peoples, and out of the consistent fear of the slaveholders that the enslaved people would end their enslavement through violent means.

Though the English cleric Hickeringill had not written directly about the enslavement of Africans in his 1661 *Jamaica Viewed*, he had proposed an approach to the enslavement of Amerindians based on his perception of the need to control both the minds and bodies of the enslaved. Hickeringill saw Jamaica's potential as an economically and strategically valuable colony of the English in the New World, but he also viewed the capitalization on this potential as possible only with a slave system that used hegemonic methods to force the enslaved to accept slavery. He was writing a virtual charter for the English slave system in Jamaica, one that he tried not to make too obvious by masking it in poetic language, but which ultimately included using the indoctrinating procedures of Christian faith through the church to which he had switched his allegiance because of the Restoration of the monarchy, the Anglican Church. This church was viewed by Hickeringill as having a crucial role to play in the domination of enslaved people, and the view that hegemony, as provided by the church, was necessary for effective domination was in use in England after the Restoration of Charles II in 1660. However, the use of church indoctrination to materialize hegemony in slaveholding British Jamaica took a long time to gain a foothold among the slaveholders. They resisted the Christian conversion of the enslaved under the impression that Christianity would encourage enslaved people to view themselves as free. Nevertheless, this perspective had to be abandoned, as Tacky's war and subsequent acts of both violent and nonviolent resistance, from the second half of the eighteenth century onward, made it even clearer that legislation and brutality were ineffective as means of suppressing the enslaved.

The change made by the slaveholders toward the adoption of the Christian conversion of the enslaved came as part of a bigger plan for the amelioration of slavery. Amelioration was an alternative means of domination, an attempt by the slaveholding people to use improvements to slavery as a way to prolong the life of the institution. Amelioration's first manifestation was in the 1784 Consolidated Act. This was a revision of the previous slave laws, which instituted harsher penalties for masters who resorted to treatment and punishments of the enslaved that were seen as brutal, backward, and unnecessary. The new law also gave the enslaved access to qualitatively and quantitatively improved medical upkeep and subsistence. This was followed some thirteen years later by the legislation passed in 1797, which was a further promotion of amelioration, but which focused more on the Christianization of the enslaved. From 1797 until the abolition of slavery in 1834, the Anglican Church was used to indoctrinate the enslaved in order to suppress resistance, and to give the impression that slavery was not the brutal, or socially and morally destructive system that it was made out to be by the abolitionist campaigners in Britain.

These campaigners, which included the famous Wilberforce, had successfully engineered the abolition of the British slave trade in 1807. But the ending of this trade had the effect in Jamaica of reinforcing the slaveholders' commitment to amelioration. It became more urgent to make sure that the institution survived without the overt extremities of past years. Every slave master had to conform, though there remained resistors among them, and the arrival of Governor Manchester in 1808 made it possible for amelioration to become arguably the most important policy-initiative of the colonial government for the next two and half decades. Manchester was an avid supporter of ameliorating slavery and never, it seemed, missed an opportunity to highlight the accomplishments of the colony in this arena. During his long tenure, which lasted until 1827, Manchester made sure that the Colonial Office was well aware of the adoption of legislation linked to the colony's amelioration plans: the curates' acts of 1813 and 1816; the new slave law of 1816; Slave Registration in 1817; the British amelioration proposals in 1824; and the use of amelioration by the enslaved people themselves throughout this period. Manchester submitted reports on the marriages of enslaved people, for instance, when slave marriage was not recognized as lawful, on the enslaved who petitioned the courts for freedom on the basis that they were illegally held as slaves, and on the manumissions in Jamaica between his arrival in 1808 and before his departure in 1827. In Manchester's hands, these were signs of the success of amelioration, but viewed from the perspective of the enslaved, they provided further evidence of slave freedom.

The one thing that the slaveholders did not take into serious consideration was how the enslaved would respond to amelioration. Slave masters believed that converting the enslaved would produce their pacification. They had been using harsh methods for many years, now it was time to take the opposite approach, and the church of state could aid in ensuring that the enslaved accepted that enslavement was not an injustice. If anything, it gave them access to British culture, through Anglican conversion and instruction, for instance, which in the minds of the slaveholders was a superior culture to the African culture and traditions of the enslaved people.

Slave Freedom in Action

Instruction and conversion went hand in hand. The first teachers of the enslaved were Anglican clerics, the first ones to provide a consistent type of schooling for enslaved people, the first ones to create a fledgling system of schooling prior to the abolition of slavery. There is no need to query whether this was real education or not. The providers saw it as an educational experience, exposure to Anglican doctrine and principles that would elevate enslaved people to the stage of civil obedience. Essentially, the Anglican Church saw its instruction and attendant conversion as ways to make the slaves better people by making them into better slaves. This was the church's ironic objective, its undeclared and underhanded role in the maintenance of slavery. The enslaved themselves made use of the chances to become literate, a preparation for life outside of slavery. In the hands of the enslaved, instruction became a way toward upward social mobility, it might not have ended their enslavement, but it gave them access to the knowledge of free society and the knowledge of its power structures with the literacy that they gained. It was a preparation for the undermining of these power structures with the very same knowledge used to support these.

In the schools, the enslaved struggled with their teachers or catechists to influence their methods and the contents of the lessons that they were taught. In the churches, they took control over how they gained access to Anglican Christianity. The catechists and the clerics recorded these acts of resistance without knowing that these were manifestations of slave agency and ultimately, slave freedom. The enslaved gave them reasons to feel motivated, reasons to feel as if they were succeeding with the amelioration plans of the slaveholding colonial regime. However, a virtual colonization of the Anglican Church was underway during the amelioration period, and by 1817, most of the members of this church were no longer slave masters, but enslaved people. The clerics had to remodel the ways that they delivered their performance as clergymen in order to accommodate the presence of the enslaved in the churches. Some complained, while others capitulated without complaint. The church was changing from the church of planters, if it ever was, into the church of the enslaved.

One planter, the absentee inheritor of two plantations in Jamaica in 1812, Matthew Lewis, discovered slave freedom when he made his first visit to his properties in 1816. Lewis did everything that the enslaved people wanted him to do, and in the end he felt betrayed. He abolished the use of the whip without investigation of the charges against the enslaved; he delayed punishments for up to a day so that nothing was done without reflection and proof. Yet, he saw none of the profitability that he expected from these allocations. His "new code of laws" produced the reverse effect. Productivity on his estates declined rather than improved. Lewis' response was to casti-gate the enslaved people, but afterward he made a more sober assessment of the outcome. He realized that the enslaved had been using him to gradually undermine their enslavement on his estates.

Enslaved people who ran away permanently did the same by removing themselves from slavery altogether. But there were enslaved people who were perpetual runaways, and through this method of resistance, reminded slave owners of their agency and their conviction that they could always find ways to circumvent the immobility imposed on them by enslavement. They were making sure that they lived as close to the manner in which they wanted to live by running away temporarily but repeatedly. Running away had a third dimension. This was seen in the report that Manchester submitted about the captured and incarcerated people who petitioned the courts for release on the basis that they were free people. These petitioners used their idea that they were free to virtually harass the colonial court system for their emancipation to be acknowledged. Only two from the list that Manchester provided relented, and one died shortly afterwards, making his reason for recanting suspicious at the very least. In other words, knowing of his impending death might have negated the need to press the court any further for his release as a free person.

The successful and unsuccessful petitioners on this list were almost equal. Sixty-nine of them gained success and were released as free people, and fifty were not successful. The list did not include most parishes, so we are limited in the assessments that can be made using the list. However, the information that was provided showed a level of determination that is worth noting. Arguably, the unsuccessful ones were more interesting, since they knew beforehand that their petitions were false, but they submitted these nevertheless. The risks involved did not prevent these petitioners from pursuing the acknowledgement that they were free using the law. This was overt resistance done while knowing that they were enslaved. It was very different from hidden resistance which showed a level of fear of the reprisals. Instead, it was barefaced and expressed a great deal of brazenness—brazenness that hidden acts of resistance could not express. It also showed the decision that these enslaved people made to contest their enslavement using the very same legal system which sought to validate their bondage. The subversion which is evidenced by this was a powerful reminder of slave freedom, an explicit rehearsal of the unwillingness to accept enslavement as valid, permanent, or socially devastating.

When an enslaved couple chose to get married, as this study has argued, before 1824 they were committing an act that was illegal. The slave laws did not address the issue of marriage by enslaved people, and because of this, the widespread view among slaveholders was that these marriages were not lawful. Marriages could not be hidden, and especially if the enslaved couples opted to marry in the church of state. The Anglican Church was the only church authorized to perform marriages, the only church that could legally solemnize a couple's union. That enslaved people chose this church was an expression of their knowledge of the church's authority in this matter, but also their willingness to expose themselves to dangerous reprisals from slaveholders who objected to the enslaved getting married. The implication of marrying was equally significant. By law, only the courts could disband a marriage and both the enslaved and their enslavers knew this. Marriages complicated the ownership of children, the ownership of property acquired by the married couples. This left slaveholders without the legal basis on which to claim ownership over children born within marriages, or over any property that the married couples might acquire. In the Bahamas, where the issue was debated around 1814, the white establishment had to admit that enslaved couples who might enter marriages also might enter a type of emancipation that made their status as slaves very problematical. Enslaved couples who were married were eroding the power of the slaveholders. More importantly, marriages represented the decision of these couples to live as they saw fit, to have stable families even across different plantations or despite the many limitations, to fashion an existence outside of the boundaries imposed by slavery, to live like free people did, even if this was only virtual freedom in the eyes of the law and the slave masters.

In this study, manumission has been presented as the endeavor of the enslaved. The crux of this perspective is that manumission under any circumstance materialized because of the sacrifices made by the enslaved people. The traditional categorization of manumission as willed or purchased does not sufficiently capture the importance of the role that the enslaved played in either case. All manumissions were achieved rather than given. The role of enslaved people was demonstrated in the time that they fulfilled in accordance with the stipulations of slaveholders, and of course, more clearly in the case of those who paid actual cash for their release from slavery. How was any of this slave freedom? Manumission was essentially the pursuit and acquisition of freedom, but then it was also much more than these. It was based on the belief that freedom was the right of all persons and that slavery was an imposed reality that, however traumatic, did not and should not mitigate the desire to be free. Furthermore, it was a demonstration of freedom as much as it might have been the pursuit of this freedom as well. Manumissions were not easily achieved and the industry created around these sent this message to the enslaved community. Both slaveholders and the colonial government profited monetarily from manumission. At the same time, the money that was used for these manumissions came from the same economy that was built around the slave system. The institution of slavery, due to the efforts of the enslaved, contributed to its own demise through manumission. The number of manumissions fluctuated but remained above 1,000 for each of the two-year periods between 1808 and 1830, except for the period 1811–1813 when the number fell to 490 manumissions. These manumissions imposed a new reality on slavery, one that showed that none of the obstacles from the slaveholders could protect slavery from the enslaved people, who were determined to have legal freedom, or to have the law manifest their freedom to the rest of the free society.

The last slave war in Jamaica, which took place between December 1831 and January 1832, played a major role in the decision by the Parliament to abolish slavery in 1833, but for this to take effect in 1834. Writing about the influence of the enslaved due to this rebellion, the "third party," as he calls them, Eric Williams states: "In 1833, therefore, the alternatives were clear: emancipation from above, or emancipation from below. But EMANCIPA-TION."[1] The enslaved had shown through the rebellion that they were still prepared to take up arms to obtain legal freedom. Amelioration did not diminish their desire for this freedom. Instead, it increased it, for the enslaved saw the powerlessness of masters in their policy to improve slavery with the hope of prolonging its existence. Amelioration was an admission of flexibility, an admission that changes could be instituted in spite of the intransigence of those slaveholders who wished to hold on to the practices of the past. But the other important message of amelioration was that it was up to the enslaved to show the slaveholders their dissatisfaction with any measure that only modified slavery. Nevertheless, when abolition came, another modification measure, known as apprenticeship, was introduced. Full freedom was delayed because of this, and the enslaved, now known as apprentices, resisted the apprenticeship as well. Self-purchase by the apprentices continued the tradition of the enslaved people who had purchased or worked for their manumissions before 1834. Apprentices complained about the attitudes of and treatment from former masters. These made apprenticeship unworkable, expressed the urgency for full freedom, and four years after its commencement, the decision was taken in Parliament to end apprenticeship with full freedom. The only group that was not ready for full freedom in 1838 was the slaveholders.

According to Christine Hünefeldt, the "inversion of the moral code" was just one of the prices that enslaved people paid for their freedom.[2] Though they were convinced that they were still free people, they also could not neglect the fact that they were enslaved. Their belief in their freedom was their motivation to resist enslavement, and they were prepared to adopt just about any measure to make this resistance effective. They were fighting against an institution that they knew to be unjust. Slavery acted against human decency in every possible way, and this justified using even what was seen as "criminal behavior" to achieve freedom under the law.[3] Slave freedom and its continuation in the agency of the apprentices were early signs of "political action," indications of the awareness among the enslaved and apprentices of the unjust distribution of resources, principally the dissemination of "power" and "goods" based on race, which needed to be eradicated for the creation of a better society in colonial Jamaica.[4] Slave freedom was the most important means through which this new society was brought into being.

Notes

1. Williams, *Capitalism and Slavery*, 207, 208.

2. Christine Hünefeldt, *Paying the Price of Freedom: Family and Labour among Lima's Slaves, 1800–1854*, Alexandra Stern, trans. (Berkeley: University of California Press, 1994), 171, 172.

3. Marvin L. Michael Kay and Lorin Lee Cary, "'They Are Indeed the Constant Plague of Their Tyrants': Slave Defense of a Moral Economy in Colonial North Carolina, 1748–1772," in *Out of the House of Bondage*, 37, 38, 39.

4. Marshall, *Slavery, Law and Society in the British Windward Islands*, 203, 204.

~

Bibliography

Manuscripts

Eighteenth Century Collections Online

ECCO, 1793, An Abridgment of the Laws of Jamaica; Being an Alphabetical Digest of All the Public Acts of Assembly Now in Force, from the Thirty-Second Year of King Charles II. To the Thirty-Second Year Of . . . George III. Inclusive, as Published in Two Volumes, . . . Jamaica. *Laws, etc.*, St. Jago de la Vega, Jamaica: printed by Alexander Aikman.

ECCO 1709, An Account of the Number of Negroes Delivered in to the Islands of Barbadoes, Jamaica, and Antego, from the Year 1698 to 1708. Since the Trade Was Opened, Taken from the Accounts Sent from the Respective Governours of Those Islands to the Lords Commissioners of Trade, *Social Sciences*, London.

ECCO 1738, Acts of Assembly, Passed in the Island of Jamaica; from 1681, to 1737, Inclusive. *Laws, etc.* London, printed by John Baskett, 1738, 1739.

ECCO, 1738 (1739), An Act to Encourage the Importation of White Men. No. 113. Acts of Assembly, Passed in the Island of Jamaica; from 1681, to 1737, Inclusive.

ECCO, 1738 (1739), An Act for the Better Regulating Slaves, and Rendering Free Negroes and Mulattoes More Useful; and Preventing Hawking and Peddling; and Enlarging the Time for the Commissioners Collecting the out-Standing Debts. No. 292. Acts of Assembly, Passed in the Island of Jamaica; from 1681, to 1737, Inclusive. *Laws, etc.*, London, printed by John Baskett.

ECCO, 1738 (1739), An Act for the Better Suppressing and Reducing the Rebellious and Runaway Negroes, *Passed in the Month of March, in the Year of our Lord One Thousand Seven Hundred and Thirty, and Which Was Continued by One Other Act Intituled,* an Act to Continue Part of Act. No. 320. Acts of Assembly, Passed in the Island of Jamaica; from 1681, to 1737, Inclusive. *Laws, etc.*, London, printed for John Baskett.

ECCO, 1738 (1739), An Act to Oblige the Several Inhabitants of This Island to Provide Themselves with a Sufficient Number of White People, or Pay Certain Sums of Money in Case They Shall Be Deficient; and for Laying a Duty Upon Shipping, and Applying the Same to Several Uses. No. 317. Acts of Assembly, Passed in the Island of Jamaica; from 1681, to 1737, Inclusive. *Laws, etc.*, London, printed for John Baskett.

Fulham Papers (Colonial Correspondence), Lambeth Palace Library, London

FP XVIII, (ii) 1740–undated (1–242), An Act to Regulate the Ecclesiastical Regimen of the Clergy, 19 November 1801.

FP XVII, Bermuda, 1695–undated (1–92), Jamaica (i) 1661–1739 (93–292), Catalogue of Books and Instructions Sent with Mr. Barrett, Jamaica, 1724.

FP XVII, Bermuda, 1695–undated (1–92), Jamaica (i) 1661–1739 (93–292), Queries to be Answered by every Minister.

FP XVII, Bermuda, 1695–undated (1–92), Jamaica (i) 1661–1739 (93–292), William Reading to Henry Maule, Palmores Hutt, Jamaica, 15 February 1723.

FP XVII, Jamaica (i) 1661–1739 (93–292), Instructions for our Trusty & well beloved Sir Thomas Lynch, Knight, Our Captain General, & Governor in Chief, in and over our Island of Jamaica—and other the Territories depending thereon, in America.—1681.

FP XVII, Jamaica (i) 1661–1739 (93–292), Instructions for Thomas Windsor, Lord Windsor, Governor of our Island of Jamaica, in the West Indies, 21 March 1661.

FP XVIII, (ii) 1740–undated (1–242), John Venn to the Bishop of London, Jamaica, 15 June 1751.

FP XVII, Jamaica (i) 1661–1739 (93–292), Lewis de Boneval (Bomeval?) to Bishop Gibson, 14 November 1739.

FP XVIII, (ii) 1740–undated (1–242), Robert Sewell, Agent for Jamaica, to the Duke of Portland, 12 April 1798.

House of Commons Parliamentary Papers

HCPP 1833 (540), *Baptist Missionaries, Jamaica*, dated 19 April 1833.

HCPP 1818 (433), *Further Papers Relating to the Treatment of Slaves in the Colonies*, 10 June 1818.

HCPP 1834 (476), *Jamaica Chapels*, 10 July 1834.

HCPP 1830–1831 (231), *Jamaica, Copy of any information which may have been relieved from Jamaica respecting an Inquiry into the TREATMENT of a FEMALE SLAVE, by the Reverend Mr. Bridges, Rector of St. Ann's, in that Island; with the MINUTES of EVIDENCE taken by the MAGISTRATES on that occasion, and the result of the Inquiry*, 10 March 1830.

HCPP 1821 (61), *Jamaica, Negroes. Copies of the Several Returns Annually Made by the Collector of the Customs in the Several West Indian Islands*, 19 February 1821.

HCPP 1814–1815 (478), *Jamaica, Papers Relating to the West Indies*, 12 July 1815.

HCPP 1831–1832 (481), *Jamaica: Religious Instruction. Copy of any Report or Reports from the Bishop of Jamaica, or of any other information in the Possession of the Government, showing the means furnished by the Colony for the Religious Instruction of the Coloured and Slave Population, the number of Churches, Chapels and other places of Worship, and the Rectors, Curates, Catechists and Schools therein*, 24 May 1832.

HCPP 1831–1832 (582), *Jamaica: Slave Insurrection*, 23 April 1832.

HCPP 1814–1815 (478), *Papers Relating to the West Indies*, 12 July 1815.

HCPP 1826–1827 (009), *Papers Respecting the Religious Instruction of the Slaves of the West Indies. Diocese of Jamaica and the Bahamas*, 1827.

HCPP 1823 (457), *Slaves at Honduras, Correspondence Relative to the Condition and Treatment of Slaves at Honduras: 1820–1823*, 16 June 1823.

HCPP 1823 (347), *Slave Population. Further Papers and Returns, presented pursuant to address, Relating to Slave Population of Jamaica, St. Christopher's, and the Bahamas*, 14 May 1823.

House of Lords Record Office, London

HLRO HL/PO/JO/10/8/981, An Account of the Estimated Expenditure of the Island of Jamaica, for the Year Ending 30th September 1831, Defrayed by Revenue Raised in That Island, and the Ways and Means for Raising Such Revenue for the Year 1831, Great Britain, *Lords Journals, Vol. LXIV*, 22 June 1832, DIAZO/3490, Reel 212.

HLRO HL/PO/PU/1/1825/6G4n338, An Act to Make Provision for the Salaries of Certain Bishops and Other Ecclesiastical Dignitaries and Ministers, in the Diocese of *Jamaica*, and in the Diocese of *Barbadoes* and the *Leeward Islands*; and to Enable His Majesty to Grant Annuities to Such Bishops Upon the Resignation of Their Offices, 25 July 1825, Great Britain, *Public General Act, 6 George IV, c. 88*, 1825, DIAZO/3489, Reel 211.

HLRO HL/PO/JO/10/8/115, Copy of Letter from Simon Taylor, Henry Shirley, George Murray, and Lewis Cuthbert, Esquires, to the Earl of Balcarres; Dated 12th December 1797; and Transmitted in His Lordship's Letter to the Duke of Portland, of December 1797, *Circular Letters to the Governors of the West India Islands, London*, 1800.

HLRO HL/PO/JO/10/8/302, Stipendiary Curates Bill, Print with MS Amendments, *Lords Journals, Vol. XLIX*, 8 April 1813.

National Library of Jamaica

NLJ MS2115/R55.7.124.2, Crop Book for the Tharp Estates, *Tharp Papers*, 1791.

The National Archives, London

TNA 548, *Howell's State Trials, Vol. 20, Cols. 1–6*, 1771–72.

University of Birmingham Archives, Birmingham
Manuscripts of the Church Missionary Society

UBA CW/012/5/1, A Few Simple Facts for the Friends of the Negro, Jamaica, 1828.

UBA CW/083/25, Bishop Christopher to Henry C. Taylor, Liguanea, Jamaica, 8 July 1826.

UBA CW/02A/1/1, Bishop Christopher, Spanish Town, Jamaica, to Rev. Edward Bickersteth, Church Missionary House, London, 5 December 1826.

UBA CW/02A/1/2, Bishop Christopher, Spanish Town, Jamaica, to Rev. Edward Bickersteth, Church Missionary House, London, 4 May 1827.

UBA CW/02A/1/5, Correspondence of Auxiliary Committee with Ecclesiastical Commissioners, Jamaica, March-July 1828.

UBA CW/056/12, Dr. James Macfayden, Certificate of Mr. Manning's Health, 3 November 1830; Society, *Register of Missionaries (Clerical, Lay and Female)*, Part One, 25.

UBA CW/025/1, Ebenezer Collins to Donald Coates, Church Missionary Society, Salisbury Square, London, 24 December 1827.

UBA CW/025/2, Ebenezer Collins to the Secretaries, Church Missionary Society, Salisbury Square, London, 13 June 1828.

UBA CW/083/14, Henry Clarke Taylor to the Secretaries, Church Missionary Society, 9 February 1827.

UBA CW/083/18, Henry Clarke Taylor to the Secretaries, Church Missionary Society, 20 December 1827.

UBA CW/083/15, Henry Taylor to the Secretaries, Church Missionary Society, London, 28 May 1827.

UBA CW/03A/12, Jamaica Auxiliary Church Missionary Society Proceedings, 26 July 1830.

UBA CW/03A/8, Mr. J.C. Sharpe to John Hylton, Accompong, 1 March 1830.

UBA CW/079/1, Rev. John Stainsby to Rev. Josiah Pratt, Church Missionary Society, Salisbury Square, London, 11 December 1820.

UBA CW/088/8, Rev. J.M. Trew to Rev. Edward Bickersteth, Church Missionary Society, London, 1 July 1828.

UBA CW/03A/13, Rev. John Stainsby to William Bullock, St. John's, 19 August 1830, On the Subject of Our Catechists Doing Militia Duty, Letter to the Governor's Secretary.

UBA CW/079/8, Rev. John Stainsby to Donald Coates, Mile Gully, Manchester, Jamaica, 10 June 1830, Jamaica.

UBA CW/079/10, Rev. John Stainsby to Donald Coates, Kingston, Jamaica, 10 March 1831.

UBA CW/02A/1/3, Letter from Rev. John M. McIntyre, Rector of St. James, Jamaica, to Bishop Christopher, Montego Bay, 24 March 1828.

UBA CW/04/1/7, Lesson Book, Jamaica Auxiliary Church Missionary Society, 1826.

UBA CW/02A/19B, Nicholas Forbes to Rev. R.C. Dallas, Maroon Town, Portland, 23 June 1832.

UBA CW/083/2, Salt Savannah, Vere, Henry Clarke Taylor to Rev. E. Bickersteth, London, 26 February 1826.

UBA CW/083/9, Salt Savannah, Vere, Henry Clarke Taylor to the Secretaries, Church Missionary Society, Salisbury Square, London, 7 June 1826.

UBA CW/080/7, Salt Savannah, William Stearn to Rev. William Jowett, Church Missionary Society, London, October (Received 2 December) 1833.

UBA CW/083/12, Taylor to the Secretaries, Church Missionary Society, Salisbury Square, London, 11 October 1826.

UBA CW/04/9/1, Thomas Jones, Return of Papine School, St. Andrew, Jamaica, 1 February 1827.

UBA CW/056/3, Rev. William Manning to Donald Coates, Church Missionary Society, Salisbury Square, London, 19 August 1828.

UBA CW/056/4, Rev. William Manning to Donald Coates, Church Missionary Society, Salisbury Square, London, 6 December 1828.

Newspapers

Daily Gleaner, March 1965.

St. Jago de la Vega Gazette, 11–18 February 1832.

The Kingston Chronicle and City Advertiser, 21 January 1833.

The Watchman and the Jamaica Free Press, 28 March 1832.

Unpublished Works

Baris Kilinc, Dogan, "Labor, Leisure, and Freedom in the Philosophies of Aristotle, Karl Marx, and Herbert Marcuse," MA Thesis, Department of Philosophy, Middle East Technical University, Ankara, 2006.

"Education for All Assessment 2000: Jamaica Country Report," Ministry of Education and Culture, Kingston, Jamaica, September 1999.

Furness, Alan E., *The Tharp Estates in Jamaica*, Kingston, National Library of Jamaica, Unpublished Manuscript.

Lindsay, John, "A Few Conjectural Considerations upon the Creation of the Human Race. Occasioned by the Present British Quixotical Rage of Setting the Slaves from Africa at Liberty. By an Inhabitant of Jamaica. The Reverend Doctor Lindsay Rector of St. Katherine's in that Island. St. Jago de la Vega," 23 July 1788, British Library Manuscript Collection.

Published Works

Alpers, Edward, Gwyn Campbell, and Michael Salman, eds., *Slavery and Resistance in Africa and Asia* (Oxon, UK: Routledge, 2005).

Anonymous (James Knight), *The State of the Island of Jamaica, Chiefly in Relation to Its Commerce, and the Conduct of the Spaniards in the West Indies* (London: H. Whitridge, 1726).

Aptheker, Herbert, *American Slave Revolts* (New York: Columbia University Press, 1943).

Arnold, David, *Colonizing the Body: State Medicine and Epidemic Disease in Nineteenth-Century India* (Berkeley: University of California Press, 1993).

Bacchus, M.K., "Education and Society among the Non-Whites in the West Indies Prior to Emancipation," *History of Education* 19:2 (1990).

——, *Utilization, Misuse and Development of Human Resources in the Early West Indian Colonies from 1492 to 1845* (Ontario: Wilfred Laurier University Press, 1990).

Barbosa, José Carlos, *Slavery and Protestant Missions in Imperial Brazil*, Trans. Fraser G. MacHaffie and Richard K. Danford (Lanham, MD: University Press of America, 2008).

Beckles, Hilary McD., *A History of Barbados: From Amerindian Settlement to Nation-State* (Cambridge, UK: Cambridge University Press, 1990).

——, "From Land to Sea: Runaway Barbados Slaves and Servants, 1630–1700," *Slavery & Abolition* 6:3 (1985): 76–94.

Bisnauth, Dale, *History of Religions in the Caribbean* (Kingston: LMH Publishing, 2006).

Blanck, Emily, "The Legal Emancipations of Leander and Caesar: Manumission and the Law in Revolutionary South Carolina and Massachusetts," *Slavery & Abolition* 28:2 (2007): 235–54.

Bloch, Marc, *The Historian's Craft: Reflections on the Nature and Uses of History and the Techniques and Methods of Those Who Write It* (Manchester, UK: Manchester University Press, 1992).

Blumer, Herbert, "Sociological Implications of the Thought of George Herbert Mead," *American Journal of Sociology* 71:5 (1966): 535–44.

——, *Symbolic Interactionism: Perspective and Method* (Berkeley: University of California Press, 1986).

Boggs, Carl, *Gramsci's Marxism* (London: Pluto Press, 1976).

Bohun, William, *The English Lawyer: Shewing the Nature and Forms of Original Writs, Processes and Mandates, of the Courts at Westminster* (London: E. Nutt, R. Nutt and R. Gosling, 1732).

Brana-Shute, Rosemary, "Approaching Freedom: The Manumission of Slaves in Suriname, 1760–1828," *Slavery & Abolition*, 10:3 (1989): 40–63.

Brathwaite, Edward, *The Development of Creole Society in Jamaica, 1770–1820* (Oxford, UK: Clarendon Press and Oxford University Press, 1978).

Bridenbaugh, Carl, and Roberta Bridenbaugh, *No Peace Beyond the Line: The English in the Caribbean, 1624–1690* (New York: Oxford University Press, 1972).

Bridges, G.W., *The Annals of Jamaica*, Vol. 2 (London: Frank Cass and Co. Ltd., 1968 [1828]).

Brown, Christopher Leslie, *Moral Capital: Foundations of British Abolitionism* (Chapel Hill: University of North Carolina Press, 2006).

Brown, Vincent, *The Reaper's Garden: Death and Power in the World of Atlantic Slavery* (Cambridge, MA: Harvard University Press, 2008).

Bryan, Patrick, "Aiding Imperialism: White Baptists in Nineteenth-Century Jamaica," *Small Axe* 14 (2003): 37–49.

Buchner, J.H., *The Moravians in Jamaica: History of the Mission of the United Brethren's Church to the Negroes in the Island of Jamaica, from the Year 1754 to 1854* (London: Longman, Brown, & Co., 1854).

Buck-Morss, Susan, "Hegel and Haiti," *Critical Inquiry* 26:4 (2000): 821–65.

———, *Hegel, Haiti, and Universal History* (Pittsburgh, PA: University of Pittsburgh Press, 2009).

Burnard, Trevor, "A Failed Settler Society: Marriage and Demographic Failure in Early Jamaica," *Journal of Social History* 28:1 (1994): 63–82.

———, *Mastery, Tyranny, and Desire: Thomas Thistlewood and His Slaves in the Anglo-Jamaican World* (Chapel Hill: The University of North Carolina Press, 2004).

———, "Powerless Masters: The Curious Decline of Jamaican Sugar Planters in the Foundational Period of British Abolitionism," The Elsa Goveia Memorial Lecture 2010, Department of History and Archeology, University of the West Indies, Mona, Jamaica.

Caldecott, Alfred, *The Church in the West Indies* (London: Frank Cass & co. Ltd., 1970 [1898]).

Carmichael, A.C., *Domestic Manners and Social Condition of the White, Coloured and Negro Population of the West Indies*, Vol. 2 (London: Whittaker and Co., 1834 [1833]).

Carretta, Vincent, "Writings of the British Black Atlantic," *Eighteenth-Century Studies* 34:1 (2000): 121–53.

Cerny, Philip G., "Dilemmas of Operationalizing Hegemony," in *Hegemony and Power: Consensus and Coercion in Contemporary Politics*, Mark Haugaard and Howard H. Lentner, eds. (Lanham, MD: Lexington Books, 2006): 67–87.

Champion, Justin, and J.L.C. McNulty, "Making Orthodoxy in Late Restoration England: The Trials of Edmund Hickeringill, 1662–1710," in *Power in Early Modern Society: Order, Hierarchy, and Subordination in Britain and Ireland*, Michael J. Braddick and John Walter, eds. (Cambridge, UK: Cambridge University Press, 2001), 227–48.

Chandler, David, "Family Bonds and Bondsmen: The Slave Family in Colonial Colombia," *Latin American Review* 16:2 (1981): 107–31.

Christopher, Emma, *Slave Ship Sailors and their Captive Cargoes, 1730–1807* (New York: Cambridge University Press, 2006).

Church Missionary Society, *Register of Missionaries (Clerical, Lay and Female), and Native Clergy from 1804 to 1904, in Two Parts, Part One* (London: Published for Private Circulation, 1896).

Craton, Michael, *Empire, Enslavement, and Freedom in the Caribbean* (Kingston, Oxford, and Princeton: Ian Randle, James Curry, and Marcus Wiener, 1997).

———, "Hobbesian or Panglossian? The Two Extremes of Slave Conditions in the British Caribbean, 1783 to 1834," *William and Mary Quarterly* 35:2 (1978): 324–56.

———, *Testing the Chains: Resistance to Slavery in the British West Indies* (London: Cornell University Press, 1982).

Crouch, Nathaniel, *The English Empire in America: Or, a View of the Dominions of the Crown of England … Illustrated with Maps and Pictures. By R. Burton*, 5th. Ed. (London: Printed for Nath. Crouch, 1711).

Daube, David, "Two Early Patterns of Manumission," *The Journal of Roman Studies* 36 (1946): 57–75.

Dayfoot, Arthur Charles, *The Shaping of the West Indian Church* (Kingston: The Press University of the West Indies and University Press of Florida, 1999).

Dick, Devon, "Role of the Maroons in the Morant Bay Uprising: You Shall Know the Truth and the Truth Shall Set You Free," St. Thomas Co-operative Credit Union Commemorative Paul Bogle Lecture, Anglican Church Hall, Morant Bay, St. Thomas, Jamaica, Wednesday, October 26, 2011.

——, *The Cross and the Machete: Native Baptists of Jamaica, Identity, Ministry and Legacy* (Kingston: Ian Randle Publisher, 2009).

Dunkley, D.A., Book Review, José Carlos Barbosa, *Slavery and Protestant Missions in Imperial Brazil*, Trans. Fraser G. MacHaffie and Richard K. Danford (Lanham, MD: University Press of America, 2008), *Church History and Religious Culture* 90:4 (2010): 723–25.

Dunn, Richard S., *Sugar and Slaves: The Rise of the Planter Class in the English West Indies, 1624–1713* (Chapel Hill: The University of North Carolina Press, 2000).

Eltis, David, "Slavery and Freedom in the Early Modern World," in *Terms of Labor: Slavery, Serfdom, and Free Labor*, Stanley L. Engerman, ed. (Stanford, CA: Stanford University Press, 1999), 25–49.

——, *The Rise of African Slavery in the Americas* (Cambridge, UK: Cambridge University Press, 2000).

Eversley, William Pinder, and William Feilden Craies, *The Marriage Laws of the British Empire* (London: Stevens and Haynes, 1910).

Fergus, Claudius, "Dread of Insurrection: Abolitionism, Security, and Labor in Britain's West Indian Colonies, 1760–1823," *William and Mary Quarterly* 66:4 (2009): 757–80.

Fergus, Howard A., *A History of Education in the British Leeward Islands, 1838–1945* (Kingston: The University of the West Indies Press, 2003).

Follett, Richard J., *The Sugar Masters: Planters and Slaves in Louisiana's Cane World, 1820–1860* (Baton Rouge: Louisiana State University Press, 2005).

Foucault, Michel, *Discipline and Punish: The Birth of the Prison* (New York: Vintage, 1995).

Fransham, John, *The World in Miniature: Or, the Entertaining Traveller. Giving an Account of Every Thing Necessary and Curious; . . .With Several Curious and Useful Tables . . . The Second Edition Much Enlarg'd: Also the Addition of a New Sett of Cutts*, 2 Vols., Vol. 1 (London: Printed, and sold by John Torbuck; Mess. Astley and Austen; T. Osborne; A. Millar; and J. Hodges and T. Harris, 1741).

Freeman, Arthur J., *An Ecumenical Theology of the Heart, the Theology of Count Nicholas Ludwig Von Zinzendorf* (Bethlehem, PA: The Moravian Church in America, 1998).

Freire, Paulo, *Education for Critical Consciousness* (New York: Continuum, 1993).

——, *Pedagogy of Hope: Reviving Pedagogy of the Oppressed*, Robert R. Barr, trans. (New York: Continuum, 1995).

——, *Pedagogy of the Oppressed*, Myra Bergman Ramos, trans. (New York: Continuum, 1994[1973]).

——, *The Politics of Education: Culture, Power and Liberation*, Donaldo Macedo, trans. (South Hadley: Bergin and Garvey, 1985).

Freyre, Gilberto, *The Mansions and the Shanties: The Making of Modern Brazil* (Berkeley: University of California Press, 1963).

Fukuyama, Francis, *The End of History and the Last Man* (New York: Free Press, 1992).

Galenson, David W., "The Settlement and Growth of the Colonies: Population, Labor, and Economic Development," in *The Colonial Era*, Stanley L. Engerman and Robert E. Gallman, eds. (Cambridge, UK: Cambridge University Press, 1996), 135–207.

Genovese, Eugene D., *Roll, Jordan, Roll: The World the Slaves Made* (New York: Vintage, 1976).

Gibson, Edmund, *Observations Upon the Conduct and Behaviour of a Certain Sect, Usually Distinguished by the Name of Methodists* (London: Publisher Unknown, 1740).

Gordon, Shirley C., *A Century of West Indian Education* (London: Longmans, 1963).

———, *Our Cause for His Glory: Christianisation and Emancipation in Jamaica* (Kingston: The Press University of the West Indies, 1998).

———, *God Almighty, Make Me Free: Christianity in Preemancipation Jamaica* (Bloomington: Indiana University Press, 1996).

———, "Schools of the Free," in *Before and After 1865: Education, Politics and Regionalism in the Caribbean*, Brian Moore and Swithin Wilmot, eds. (Kingston: Ian Randle Publishers, 1998), 1–12.

———, "The Negro Education Grant, 1835–1845: Its Application in Jamaica," *British Journal of Educational Studies* 6:2 (1958): 140–50.

Goveia, Elsa V., *A Study on the Historiography of the British West Indies to the End of the Nineteenth Century* (Washington, DC: Howard University Press, 1980).

Gragg, Larry, *The Quaker Community on Barbados: Challenging the Culture of the Planter Class* (Columbia: University of Missouri Press, 2009).

Gramsci, Antonio, *Selections from the Prison Notebooks*, Quintin Hoare and Geoffrey Nowell Smith, eds. and trans. (London: Lawrence and Wishart, 1971).

Gray, Obika, *Demeaned but Empowered: The Social Power of the Urban Poor in Jamaica* (Kingston: University of the West Indies Press, 2004).

Green, Cecilia A., "'A Civil Inconvenience?' The Vexed Question of Slave Marriage in the British West Indies," *Law and History Review* 25:1 (2007): 1–59.

Green, William A., *British Slave Emancipation: The Sugar Colonies and the Great Experiment, 1830–1865* (London: Oxford University Press, 1976).

Haggis, Sheila M., *Science and Technology Education in Jamaican Schools* (Paris: UNESCO, 1984).

Hall, Douglas, "The Apprenticeship Period in Jamaica, 1834–1838," *Caribbean Quarterly* 3:3 (1953): 142–66.

———, *In Miserable Slavery: Thomas Thistlewood in Jamaica, 1750–86* (Kingston: The University of the West Indies Press, 1999).

Hart, Richard, *Slaves Who Abolished Slavery, Volume 2: Blacks in Rebellion* (Kingston: Institute for Social and Economic Research, University of the West Indies, 1985).

Haugaard, Mark, "Conceptual Confrontations," in *Hegemony and Power: Consensus and Coercion in Contemporary Politics*, Mark Haugaard and Howard H. Lentner, eds. (Lanham, MD: Lexington Books, 2006), 3–20.

Hawthorne, Walter, "'Being Now, as It Were, One Family:' Shipmate Bonding on the Slave Vessel *Emilia*, in Rio De Janeiro and Throughout the Atlantic World," *Luso-Brazilian Review* 45:1 (2008): 53–77.

Hegel, G.W.F., *Hegel's Science of Logic* (London: Allen and Unwin, 1812).

Heuman, Gad, *Between Black and White: Race, Politics, and the Free Coloured in Jamaica, 1792–1865* (Westport, CT: Greenwood Press, 1981).

——, ed., *Out of the House of Bondage: Runaways, Resistance, and Marronage in Africa and the New World* (London: Frank Cass, 1986).

——, "Runaway Slaves in Nineteenth-Century Barbados," *Slavery & Abolition* 6:3 (1985): 95–111.

——, "The Free Coloreds in Jamaican Slave Society," in *The Slavery Reader*, Gad Heuman and James Walvin, eds. (London: Routledge, 2003), 664–67.

Hickeringill, Edmund, *Jamaica Viewed: With All the Ports, Harbours, and Their Several Soundings, Towns, and Settlements Thereunto Belonging. Together with the Nature of Its Climate, Fruitfulness of the Soil, and Its Fruitfulness to English Complexions*, 3rd. ed. (London: Benjamin Bragge, at the Blew Ball, in Ave-Mary Lane, 1705 [1661]).

——, *The Ceremony-Monger, His Character in Five Chapters* (London: Reprinted the Year 1703, Humbly proposed to the consideration of the Parliament, 1703).

Higman, B.W., *Plantation Jamaica, 1750–1850: Capital and Control in a Colonial Economy* (Kingston: University of the West Indies Press, 2005).

——, *Proslavery Priest: The Atlantic World of John Lindsay, 1729–1788* (Kingston: University of the West Indies Press, 2011).

——, *Slave Population and Economy in Jamaica, 1807–1834* (Kingston: The Press, University of the West Indies, 1995).

——, "The Slave Family and Household in the British West Indies, 1800–1834," *Journal of Interdisciplinary History* 6:2 (1975): 261–87.

Hindle, Steve, "Exhortation and Entitlement: Negotiating Inequality in English Rural Communities, 1550–1650," in *Power in Early Modern Society: Order, Hierarchy, and Subordination in Britain and Ireland*, Michael J. Braddick and John Walter, eds. (Cambridge, UK: Cambridge University Press, 2001), 102–22.

Hollingsworth, Rev. N.J., *An Address to the Public, in Recommendation of the Madras System of Education, as Invented and Practiced By the Rev. Dr. Bell, F.A.S.S. F.R.S. ED. With a Comparison between His Schools and those of Mr. Joseph Lancaster* (London: Printed by Law and Gilbert, 1812).

Holt, Thomas C., *The Problem of Freedom: Race, Labor, and Politics in Jamaica and Britain, 1832–1938* (Baltimore, MD: The Johns Hopkins University Press, 1992).

Hünefeldt, Christine, *Paying the Price of Freedom: Family and Labour among Lima's Slaves, 1800–1854*, Alexandra Stern, trans. (Berkeley: University of California Press, 1994).

Hunte, Keith, "Protestantism and Slavery in the British Caribbean," in *Christianity in the Caribbean: Essays on Church History*, Armando Lampe, ed. (Kingston: University of the West Indies Press, 2001), 106–15.

Hutton, Joseph E., *A History of the Moravian Church* (Grand Rapids, MI: Christian Classics Ethereal Library, 2000 [1872]).

Ivamy, E.R. Hardy, *Mozley and Whiteley's Law Dictionary* (London: Butterworth and Co., 1988).

Jarman, T.L., *Landmarks in the History of Education* (London: John Murray, 1970).

Jobson, Richard, *The Discovery of River Gambia* (London: Hakluyt Society, 1999 [1623]). Also see this later work by John Watts, *A True Relation of the Inhumane and Unparallel'd Actions and Barbarous Murders of Negroes or Moors, Committed on Three English-Men in Old Calabar in Guiny . . .* (London, 1672 [1668]).

Johnson, Lyman L., "Manumission in Colonial Buenos Aires, 1776–1810," *The Hispanic American Historical Review*, 59:2 (1979): 258–79.

Kay, Marvin L. Michael, and Lorin Lee Cary, "'They Are Indeed the Constant Plague of Their Tyrants': Slave Defense of a Moral Economy in Colonial North Carolina, 1748–1772," in *Out of the House of Bondage: Runaways, Resistance, and Marronage in Africa and the New World*, Gad Heuman, ed. (London: Frank Cass, 1986), 37–56.

Klein, Herbert S., and Clotilde Andrade Paiva, "Freedmen in a Slave Economy: Minas Gerais in 1831," *Journal of Social History* 29:4 (1996): 933–62.

Knaplund, Paul, "Great Britain and the British Empire," in *Material Progress and World-Wide Problems 1870–1898*, F.H. Hinsely, ed. (Cambridge, UK: Cambridge University Press, 1962), 383–410.

Koot, Christian J., *Empire at the Periphery: British Colonists, Anglo-Dutch Trade, and the Development of the British Atlantic, 1621–1713* (New York: New York University Press, 2011).

Kopytoff, Barbara Klamon, "Colonial Treaty as Sacred Charter of the Jamaican Maroons," *Ethnohistory* 26:1 (1979): 45–64.

Lambert, David, "The Glasgow King of Billingsgate: James Macqueen and an Atlantic Proslavery Network," *Slavery & Abolition* 29:3 (2008): 389–413.

Lancaster, Joseph, *Tracts on Education, 1776–1880* (London: Printed at the Royal Free School Press, 1811).

Lawson, John, and Harold Silver, *A Social History of Education in England* (London: Methuen and Co. Ltd., 1978).

Leslie, Charles, *A New and Exact Account of Jamaica...* 3rd Ed. (Edinburgh: R. Fleming, 1740).

Levo, John E., *The Romantic Isles: A Sketch of the Church in the West Indies* (London: SPG and SPCK, 1937).

Lewis, Matthew, *Journal of a West India Proprietor*, Judith Terry, ed. (Oxford, UK: Oxford University Press, 1999 [1833]).

Lister, Thomas Henry, *The Life and Administration of Edward, First Earl of Clarendon; with Original Correspondence and Authentic Papers Never Before Published. In Three Volumes, Vol. 1* (London: Longman, Orme, Brown, Green, and Longmans, 1838).

Locke, John, *Two Treatises of Government: In the Former, The False Principles and Foundation of Sir Robert Filmer, And His Followers, are Detected and Overthrown. The Latter is an Essay concerning The True Original, Extent, and End of Civil-Government* (London: Printed for Awnsham Churchill, 1690 [1689]).

London, Norrel A., "Policy and Practice in Education in the British West Indies During the late Colonial Period," *History of Education* 24:1 (1995): 91–104.

Long, Edward, *The History of Jamaica. Or, General Survey of the Antient and Modern State of That Island: With Reflections on Its Situation, Settlements, Inhabitants, Climate,*

Products, Commerce, Laws, and Government, Vol. 2 (London: Printed for T. Lowndes, 1774).

Luster, Robert E., *The Amelioration of the Slaves in the British Empire, 1790–1833* (New York: Peter Lang, 1995).

Marshall, Bernard, *Slavery, Law, and Society in the British Windward Islands, 1763–1823: A Comparative Study* (Kingston: Arawak Publications, 2007).

Matison, Sumner Eliot, "Manumission by Purchase," *The Journal of Negro History* 33:2 (1948): 146–67.

Matthews, Gilien, *Caribbean Slave Revolts and the British Abolition Movement* (Baton Rouge: Louisiana State University Press, 2006).

McDonald, Roderick A., "Measuring the British Slave Trade to Jamaica, 1789–1808: A Comment," *The Economic History Review* 33:2 (1980): 253–58.

——, *The Economy and Material Culture of Slaves: Goods and Chattels on the Sugar Plantations of Jamaica and Louisiana* (Baton Rouge: Louisiana State University Press, 1993).

McNulty, J.L.C., Hickeringill, Edmund (*Bap.* 1631, *D.* 1708), *Oxford Dictionary of National Biography*, (www.oxforddnb.com/view/article/13200, Accessed January 21, 2009).

Metcalfe, Alida C., *Family and Frontier in Colonial Brazil: Santana De Paraiba, 1580–1822* (Berkeley: University of California Press, 1992).

Mintz, Sidney, "Slave Life on Caribbean Plantations," in *Slave Cultures and the Culture of Slavery*, Stephan Palmié, ed. (Knoxville: The University of Tennessee Press, 1995), 40–54.

Moister, William, *The West Indies, Enslaved and Free* (London: T. Woolmer, 1883).

Moitt, Bernard, "Freedom from Bondage at a Price: Women and Redemption from Slavery in the French Caribbean in the Nineteenth Century," *Slavery & Abolition* 26:2 (2005): 247–56.

Monteith, Archibald John, "Archibald John Monteith: Native Helper and Assistant in the Jamaica Mission at New Carmel," *Callaloo* 13:1 (1990): 102–14.

Montesquieu, Baron de (Charles de Secondat), *The Spirit of the Laws*, 2 Vols. (London: G. Bell & Sons, Ltd., 1914 [1748]).

Morgan, Edmund S., *American Slavery, American Freedom: The Ordeal of Colonial Virginia* (New York: W.W. Norton and Co., 2003).

Morgan, Kenneth, *Slavery and the British Empire: From Africa to America* (Oxford, UK: Oxford University Press, 2007).

Morrill, John, Cromwell, Oliver (1599–1658), *Oxford Dictionary of National Biography*, (www.oxforddnb.com/view/article/13200, Accessed January 21, 2009).

Moreton, J.B., *Manners and Customs in the West India Islands. Containing Various Particulars Respecting the Soil, Cultivation, Produce, Trade, Officers, Inhabitants, &C., &C. With the Method of Establishing and Conducting a Sugar-Plantation; in Which the Ill-Practices of Superintendents Are Pointed Out. Also the Treatment of Slaves; and the Slave-Trade* (London: J. Parsons, W. Richardson and J. Walter, 1793 [1790]).

M'Queen, James, *The West India Colonies; the Calumnies and Misrepresentations Circulated against Them by the Edinburgh Review, Mr. Clarkson, Mr. Cropper, Etc.* (London: Baldwin, Cradock, and Joy, 1824).

Olwell, Robert, "Becoming Free: Manumission and the Genesis of a Free Black Community in South Carolina, 1740–90," in *Against the Odds: Free Blacks in the Slave Societies of the Americas*, Jane G. Landers, ed. (New York: Routledge, 1996), 1–19.

O'Shaughnessy, Andrew Jackson, *An Empire Divided: The American Revolution and the British Caribbean* (Pennsylvania: University of Pennsylvania Press, 2000).

Paine, Thomas, *Common Sense* (Philadelphia: Independence Hall Association, 1995 [1776]).

Paton, Diana, *No Bond but the Law: Punishment, Race, and Gender in Jamaican State Formation, 1780–1870* (Durham, NC: Duke University Press, 2004).

Patterson, Orlando, *Freedom in the Making of Western Culture*, Volume 1 (London: I.B. Tauris & Co. Ltd., 1991).

———, *Slavery and Social Death: A Comparative Study* (Cambridge, MA and London: Harvard University Press, 1982).

Periodical Accounts Relating to the Missions of the Church of the United Brethren, Established among the Heathens. Vols. II, VI, VIII, X, IX (London: W.M. McDowell, for the Brethren's Society for the Furtherance of the Gospel Among the Heathen, 1796, 1814, 1821, 1823, 1826).

Perrin, Frances Rosemary, *For Christ and His Church: Twelve Lessons on the Church in the West Indies for Boys and Girls of 8–11* (London: The Society for the Propagation of the Gospel in Foreign Parts, 1952).

Petley, Christer, "Gluttony, Excess, and the Fall of the Planter Class in the British Caribbean," *Atlantic Studies* 9:1 (2012): 85–106.

———, *Slaveholders in Jamaica: Colonial Society and Culture during the Era of Abolition* (London: Pickering & Chatto Ltd., 2009).

Phillippo, James Murcell, *Jamaica, Its Past and Present State* (London: John Snow, 1843).

Porter, Andrew, *Religion versus Empire? British Protestant Missionaries and Overseas Expansion, 1700–1914* (Manchester, UK: Manchester University Press, 2004).

Rousseau, Jean-Jacques, *Discourse on Inequality*, G.D.H. Cole, trans. (Whitefish, MT: Kessinger Publishing, 2004).

———, *The Social Contract or Principles of Political Right*, H.J. Tozer, trans. (Hertfordshire, UK: Wordsworth Editions, 1998).

Russell, Horace, "The Emergence of the Christian Black: The Making of a Stereotype," *Jamaica Journal* 16:1 (1983): 51–58.

Ryden, David, *West Indian Slavery and British Abolition, 1783–1807* (Cambridge, UK: Cambridge University Press, 2009).

Satchell, Veront M., "Colonial Injustice: *The Crown v. the Bedwardites*, 27 April 1921," in *The African-Caribbean Worldview and the Making of Caribbean Society*, Horace Levy, ed. (Kingston: University of the West Indies Press, 2009), 46–67.

Scott, James C., *Weapons of the Weak: Everyday Forms of Peasant Resistance* (New Haven, CT: Yale University Press, 1985),

Scott, Rebecca J., *Degrees of Freedom: Louisiana and Cuba after Slavery* (Cambridge, MA: Belknap Press of Harvard University, 2008).

Sellin, J. Thorsten, *Slavery and the Penal System* (New York: Elsevier Scientific Publishing, 1976).

Senior, Bernard, *Jamaica, As It Was, As It Is, And As It May Be* (London: T. Hurst; Edinburgh: Grant and Son, 1835).

Sensbach, Jon, *A Separate Canaan, the Making of an Afro-Moravian World in North Carolina, 1763–1840* (Chapel Hill and London: University of North Carolina Press, 1998).

Shepherd, Verene A., *Livestock, Sugar, and Slavery: Contested Terrain in Colonial Jamaica* (Kingston: Ian Randle Publishers, 2009).

Sheridan, Richard B., "The Jamaican Slave Insurrection Scare of 1776 and the American Revolution," *The Journal of Negro History* 61:3 (1976): 290–308.

Smith, Adam, *An Inquiry into the Nature and Causes of the Wealth of Nations*, Vol. 2 (Hartford: O.D. Cooke, Lincoln and Gleason Printers, 1804[1776]).

Spivak, Gayatri Chakravorty, "Can the Subaltern Speak?" in *Marxism and the Interpretation of Culture*, C. Nelson and L. Grossberg, eds. (Basingstoke, UK: Macmillan Education, 1988), 271–313.

Stalley, R.F., "Plato's Doctrine of Freedom," *Proceedings of the Aristotelian Society* 98 (1998).

Stewart, John, *A View of the Past and Present State of the Island of Jamaica* (New York: Negro Universities Press, 1969[1823]).

Stoler, Ann Laura, "Colonial Archives and the Arts of Governance," *Archival Science* 2 (2002): 87–109.

Sturge, Joseph, and Thomas Harvey, *The West Indies in 1837; Being the Journal of a Visit to Antigua, Montserrat, Dominica, St. Lucia, Barbados, and Jamaica; Undertaken for the Purpose of Ascertaining the Actual Condition of the Negro Population of those Islands* (London: Hamilton, Adams, & Co. Paternoster Row, 1838).

Sweet, James H., "Manumission in Rio De Janeiro, 1749–54: An African Perspective," *Slavery & Abolition* 24:1 (2003): 54–70.

Taylor Holmes, Stephen, "Aristippus in and out of Athens," in *Aristotle's Politics: Critical Essays*, Richard Kraut and Steven Skultety, eds. (Lanham, MD: Rowman & Littlefield Publishers, 2005).

Thome, James A., and Joseph H. Kimball, *Emancipation in the West Indies: A Six Months' Tour in Antigua, Barbadoes, and Jamaica, in the Year 1837* (New York: The American Anti-Slavery Society, 1838).

Thompson, Benita P., S. Joel Warrican and Coreen J. Leacock, "Education for the Future: Shaking off the Shackles of Colonial Times," in *Readings in Caribbean History and Culture: Breaking Ground*, D.A. Dunkley, ed. (Lanham, MD: Lexington Books, 2011), 61–86.

Thompson, E.P., "The Moral Economy of the English Crowd in the Eighteenth Century," *Past and Present* 50:1 (1971): 76–136.

Thompson, Henry Paget, *On the Other Side: The Story of the Church in the West Indies* (London: Junior Work Department, the Society for the Propagation of the Gospel in Foreign Parts, 1929).

Trouillot, Michel-Rolph, *Silencing the Past: Power and the Production of History* (Boston: Beacon Press, 1997).

Turner, Mary, "Planters Profits and Slave Rewards: Amelioration Reconsidered," in *West Indies Accounts: Essays on the History of the British Caribbean and the Atlantic Economy in Honour of Richard Sheridan*, Richard B. Sheridan and Roderick A. McDonald, eds. (Kingston: The Press, University of the West Indies, 1996), 232–52.

———, *Slaves and Missionaries: The Disintegration of Jamaican Slave Society, 1787–1834* (Urbana: University of Illinois Press, 1982).

United Brethren in Christ, *Instructions for Members of the Unitas Fratrum, Who Minister in the Gospel among the Heathens* (London: Printed for the Brethren's Society, for the furtherance of the Gospel among the Heathens, 1784).

Vaughan, Megan, *Creating the Creole Island: Slavery in Eighteenth-Century Mauritius* (Durham and London: Duke University Press, 2005).

Waldron, Jeremy, *God, Locke, and Equality* (Cambridge, UK: Cambridge University Press, 2002).

Ward, J.R., *British West Indian Slavery, 1750–1834: The Process of Amelioration* (Oxford, UK: Clarendon Press, 1988).

Warner-Lewis, Maureen, *Archibald Monteath: Igbo, Jamaica, Moravian* (Kingston: University of the West Indies Press, 2007).

Williams, Eric, *Capitalism and Slavery* (London: André Deutsch Ltd., 1993).

Wood, Ellen Meiksins, *The Origin of Capitalism: A Longer View* (New York: Verso, 2002).

Woods, Ralph Louis, *Famous Poems and the Little-known Stories Behind Them* (Portland, OR: Hawthorn Books, 1961).

Wright, Philip, ed., *Lady Nugent's Journal of Her Residence in Jamaica from 1801 to 1805* (Kingston: The University of the West Indies Press, 2002).

Index

~

About the Author

Daive (D.A.) Dunkley teaches history in the Department of History and Archaeology at the Mona campus of the University of the West Indies in Jamaica. He was educated at the University of Warwick, England, where he obtained his PhD in history in 2009, and at the University of the West Indies, Jamaica, where he gained his BA and MA degrees. He is the editor of *Readings in Caribbean History and Culture: Breaking Ground*, published in 2011, and has authored a number of book chapters as well as journal articles for *Caribbean Quarterly* and other international journals. He specializes in the histories of power and resistance—which is better termed as agency—both during and after slavery in the Caribbean and the wider Atlantic world.